The Lives of Chang and Eng

THE LIVES OF
Chang & Eng

Siam's Twins
in Nineteenth-Century America

JOSEPH ANDREW ORSER

The University of North Carolina Press Chapel Hill

This book was published with the assistance of the
Anniversary Endowment Fund of the University of North Carolina Press.

© 2014 THE UNIVERSITY OF NORTH CAROLINA PRESS

All rights reserved. Set in Miller and Letterpress by codeMantra.
Manufactured in the United States of America. The paper in this book meets
the guidelines for permanence and durability of the Committee on Production
Guidelines for Book Longevity of the Council on Library Resources.

The University of North Carolina Press has been a member
of the Green Press Initiative since 2003.

Jacket illustration: Eng and Chang. Photograph c. 1860.
Wellcome Library, London.

Library of Congress Cataloging-in-Publication Data
The lives of Chang and Eng: Siam's twins in nineteenth-century America /
Joseph Andrew Orser.
pages cm
Includes bibliographical references and index.
ISBN 978-1-4696-1830-2 (cloth : alk. paper) — ISBN 978-1-4696-1831-9 (ebook)
1. Bunker, Chang, 1811–1874. 2. Bunker, Eng, 1811–1874. 3. Conjoined twins—United States—
Biography. 4. Conjoined twins—United States—History—19th century. I. Title.
QM691.B86O77 2014
616'.043—dc23
2014015419

18 17 16 15 14 5 4 3 2 1

CONTENTS

ILLUSTRATIONS

ACKNOWLEDGMENTS

I want to take this opportunity to recognize those who supported and encouraged me as I undertook this study of the lives of Chang and Eng. A number of colleagues deserve special acknowledgment. Judy Wu and Alan Gallay encouraged me to take on this project and offered important reassurance at every stage of my research and writing. John Brooke, Kevin Boyle, and Mytheli Sreenivas were inspiring teachers and enthusiastic critics. Jeff Dow, Sean Ford, and Louisa Rice have provided valuable advice and motivation at crucial moments. In addition to their thorough and detailed criticism of the manuscript, my editors at the University of North Carolina Press, David Perry and Brandon Proia, proved to be extraordinarily patient with an author who was dilatory in his revisions.

Financial support from Ohio State University and the University of Wisconsin–Eau Claire was essential. I am especially grateful for travel funds awarded by UWEC's Academic Affairs Professional Development Program Grant and research fellowships awarded by OSU, namely, the College of Humanities Summer Research Award and the Henry H. Simms Award. A U.S. Department of Education grant allowed me to spend a summer in Thailand engaging in language study and research.

Descendants of the Bunkers provided assistance that no one else could. Tanya B. Jones, executive director of the Surry Arts Council in Mount Airy, was generous with her time and expertise, as was family genealogist Jessie Bunker Bryant. Tom Atkins shared with me his personal collection of family letters and documents that he has worked to assemble. Though not a Bunker, Amy Snyder of the Mount Airy Museum of Regional History proved helpful on multiple occasions.

I have benefited from the kindness of friends and family. Colleen Flannery, Erin Greenwald, and Gary and Wipha Risser opened their homes to me on research trips, as did my dear cousins Jennifer and B. L. Morris. My parents, Frank and Lawan Orser, have always been supportive and more than ready to share their opinions on the direction my thinking should take. Even though we disagreed more often than not, I am forever grateful and profoundly touched by their commitment to my success. My greatest debt is to my wife, Nick, and our son, Will, who allow me every day to leave behind my work and enter a world where discussions revolve around soccer, food, and other "diversions" that are, actually, the essence of life. Thank you for sticking with me through all of this. Your love, laughter, and encouragement have been my greatest inspirations.

The Lives of Chang and Eng

The Monster Now before Us

When, in February 1874, surgeons at Philadelphia's College of Physicians reported the findings of their postmortem examination of conjoined twins Chang and Eng Bunker, the world-famous "Siamese twins," they spoke of "the monster now before us." The good doctors meant this quite literally. The twins had long been classified in the field of teratology—*teras* was Greek for "monster"—as *Xiphopages*, which Dunglison's definitive *Medical Lexicon* identified as "a monstrosity in which twins are united by the epigastrium, as in the case of the Siamese twins." Additional specialization in the field of "diploteratology"—the study of "compound human monsters"—further categorized the twins as *Xiphopages* of the third order: *terata anacatadidyma*. The twins were monsters; great books and learned men said so.[1]

And yet, it should go without saying, they were not monsters. They were men, individuals, who were joined from birth at the chest by a band of flesh and cartilage.

Chang and Eng were born in Siam in 1811, in a village sixty miles southwest of Bangkok. Their father was a migrant from China; their mother likely had a Chinese father and Siamese mother. In the mid-1820s, a British merchant saw them playing in a river. At first, he thought they were some sort of creature, but then, realizing they were boys, he recognized he might make a fortune exhibiting them and what he considered their monstrous bodies. In 1829, when the brothers were eighteen, the merchant teamed with an American sea captain to contract their services to travel to the United States and Europe and display their physical anomaly. The brothers believed they would be gone for a short while; instead, they spent the rest of their lives in the West, in the public eye, as part of a larger trade in freaks of nature and Oriental curiosities.

In the 1830s, they traveled throughout the United States, to Canada and Cuba, and across Britain and western Europe. In 1839, at the age of twenty-eight, they withdrew from public performance, settling in North Carolina as farmers, taking the oath of American citizenship, adopting the last name of Bunker, marrying white sisters, becoming slaveholders, and, over the course of their lives, fathering at least twenty-one children between them. By 1849, with rising expenses to support two growing families, the thirty-eight-year-old twins returned to show business. For the next twenty-five years, until their deaths in 1874 at the age of sixty-two, Chang and Eng toured off and on, almost always taking along a pair of their offspring, sharing the stage with their children.[2]

Throughout their lives in America, the brothers made claims of normality. Culturally, they spoke English and attended church. Politically, they voted as Southern Whigs into the 1850s, and then, when the Union faced its gravest political crisis, they sided with their white neighbors and backed the Confederacy. Economically, they were masters of other men and women even as they forged networks within an emerging southern middle class. Biologically, they showed again and again and again their reproductive prowess. Yet the necessity to prove themselves normal in the public eye undermined any such claims of normality. In attempting to demonstrate just how normal they were, Chang and Eng instead exhibited their difference.

Their difference, however, was not limited to any single category such as national origins, skin color, religious beliefs, political allegiance, or, most obvious, physical anomaly. Rather, the most apt description was monstrosity, both then and now. Nineteenth-century Americans gave concrete meaning to "monstrosity" and made wide use of the term in medical and cultural arenas in ways that audiences today, sensitive to its derogatory and marginalizing influence, do not. Nevertheless, scholars today have borrowed the concept of the monster to offer insightful analysis of the ways societies have organized and monitored their members.[3] Monstrosities defied easy categorization because they existed at the extreme margins of many categories, as did the twins. Monstrosities exhibited striking differences from societal norms but had enough of the familiar to register on mental maps of normality, as was the case with the twins. And it was this recognition of a common ground that so unnerved observers and audiences, driving them to react with ridicule, disgust, fear, and menace. Ultimately, it was observers— the public—who determined the monster. The twins' "monstrous" characteristics were nothing but projections cast upon them of American fears, evidence of the public's recognition that American society had its own monstrously ambivalent qualities. These examples of ambivalence in America— slavery in a land of liberty, sectionalism in a grand union, miscegenation in a white republic, to name just three—are as central to the narrative and analysis of this book as the twins are.

Situated precariously at the margins of performance and being, discourse and the material, monstrosity and humanity, this book attempts a balancing act between analytic categories that resemble the monster it aims to explicate. In pursuing this line of inquiry, I am also entering contentious terrain. In the mid-1990s, an insightful essay analyzing Chang and Eng through a lens of monstrosity received a tongue-lashing from a reviewer, who called it a "stunningly dehumanizing essay on two inoffensive North Carolina farmers."[4] So let me be clear: Acknowledging that the twins were considered monsters does not condone this fact, and ignoring this fact does not change it. Yes, the twins were men, and this book explores the very human strategies they followed to express their humanity to the world. But to many, if not most, observers, they were not men but objects, commodities, curiosities, freaks, and monsters. To acknowledge this is not to embrace it but to recognize it, and making this acknowledgment is the first step toward exploring the lessons Chang and Eng offer about the America in which they lived. It is also to recognize that they *were* seen by many as men—as humans—and to investigate what Siam's twins reveal about nineteenth-century America.

Siam's Twins and America's Monsters

The Lives of Chang and Eng examines the social and cultural spaces the Bunkers occupied, interrogating the unexpected insights their experiences offer into nineteenth-century ideas of race, deformity, gender, and sexuality. The twins, and their families, straddled the divide between subject and citizen, feminine and masculine, alien and American, nonwhite and white, disabled and able-bodied. The twins' otherness, their children's mixed-racedness, the family's high profile, and their lengthy careers touring the nation and world allow for the comparison and contrast of norms of race, respectability, gender, and family across space and time. In this way, Siam's twins reveal America's monsters.

In his 1868 work on diploteratology, George Jackson Fisher offered a quotation from Goethe: "It is in her monstrosities that nature reveals her laws."[5] So it could be said of the United States and its monstrosities. Chang and Eng were not born "monsters." Rather, they came to be perceived as such, and this perception—and the many guises the twins' monstrosity took—says everything about the people who projected certain values onto the brothers and little, if anything, about the two men themselves. As a result, this book is organized around various "monsters."

For one, the twins reinforced and challenged American ideas about race and slavery, as Asian immigrants and American citizens, and as bonded labor and slaveholders. Chang and Eng traveled about freely, engaging in activities of leisured respectability, and yet they were thought of as the property of a northern sea captain, sold by their mother. Later in their lives, as slaveholders of Asian origins, they complicated people's understanding of slaveholding as a white institution, and they served as an illustration of the argument that slavery was much more diverse than Americans had come to accept.

The twins became part of a debate over who could be a citizen, naturalizing in the aftermath of Jacksonian popular democracy, at a time when naturalization was supposed to be limited to whites, a point that commentators made note of during the nativist 1850s. Their conjoined status also provided fodder for those who believed the twins as citizens made a mockery of citizenship: dependent on and bound to each other as they were, how could they even pay lip service to being independent, self-governing citizens? Democracy and political citizenship were not monsters themselves, but in the wrong hands—foreign born, nonwhite, dependent—there was the threat of becoming monsters, at least in the eyes of many Americans.

Notions of the family also underwent a great deal of tumult in the mid-nineteenth century, and the twins and their wives and children often found themselves in the middle of these debates, even as they tried to present themselves as normal American families. The relationships that governed domestic life—husband and wife, parent and child—provided order to the twins' everyday existence and gave them the currency to engage neighbors, community, and country on a common ground. That the twins constructed roles as husbands and fathers reveals their embrace of the racial and gender order of nineteenth-century America.

In all this, the intimacy of the family was contested in public. It was not the individuals who lived, ate, and slept together that determined their family-ness; rather, the public sanctioned the organization as a family. And families inhabited a problematic space, existing at the borders of numerous social categories—public and private, individual and society, man and woman, adult and child—and this positioning meant that family itself might become monstrous, a potent mix of the familiar and the deviant. The twins' marriages provoked images of bestiality, adultery, polygamy, and interracial sex. And their offspring, born to Asian fathers and white mothers and placed on a public stage for all to see, forced Americans to talk about mixed-race children at a time when such topics were preferably ignored.[6]

In considering the American monsters that Chang's and Eng's everyday lives reveal, the spaces the Bunkers crafted for themselves and the discursive, symbolic worlds they inhabited, I build on research that interrogates relationships between legal and popular understandings of race, the interrelatedness of race and disability/deformity, and the politics of family and sexuality. Defining race as a socially constructed hierarchy of power relations based on physical characteristics such as skin color,[7] this examination of Chang's and Eng's lives reveals a disjuncture between legal and popular understandings of race in the nineteenth century. The public viewed the twins as different; aside from their conjoined state, their skin color and facial features drew comments. But the law treated them as white; they became U.S. citizens, appeared in the census as white, and married two white women. The ability of the twins to enjoy these rights and privileges of whiteness was rare among Asians in America; my look at the dissonance between legal and lived experiences of race reveals the capriciousness with which authorities marked individuals as one race or another and the impact such decisions had on the people thus marked.

Like race, ideas of disability and deformity built upon physical characteristics and separated people into categories of normal and abnormal. Bodily and racial differences played off each other, heightening public perceptions of physical anomalies. By midcentury, experts routinely connected nonwhite races to people with disabilities. Down's syndrome was first identified in 1866 as Mongolism; the Siamese twins, too, bore a name that conveyed both racial and bodily anomalies. That the twins could claim the advantages of legal whiteness sheds light on local and national understandings of race and disability and how the individuals who inhabited these bodies negotiated such cultural expectations.[8]

Throughout their lives, Chang and Eng were a frequent topic of conversation, and the public's fascination with them revolved around the ways these two men constructed "normal" lives in spite of their monstrous bodies. This intrigued people, and it scared them. Through the adoption of citizenship, family, slaves, and the like, the twins at once reinforced normative values that favored republican values, marriage between man and woman, the raising of a robust family that embraced education and urbanity, and the exercise of power over a racial underclass. And as each of these steps reinforced these normative values, it also challenged them. What did it mean that these two "monsters" could lead such mundane lives, that this spectacle could be so ordinary? Even the most mundane institutions could become monstrous, recognizable but hideously so. And the characteristics of the twins that came to be regarded as monstrous were, ultimately, those very characteristics that made them American, or at least legible to an American audience and, as a result, threatening to that audience.

Cultural and Social Worlds

This book brings abstract symbolic discourse into conversation with specific, on-the-ground, everyday lives. I use promotional literature, newspaper items, and visual images, as well as diplomatic reports, census data, tax lists, court cases, church records, letters, diaries, and household budgets, to try to re-create the places the twins lived and visited but also to read the sources discursively, to analyze the language used and to seek significance in word choice, suggestive images, and silences. These two methods allow the materiality of lived experience to be brought together with the symbolism of larger cultural forces to appreciate fully the nuance and complexity of the social and cultural worlds that the twins and their families occupied.

At one level, these social worlds were very closely linked to physical places on a map. Normative ideals of race, gender, and the family in the nineteenth century often derived from local standards, and different parts of the United States reacted to the twins in distinct ways. These differences rested partly in each region's distinct economic and labor systems. But the twins' journeys did not simply identify disparities across space; rather, they show how everyday lives, as well as discourses of race, deformity, gender, and sexuality, were mutually constitutive across disparate regions. For example, California's growing Chinese population during the 1850s raised questions in the East about where Chang and Eng should fit into U.S. legal and political categories. Meanwhile, the journey of the "Americanized" twins and children to California in 1860 suggested to white westerners a potential for Chinese assimilation. Similarly, their experiences in the North, where they engaged in a struggle for their independence from bonded labor and, once free, were condemned as "niggers," contrasts sharply with their experience in the South, where they made their claims to white by becoming American citizens, marrying white women, and owning slaves.[9]

At another level, the cultural worlds the twins occupied were conceptual. Here, my study is influenced by the analysis of discursive representations done by Edward W. Said, John Kuo Wei Tchen, and Robert G. Lee. Their examinations of Western policy statements, travel accounts, literature, and popular culture show the ways in which cultural differences between East and West became essentializing representations of opposition between the self and the other. The Orient came to be described as irrational and backward; the West was the mirror image, rational and progressive. Through the creation of representational systems such as this, the West came to control public perceptions of East and West, even among the "Oriental."[10]

The attempt to bridge the gaps between social and cultural—to determine what "really" happened as opposed to making sense of why people talked about the twins in the ways that they did—required me ultimately not to frame my discussion simply in terms of the twins' experience but rather to focus much of my analysis on *the historian's* (or more precisely, *my*) attempt to determine their experience, or more specifically, to determine the processes they pursued to produce an identity, to establish their position in society.[11] Take, for instance, any attempt to delineate the discourse surrounding Chang and Eng from their actual everyday experiences or, even more tricky, any attempt to find their voice. The primary evidence *about* the twins is voluminous; the evidence *by* them is minuscule. Instead, what we have are letters written on their behalf by managers; exhibition pamphlets that purposely exaggerate and fictionalize even as they offer some factual information; news reports that include purported interviews with the twins; alleged court testimony of the twins and other court records that are more incomplete than complete; and scientific studies that treat the twins as specimens. All these sources are mediated by outside parties to a degree that left me uncomfortable looking for a chance to let the twins speak.

Faced with circumstances such as these, with sources that claim—some perhaps with more validity than others—to speak for a certain person but in practice speak in place of that other person, some scholars have argued that it is impossible to know what went on in the minds of these silent/silenced others, and it is inappropriate to place words in their mouths.[12] To the extent that it is impossible to know anything, of course they are correct. Even texts whose author is undisputed are not necessarily accurate of that person's thoughts; any source—written or unwritten—is mediated by outside concerns to some extent. Yet rather than wave a white flag and wash my hands of the mess, the attempt to discern what the twins thought about their circumstances, how they understood them, and the ways in which they decided to bring about change—the various processes that made up their experiences—offers insight into the positions they occupied in society and the role they played in shaping their worlds, in situating themselves.

Further, understanding their process of pushing back against the economic, racial, and gendered systems that they faced also allows us to more completely understand the constraints these systems placed on individuals and the avenues for change that presented themselves, at least to these two men.

It is impossible simply to accept without scrutiny statements and actions attributed to the twins. Certain questions must guide the reading of these documents. For instance, under what circumstances and for what purposes were the twins made to speak? To what extent did opportunities to speak reflect the desires of others—scientists or journalists, for example—and to what extent did these opportunities represent the independent volition of the twins? What interests were at stake for the twins, and what interests were at stake for the mediator? How did the mediators frame these opportunities for the twins to speak, and how did the twins frame these opportunities, if, in fact, they did? And, finally, what common threads became evident, and what did these reveal about the twins and about U.S. society at various points in time? In the end, an accumulation of evidence from a diverse set of sources revealed a consistent voice that, I argue, represents the twins' efforts—with varying levels of success—to place themselves in positions that maximized their chances for respect, profit, and self-determination. In so doing, Chang and Eng worked to assert themselves as men and not monsters.

CHAPTER ONE

In and Chun

"Susan, I have two Chinese Boys, 17 years old, grown together they enjoy extraordinary health. I hope these will prove profitable as a curiosity." So wrote American sea captain Abel Coffin in the summer of 1829, as his ship, the *Sachem*, approached St. Helena on its way home from Siam to Newburyport, Massachusetts. Aside from the unnamed "Chinese Boys," the *Sachem* carried a cargo of sugar, an international crew of eighteen, and British merchant Robert Hunter, who claimed to have discovered the twins and who, Coffin wrote, "owns half" of them. (Unmentioned was the presence of another Siamese man who acted as translator for the twins in their first months in the United States and then Britain.) Coffin also carried with him a written plea from English missionary Jacob Tomlin for his "American brethren" to come to Siam and do the work of Christ.[1]

As the ship's captain, Coffin saw himself as father to his crew, a role that influenced his relationship with the twins at sea and, ultimately, on land but also with the other men who sailed under him. In good times, Coffin celebrated their successes—he boasted to Susan of a crew member named Ezra Davis who stayed in Bangkok to manage a European business venture. And in bad, he mourned their losses. The drowning of German crew member Henry Monk in late July, before the ship reached Bermuda, served as a grim reminder to Coffin of the responsibility for each of his men that he projected on himself. "All the crew naturally look to me as children to a parent, and when I saw the sorrow of their feelings, it pearsed me to the heart," he wrote to Susan. Coffin, as captain, was able to articulate the relationships between him and others on the vessel with an authority—or simply a voice—that no one else possessed. He was the parent, and crew members were the children, because he said so. When he and the twins arrived in North America, he would similarly name their relationship.[2]

For the "Chinese Boys," later reports claimed, the ship was a playground on which the twins could run and jump and show off an agility that belied their conjoined state. One brother—which one was not made clear—sometimes climbed the ship's mast, "the other following as well as he could without complaining." The two ascended the masthead "as fast as any sailor aboard the ship." They raced about the *Sachem's* deck, sometimes at their peril, such as the time they escaped "probable" death by leaping together at the last moment over a hatchway that had been inadvertently left open. It was not unheard of for the boys to quarrel over petty affairs, such as the temperature of their bathwater, but in those instances the captain intervened and reconciled the two in short order, as any good parent would, the published reports remarked.[3] Sometimes, the brothers thought of their home and the mother they had left behind, even though they expected to return in the not-too-distant future; at other times they looked north and west across the ocean waters, toward their unknown destination, and dreamed of the day they might captain a ship of their own.[4]

This particular ship, bearing as its name a Native American word for "chief," carrying curious young men from Siam, and manned by a Massachusetts sea captain and an international crew, served as much as any other commercial vessel to bring together different worlds and create new meanings. The early nineteenth century was a period of peoples in constant motion. European powers consolidated empires across Asia, and on a lesser scale, the United States played increasing commercial and cultural roles in distant regions of the globe. Agents of empire—sailors, merchants, missionaries, soldiers, and government officials—encountered new lands, new peoples, and new ways of living, and they worked mightily to articulate these new worlds in a manner that they and their compatriots back home might readily comprehend.[5]

By engaging in such acts of naming, these men were defining the "Orient" by its difference from the West—what the West was *not*—and in so doing tied cultural representations with political and commercial interests. As these (mis)representations became embedded in the popular imagination and official policy planning, inhabitants of the East became, or remained, invisible.[6] Similar acts of naming through cultural representations occurred in the case of the twins. In and Chun became Chang and Eng; the "Chinese Boys" achieved fame as the "Siamese Twins"; and journalists, physicians, and philosophers struggled to articulate the worlds that the brothers occupied from birth through their initial encounter with the American public in the late summer and early fall of 1829 and their subsequent journey to England in late 1829 and in 1830. The practice of naming is extraordinarily fickle, yet the power that names carry can be both tenacious, marking a person for life despite changes in circumstances that might render a name anomalous, or transitory, tossed away as new circumstances and new names take the place of the old. To trace the naming of these two brothers is also to identify a host of new circumstances that made possible the phenomenon of what would become the "Siamese Twins." These included the opening of Siam to trade relations with the West; the proliferation of travel narratives employing ever cruder descriptions of non-Western (and here, specifically, Asian) peoples; the development of scientific knowledge of the human body, both the functions of its inner organs (physiology) and the descriptions of its outer appearance (racial "sciences" such as physiognomy and phrenology); and the emergence of increasingly sophisticated print technology necessary to ensure that such travel and medical writings enjoyed wide circulation and consumption.

Stories of their birth and childhood lacked any material grounding; no birth records exist, and no documentation of their early lives has turned up.[7] But newspaper accounts of their arrival in Boston carried significant weight in how the public received the twins, both in their initial years abroad and later in their lives. The earliest report of the twins, a *Boston Patriot* article published in August 1829, offered May 1811 as the twins' birth date, a date that ultimately was accepted as official.[8] Their father, a fisherman who with thousands of others had migrated from China to Siam, died while the brothers were young, reportedly in a smallpox epidemic that struck Siam in 1819. Their mother, born in Siam but of uncertain ethnic heritage, worked hard to support her children. Like her famous sons, she was characterized as an oddity. Narratives reported she gave birth to as many as seven sets of twins and one set of triplets (though In and Chun were the only conjoined pair in these stories). More likely were the reports—including those in the exhibition pamphlets that accompanied their early tours—that while she had a number of other children, several of whom died during the same outbreak that claimed their father, none were twins.[9]

In the years after the father's death, the twins' family raised ducks to support itself. But with money scarce, the opportunity to earn money through the exhibition of the brothers in the United States and Europe proved too good to pass up. The characterizations of the transaction that followed varied; physician reports announced that their mother sold the twins to Coffin, while exhibition pamphlets stated that she had simply placed them in Coffin's trust with the promise of monetary remuneration and the return of the twins within a short period of time. Were they slaves? Did they belong to Coffin? Or were they their own men? The different articulations of this transaction also proved significant in the twins' lives down the road. For the moment, the important thing to take from the representations of their youth were the financial hardships the twins' family faced, the relief that the American Coffin and the British Hunter offered the twins and their family, and the commoditization of the twins' story and their lives. The "Siamese Youths," or "Siamese Boys," or "Siamese Twins," or Chang and Eng, or Chang-Eng, as newspapers variously called them, became huge commodities in a flourishing American market in Oriental curiosities.[10]

These Siamese twins, as commodities, were very much a product of the engagement between Siam and Britain and other Western countries that started in the early 1820s. Siam was a kingdom located on a peninsula between China and India that Europeans and Americans variously called the "Land beneath the Winds," "India beyond the Ganges," "Hindu-China," or "Southern and Eastern Asia." The country now is called Thailand in English, located in Southeast Asia. Contemporaries were aware of the imprecision of these names and the creative stage at which the naming process stood. An 1824 article published in the *Singapore Chronicle* opened with the lines, "The term Hindu-Chinese was, we think, first employed by Dr. Leyden, and it is certainly more appropriate than the vague and clumsy one of the old geographers 'India beyond the Ganges.'"[11]

Since 1782, the seat of Siamese royal power had rested in Bangkok. Though heavily involved in tributary trade with China, Siam remained relatively isolated from Western eyes in the first two decades of the nineteenth century. Diplomatic contacts with Portugal resumed in 1818, several American ships received a warm welcome from 1818 to 1821 because they brought arms, and a British embassy led by John Crawfurd visited in 1821 hoping to encourage free trade. None of these resulted in commercial treaties or in sustained relations, although accounts published by Crawfurd, a colonial administrator for the British East India Company, gave his embassy a prominent place in the public's understanding of the region. Not until war between Britain and Burma broke out in 1824 did Siam become serious about formally engaging with the West. Alarmed by the ease with which the British disposed of the kingdom's neighbor and greatest rival, Siam signed a trade treaty with Britain in 1826, which also opened the doors for more active commercial activity with other Western merchants. Throughout the 1820s, however, until the twins arrived in 1829, most Americans remained ignorant of the country.[12]

Robert Hunter, the man credited with "discovering" the brothers, was one of the earliest European merchants in Siam. He arrived in Bangkok in

August 1824, apparently at the request of Crawfurd. In addition to setting up shop—he sold imported goods, such as fabrics from Europe and India, Western medicines, opium, and weapons—Hunter and an early business partner reported to the British government on the royal palace, Siamese culture, and prospects for trade. Hunter also became a trusted partner in trade with the Siamese government, receiving the official title of Luang Awutwiset in 1831. To early protestant missionaries he played host and protector, showing them around coastal regions, having them over to dine, and interceding on their behalf when the Siamese government wanted to expel them from the kingdom.[13]

Hunter's semiofficial status also allowed him to travel more freely than other foreigners, and in 1824, while on a fishing boat in the Menam River, he first saw the twins. "They were naked from the hips upwards, were very thin in their persons, and it being then dusk, he mistook them for some strange animal," reports the earliest account of this encounter. Hunter soon became eager to learn all he could about these boys, who would have been twelve or thirteen years old at this point. The story he later told of the twins' childhood was that Siam's king, wed to superstition and barbarism, initially ordered the death of the twins upon learning of their birth, "conceiving them to be monsters, and imagining that the existence of such beings portended evil to his kingdom." The twins were ultimately spared, and while perceived as a threat to the Siamese king, they offered economic opportunity to the British trader. Hunter tried without success for the next five years to receive permission to take the twins abroad until he paired up with the American Abel Coffin.[14]

Coffin was a veteran mariner who had captained several missions to China and the East Indies. He was one of many Yankee traders who in the 1820s tried to make their fortunes in the Far East. In 1824, for example, forty-seven American vessels visited the ports of Sumatra, Borneo, and the Malayan peninsula—the "Spice Islands." They imported a portion of their cargoes to the United States and took the rest to supply a lucrative European market. Coffin most often dealt in tea from China or sugar from Siam. In Siam, Coffin managed his own affairs; there was no U.S. consul in place to help American traders. He fell in with two protestant missionaries, Jacob Tomlin and Karl Gutzlaff, and on a number of occasions asked Tomlin to preach to his crew. With Tomlin, Coffin made trips into the city's walls to view "half-naked" Siamese on display, white elephants tied up in stalls, and the captured royal family of Laos, the king and his children encaged with chains round their necks and legs. Through Robert Hunter, Coffin became acquainted with one more curiosity: twins connected just above the waist.[15]

The efforts of Robert Hunter and Abel Coffin to bring the brothers to the West in 1829 provided the American public with a fuller picture of Siam than any it had enjoyed before, albeit one much influenced by stereotypes of an exotic Orient. Siam and its twins came to occupy a prominent spot in the way Americans imagined the Orient. The twins' arrival in Boston also gave Americans new ways to consider physical questions about the human anatomy and metaphysical questions about the nature of the self. The twins—their origins and their bodies—allowed Americans to create knowledge and, in so doing, to shape the reality they appeared to describe.[16]

Their Origins

At some point between Coffin's letter to his wife in June 1829 and the brothers' introduction to the American public on August 17, 1829, a decision was made to call the twins "Siamese." Almost half a century later, James W. Hale, who managed the twins during their initial years on tour, claimed credit for this decision. "Their father and mother and all their ancestors were Chinese," Hale wrote after the twins' deaths in 1874, "but as they were born in Siam, which country was but little known to us in 1829, the 'boys' . . . were announced to the public by me as the 'Siamese Youths,' as being more likely to attract attention than by calling them Chinese."[17] Whether we accept Hale's self-serving account or not, the decision to refer to the twins as Siamese rather than Chinese offers two points for further consideration. The first deals with the role the twins played in educating the American public about this far-off, exotic kingdom of Siam; the second speaks to a particular articulation of race emerging in the United States.

Other descriptions of the twins and the world from which they came served to educate audiences about their homeland, although the significance attached to these elements offers more insight into Americans than into Siam. At the center of this consideration was the question over their "Chinese" or "Siamese" origins. The first report of the twins' arrival in the United States described the brothers as "about five feet in height" with "well-proportioned frames," in short "exhibiting the appearance of two well made Siamese youths." Ten days later, the physician who examined them on arrival made his findings known in newspapers, again referring to their height, but also to their "Chinese complexion and physiognomy."[18] Neither of these reports went into any detail about what qualities comprised a well-made Siamese youth or a Chinese complexion and physiognomy, so these statements, and many others like them, were in and of themselves meaningless. They served in no way to describe what the twins actually looked like—their facial features, their hair, or their dress. (As we will see, however, descriptions of the twins' bodily anomaly abounded.) And yet, these words—Siamese and Chinese, the latter likely more than the former—evoked a rush of meaning for American consumers. The problem of articulation as a creative act or as a lazy act becomes relevant here. To what extent were these labels simply building off a vernacular already in wide use? To what extent did the distinction rest in attention to detail, and to what extent was it simply an attempt to avoid meaningful enlightenment with overly broad tropes of description? And what impact did the discrepancy—Siamese label, Chinese parentage—have on how Americans received the twins?

After the twins arrived in the United States, reporters tried to make their parentage clear to the public. Soon, all accounts agreed that the twins were born to a Chinese father and a mother who was Siamese, or Chinese, or part Chinese and part Siamese, or part Chinese and part Malay.[19] Descriptions of "well made Siamese youths" quickly gave way to "their general appearance is indeed rather Chinese than Siamese." This transformation went beyond descriptions of their appearance. Accounts modified the identification of their nationality or race: "they were not Siamese, but Chinese." A similar transformation occurred with the young interpreter traveling with the twins. Initially, he was identified as Siamese, "of a much darker complexion, [and] has no Chinese features about him." He soon became "the son of a Chinese merchant and a Siamese lady" and then simply Chinese.[20]

These dual—or dueling—identities continued to mark the twins throughout their lives.[21] Indeed, as the twins became experienced performers, they drew on ideas of Chineseness to present themselves to the public. This is to say that, from their initial appearance in the United States in 1829 to their deaths in 1874, a distinction between Siamese and Chinese was drawn, by others and by the twins.[22] What is not as clear, however, is just what this distinction meant to an Anglo-American sensibility in the second quarter of the nineteenth century.

Siam was an independent kingdom and a tributary state of the Chinese empire. It was at once separate from and connected to China. Within Siam, there had long been a Chinese community, but with the rise of a Bangkok empire in the late eighteenth century, the Chinese role—both in numbers and in political influence—grew. The Thonburi king Taksin, who reestablished a Siamese government after the sack of Ayutthaya by the Burmese in 1767, was the son of a Chinese father and a Siamese mother. The first two kings of the current Chakri dynasty, born in the first half of the eighteenth century, had a Chinese mother. Other leading families also had Chinese connections. Trade with China grew during the late eighteenth and early nineteenth centuries, providing an economic lifeline for the early Bangkok empire. Chinese junks and merchants dominated this trade, introducing a rising Chinese economic elite to the kingdom. At the same time, the kings of early Bangkok welcomed Chinese migrants; wars with Burma in the late eighteenth century had depleted Siam's population, and immigration served to increase numbers and provide manpower, not only in shipping and commerce but also in commercial agriculture. The cultivation of sugar, for instance, rested with Chinese labor. According to a contemporary observer, about seven thousand Chinese immigrated to Siam annually by the end of Rama II's reign in 1824.[23]

Most British and American reports from Siam—published or not—discussed the kingdom's Chinese population at length. In part because the observers were in Bangkok, which as the kingdom's center of trade had a large Chinese presence, population estimates often had Chinese outnumbering Siamese. The Tomlin letter that accompanied Coffin and the twins in 1829 estimated that Bangkok's population included (out of a total of 401,300) 8,000 Siamese, 50,000 descendants of Chinese, and 310,000 Chinese. Tomlin wrote that these numbers came from an 1828 census done by the Siamese government, and since the Siamese "should [not] underrate themselves and over-rate the Chinese, . . . we cannot reject it as incorrect." In fact, the numbers came from a Dutch trade mission, and scholars have since rejected them as outrageously incorrect, but no such attempts were made at the time, and for many these numbers represented an accurate picture of Bangkok and Siam.[24]

The issue that concerned observers of the Siamese twins, however, was not the political or economic relationship between Siam and China, nor was it the fact of a Chinese presence in Siam. Rather, the issues at hand were the racial traits—behavioral, cultural, and physical—that distinguished Chinese and Siamese and the indelible mark left on the twins by the fact of their father's birthplace. After all, despite a mother who was born in Siam, despite having lived only in Siam, despite speaking the Siamese language, "the twins [were] in no sense Siamese, except that they were born in Siam."[25]

Distinctions between Chinese and Siamese were real enough, although those drawn by European and American observers—either those who had been to Asia or those who had simply read about it and were now reading these differences onto the twins—rarely had much grounding in fact. Sources agreed that there was a Chinese commercial elite, whose hardworking members and orderly shops provided a stark contrast to lazy and filthy Siamese. Similarly, European and American observers noted that the Chinese avoided corvée labor through the payment of a tax every three years, while Siamese subjects to the crown had to serve a lord at least three months every year. In truth, though, there was no monolithic "Chinese" in Siam and no monolithic "Siamese." In class terms, there were, very roughly speaking, two divisions of Chinese in Siam. Those who experienced great economic success were able to penetrate the Siamese social and economic order, taking a position near the top, either as members of the court or as masters or lords in the corvée labor system. They typically assumed Siamese ways and eschewed Chinese ways in such acts as cutting off their queues. Chinese who remained in ethnic enclaves, who did not necessarily learn the Siamese language, and who kept their pigtails were not as successful economically, although they were able to use their Chineseness to remain outside the Siamese system of corvée labor.[26]

Despite their ability to speak Siamese, the twins apparently came from this latter group. The meaning of this group's Chinese identity is not clear. It is possible that their Chineseness was a prized identity, their pigtails a sign of loyalty to their emperor, their continued use of a Chinese dialect a nod to their heritage.[27] It is also possible that their Chineseness was imposed upon them by Siam's rulers, that their pigtails were a marker of a different status, that their regional dialects symbolized also a decentralized identity, and that their continued isolation from Siamese ways was the price they paid for their independence from forced labor.[28] In either case, some Chinese did strip themselves of their Chinese identity—and cut the queue—to join the sakdina order, both as masters and laborers, and some Siamese did don the queue, with the knowledge of the kingdom's rulers, and opt out of the Siamese labor system, instead paying the triennial tax while also losing the protection of their master.

All of this suggests a level of fluidity—racial, cultural, or economic—that most discussions of Chinese in Siam have not acknowledged, a shortcoming that has also characterized representations of the Siamese twins.[29] Under shifting guises of economic status, clothing fashions, hairstyles, and tattoos or bracelets, Chinese became Siamese and Siamese became Chinese, but acceptance of an in-between status was very rare within the Siamese context. Meanwhile, Europeans saw the fluidity of Siamese society, but they did not accept the changes in social status so readily. Siamese did not become Chinese but rather mimicked a higher race. The Chinese possessed "industry, . . . superior intelligence, and knowledge of the arts," wrote one

British observer. "It is to the Chinese nation that they [the Siamese] are indebted for whatever knowledge they possess." And Chinese did not become Siamese but rather degraded themselves by adopting the habits of a lower people. These Chinese "delight to live in wretchedness and filth and are very anxious to conform to the vile habits of the Siamese."[30]

Did clothes make the man? Or did physical characteristics more accurately reflect his nature? Could a claim for certain status be based on lineage and the presence of distinguished blood in one's veins? Or did prestige flow only from the power dynamics of the present, from the respect one demanded as a matter of course? Rather than seek answers that featured nuanced complexity, the American public paid attention to simplistic views that drew broad distinctions between racial groups or nations—Siamese versus Chinese versus Europeans, for instance. Crude considerations such as these certainly resembled discussion about the twins. Two examples of the forms these articulations took emerged from the 1822 Crawfurd mission, each of which received play in American newspapers and appeared on the shelves of American booksellers. In the eyes of these Western observers, the commercial success and privilege enjoyed by the Chinese rested on a civilizational superiority that often found articulation in descriptions of their physical qualities.

The memoirs of George Finlayson, who served as surgeon on the Crawfurd mission, appeared in 1826. Finlayson described a great Mongol race, to which belonged the Chinese and also the people of Ava and Pegu, Cambodia, Cochin China, and Siam. (To these he also added Malays.) In all things, the Chinese were the "prototype of the whole race," and the rest were copies, but with clear deviations and of lesser quality.[31]

As for the Siamese appearance, while it did not "possess, in the most acute degree, the peculiar features of the original"—that is, the Chinese— "they are at least stamped with traits sufficiently just to entitle them to be considered as copies." The Siamese were, in other words, a duller replica of the Chinese. This dulled nature extended to commerce, culture, and physical appearance. It meant that the Chinese, on the one hand, were taller (though shorter than the Europeans), their skin was of a lighter color (though yellow), their physique was more muscular (though lacking the "hardness" and "elasticity" of Europeans), and their facial features more "acute." The Siamese, on the other hand, were shorter, darker, and fatter, and they had "moderately linear" facial features.[32]

For Finlayson, these physical features carried the most significance, and this significance related closely to British interests in the region. The

Siamese, he said, had foreheads that were broad laterally but narrow vertically, cheekbones that were "large, wide, and prominent," and lower jaws of "uncommon breadth." Indeed, the Siamese, according to Finlayson, appeared to be malformed. "The head is peculiar," he wrote, and while the facial features were uncommonly large—the size of the lower jaw made it appear that the Siamese "were all affected with a slight degree of *goiter*"—the diameter from the top of the head to the nape of the neck was uncommonly short, "nearly a straight line." And while their trunks were square and their bodies stout, their arms were "uncommonly long" and "rather disproportionate in length to the body." Their form and their frame suggested their physical aptitude for toilsome labor but a mental propensity for laziness.[33]

Finlayson's methods drew on the emerging sciences of physiognomy and phrenology, taught since the turn of the century at medical colleges in Britain and becoming popularized in the 1820s. People in these disciplines, along with anatomists and natural scientists, tried to determine— and rank—the characteristics of men and women through the observation and measurement of facial features and the shape and size of skulls (and, hence, brains). Practitioners stated explicitly their intentions to determine the dispositions of nations through comparative examination of these features, and scholars today recognize the racialized nature of the endeavor; too often, head measurements simply served to reinforce previously held stereotypes.[34] Yet medical men themselves could not reach a consensus as to the racial implications of these sciences. Some, such as Crawfurd, who trained as a surgeon, dismissed these "structural" examinations in favor of something more readily apparent: skin color.

"Writers on the natural history of man, judging from the remote analogy of plants, have been disposed to undervalue colour as a discriminating character of the different races," he wrote in his journal, which was published in 1828 and excerpted widely in the United States starting in 1829, coincidentally just as the twins reached American shores. "But still I am disposed to consider it as intrinsic, obvious, and permanent a character, as the form of the skull, or any other which has been more relied upon." Then he proceeded to describe the color of the Siamese. "Their complexion is a light brown, perhaps a shade lighter than that of the Malays, but many shades darker than that of the Chinese. It never approaches to the black of the African negro or Hindoo." He did not actually state here the significance of these colors, but in other sections, drawings offered a graphic illustration of his proposed racial hierarchy. The Chinese, the lightest skinned, were the most civilized in the region, followed closely (in skin color) by the Annamese, who he said at one time had likely been more similar to other peoples in the region—that is, with darker skin—but who, because of their close contact with and subjugation to the Chinese, had had "stamped upon [them] to so great a degree the type of the Chinese character." The Siamese, "one of the most considerable and civilized of the group of nations inhabiting the tropical regions, lying between Hindostan and China," were next, alongside the Burman and Peguan. Then came the Cambodian, Lao, and Arakanese and, last, the Kyen, Karian, Law'a, K'ha, Chong, and Moi, of a "savage or half-savage state," and who are drawn as such, rivaling Africans for darkest.[35]

The earliest descriptions of the twins revealed the variety of ways in which Europeans and Americans "read" race. Some attributed physical characteristics to the tropical climate from which they had come, while others described their appearance in terms of deformity and disease. One American publication based out of Boston did not identify any Chinese heritage, saying the Siamese brothers shared a "dark and sallow" complexion, like other "natives of the torrid zone"—fitting easily into earlier descriptions of the Siamese. But then it added that the twins had long hair that was shaven from the top of their head, following "the custom of their country," even though this was not at all the "custom of their country"—Siam. "They resemble the Chinese in their general features; and their country is very near to the Chinese empire," the article concluded.[36]

That initial American reports on the twins commented on their "Chinese complexion and physiognomy" without any elaboration on just what these terms meant reflects a certain inexperience when it came to articulating Chineseness. London papers, covering the twins' arrival in Britain in November 1829, offered a level of description that likely was possible because of the extended history Britain already had in Asia and that Asians had in Britain. The twins spoke a Chinese dialect spoken in Siam, papers reported; one had the features of a "Mongol Tartar," the other not so much; and "the persons of these boys exactly resemble the figures of the Chinese, which may be frequently seen in the shops in London."[37] It would be another several decades before the Chinese population in the United States was significant enough to color the ways that Americans "read" the twins' race. Nevertheless, the specificity of the language produced in England was consumed in the United States.

The discussion of Asian bodies emphasized the distance from the common European body, not only in skin color but also in the shape of the nose and lips, the style of the hair, and the clothes—or lack of clothes—worn. And even though Crawfurd, among others, created an Asian hierarchy in which the Chinese occupied the top position, inhabitants of the Orient occupied a position entirely distinct from, and below, the European. (In another work, for instance, Crawfurd wrote that "whatever is ennobling, or bears the marks of genius and enterprise in the civilization of the Asiatic nations, may be fairly traced to the European race.") And so, when the twins arrived in the West in 1829, first in the United States, then in Britain, discussion of their physical features similarly served to set them apart. Published accounts made clear that this curiosity was both exotic and a freak of nature. "They excite the attention of people here for two reasons," one publication announced. "One is, that they are natives of a very distant country, whose features, and language, and manners, are very different from ours. The other reason is, that these boys are bound or tied together, and have been so from their birth."[38] The question for us is to what extent, and in what ways, were these two reasons connected.

Their Bodies

Phrenology and physiognomy also had an impact on the medical men who examined the twins. John Collins Warren, a renowned American surgeon and the first dean of Harvard Medical School who was also one of the first doctors to examine the twins, wrote that, because of a "malformation," their foreheads were "more elevated" and "less broad" than that of the Chinese. This type of comment speaks to the presence in Warren's mind of a single, ideal type of Chinese physiognomy, and any deviation from this type became a "malformation." But what caused this departure? Was it simply that no two heads are alike? (He noted that the twins, while resembling each other, harbored "various points of dissimilarity" if an observer looked closely enough.) Or was he noticing the mixed-race heritage of the twins, apparently without being aware of it? Or intimating additional defects in these already deformed bodies?[39]

At this stage, nothing indicates that doctors or the public saw the twins' specific physical anomaly, their conjoined state, as racial in any way. Indeed, the occasion of the twins' visit gave medical experts the opportunity to recount earlier instances of conjoined twins, none of whom were Asian, and some of whom were English or Anglo-American. In 1748 and again in 1752, united twins were stillborn in England. Within two weeks of the twins' arrival, American newspapers reported that Cotton Mather and Samuel Sewell had witnessed a similar set of twins conjoined at the chest in Boston in 1713. Mather recorded the "monster" in a letter to the Royal Society;

Sewell memorialized the "rare and awfull sight" in his diary. In this case, as in most others, the children died at birth. It also was not unusual for conjoined twins to be known by some national nomenclature. The "Hungarian sisters," joined at the lower part of the back, lived for twenty-two years, from 1701 to 1723, which, at the time of Chang's and Eng's arrival, was longer than the brothers had been alive. In March 1829, just one month before the twins left Siam for the United States, conjoined twins were born in Sardinia, and by May their father planned to take them to Milan, then Geneva. They died a year later, in France. "In the Philosophical Transactions and various other works," Warren wrote, "a multitude of similar monstrosities are recorded; most of them born dead, or dying soon after birth."[40]

The twins' longevity, in an age when newspapers proliferated more than ever before and improved transportation enabled wide dispersal of information, meant that they soon came to provide an easy frame of reference to articulate future conjoined births. In October 1829, just two months after the twins were introduced to the American public, reports used the phrase "like the Siamese boys" to describe conjoined twin girls born in Ohio. (The girls lived two days.) This phrasing—it would eventually evolve to "like the Siamese twins"—became common to illustrate such births, although it would take decades until conjoined twins came to be called "Siamese twins" outright. Nevertheless, the twins' arrival in the United States reinforced claims that the Orient was home to all kinds of freaks of nature or monsters. Race, or nationality, was often viewed as implicit with deformity. Just as Finlayson had used a physical deformity—goiter—to describe the facial features of the Siamese, some people argued that the twins' deformity was more common in Asia. In 1830, the *Edinburgh Journal of Science* reported that, "especially in the East, . . . *lusus naturae* are, perhaps, more frequent than in other parts of the world." To support this claim, the journal referred to a pair of twins joined at the chest that a British colonial official had encountered in India in 1807.[41]

Illustrations of the twins also highlighted their exoticness, Chinese-ness, or otherness, by featuring long hair braided into wreaths around their heads, loose-fitting costumes made to resemble the clothes worn in their native land, and facial features intended to evoke images of the Chinese but, across the various pictures, displaying such a variety of looks that clearly they were based on the artists' imagination and not the originals. Naturally enough, these images, intended to attract attention to the twins and draw in visitors, sell pamphlets, and cash in on these Oriental commodities, highlighted the twins' connection. This ligature, however, did not present itself to graphic illustration. It was, after all, simply a band of flesh that attached each to the other. The first illustration of the twins, a crude lithograph that accompanied a doctor's report on the twins, left much to the imagination. Although it was reproduced with some regularity, in an era before photographs, verbal descriptions provided greater details for those who had no opportunity to see the twins.[42]

To provide the most authoritative description, Abel Coffin employed doctors. Medical men examined the twins, often in very intimate and invasive ways, then vouched for the authenticity of the deformity in widely reprinted pamphlets and letters to newspapers. These reports often became part of the advertisements for the twins' exhibitions. As part of this publicity function, experts invariably attested to the harmlessness of the twins, that women and children could view them safely without harm or offense. Yet these examinations offered medical specialists the opportunity to study a condition that, while with precedent, had not been studied with any thoroughness. For these men, the twins offered a chance to bring their disparate expertise together and postulate about a condition they had never seen and, without killing the twins, could not fully confirm. And, unlike consideration of the brothers as Chinese, which seemed to deny the possibility of acceptance as equal beings, they at least asked the question, Could these "monstrous" twins become "normal" individuals?

Fittingly, newspapers gave the most colloquial articulation of the twins' condition. Initial reports described the connecting substance itself simply as about four inches long. As medical reports entered the media, though, it became clear the band was not uniformly so; along the top, it was only about two inches long, while the bottom edge ran about five inches long. From top to bottom, it measured about four inches, and from front to back about two. The band's top emerged from the area of their lower breastplate, and the bottom emerged from around their stomach. Some described it as having an hourglass shape, and others compared it in size to a man's hand. The connective tissue was covered by skin, "exhibiting the same external appearance as the rest of the skin." It showed no discoloration or blemishes, save for a single umbilicus, which the two brothers shared, and which was "with curious precision . . . an equal distance between the two bodies." (The thrill of two men sharing a single navel was amplified by reports that this, too, was malformed, bearing "little resemblance to that usually left by division of the umbilicus." It was, instead, longer and more even than doctors had before seen. Perhaps the years of pulling on this connective mass had drawn it out, a journal speculated, or perhaps the Siamese had a different method for removing the umbilical cord than did Americans.)[43]

The band had some degree of elasticity. Even though the natural position for the twins was face to face, they were able to walk, stand, and sleep side by side. Yet, at the same time, most reports made the point that the band itself was very hard, "apparently bony or cartilaginous"—other newspapers used the word "gristle." "Nevertheless," one reporter wrote, "it has nothing of the dried feel of parchment, or a feverish surface, but the soft and natural feeling of flesh in healthful circulation."[44]

What actually was inside the band, however, was a matter of great debate for medical professionals. Just as early observers used their understandings of the Chinese and the Siamese and the European to name the characteristics they believed the twins ought and ought not to possess, doctors used their experience with normal and abnormal anatomies to postulate what the structure of the band contained. Breastbone appeared to give way to ensiform cartilage along the top of the band, similar to a rib. Where the cartilage from each met in the middle, it gave way to ligaments at a joint that could flex up and down, back and forth. When the twins faced each other, causing the band to be at its loosest, doctors who placed one hand above the curvature where the ligaments met and placed another hand below found that by pressing the hands toward each other they were almost able to come together. The cartilage that ran across the top of the band was concave, and under the cartilage ran a cord that seemed to connect the twins internally. "There can be no doubt of a communication of some sort between the two boys through the internal part of this ligament," doctors reported, but none of the medical men "could discover the least pulsation in it—a fact which negatives the possibility of arterial communication."[45]

This question of circulation between the two brothers drove one line of inquiry, which was largely experimental. Running a battery of exams, the doctors postulated that, at some level, something must pass between the twins. Two examiners from New York believed that a canal in the band "communicated" with the abdominal cavities of both brothers. George Buckley Bolton, their personal physician in London, argued that capillary blood vessels from each "unquestionably inosculate" in the band, concluding that it was obvious that some diseases and medicines would pervade both twins. Warren, in Boston, was more circumspect. "There is, no doubt, a network of blood vessels, lymphatics and some minute nerves passing from one to the other," he wrote. "How far these parts are capable of transmitting the action of medicines, and of diseases, and especially of what particular medicines, and what diseases, are points well worthy of investigation." He speculated that diseases that could spread through absorbent or capillary blood vessels—such as deadly poisons, syphilis, cowpox, and smallpox—would pass easily from one to the other.[46]

Bolton undertook experiments designed to see the extent to which the twins' bodies communicated through their common bond. Hoping to find the point where the inosculation of one with the other took place, Bolton made a series of punctures with a needle into the band; he discovered that both boys drew away from the punctures at the middle of the band, whereas at half an inch or more from the center, only the twin on that side felt the pain. He concluded that the skin that the twins shared covering the band "maintain[ed] a sensitive communication with each of the two youths," that both twins shared certain "distempers" even as they maintained "peculiarities" between the two of them. He also inferred that similar communication between small arteries and veins likely occurred. Another of his tests showed that when one brother experienced a sour taste in his mouth, the other did as well, proving "that the galvanic influence passes from one individual to the other, through the band which connects their bodies." Bolton also learned, however, that the distinctive smell that marked the urine of people who consume asparagus only affected the urine of that twin who ate asparagus, revealing that "the sanguineous communication between the united twins is very limited."[47]

Doctors in New York and London, hoping to learn something of the canal they believed existed in the band, observed that every time one of the twins coughed or exerted himself, a "protrusion of viscera," or a hernia, occupied almost half of the cavity.[48] That this portion of internal organ—possibly intestine, liver, stomach, or spleen because all these occupied places close to the opening—penetrated the connective band gave doctors pause about the other key question that guided their examinations: Could the twins be separated? Or, put another way, should the twins be separated? The differences between these two questions came to represent diverse approaches to articulating their condition, differences between the physical and the metaphysical, between medicine and philosophy.

The medical cases made both for keeping the twins as they were or for separating them were exercises in speculative medicine. None of the doctors had before examined any other conjoined twins, and the descriptions of the band's interior were made solely on the sensory information gained by pokes and prods and by the application of knowledge of the human anatomy to these two bodies that, clearly, deviated from the anatomical norm. The earliest medical discussions on the ability to separate the twins produced no consensus. Warren wrote that there was nothing to indicate that an operation to separate the twins would prove fatal. There might be complications—he specifically identified the probability that the perito-neum might extend from abdomen to abdomen—but even these would not be too dangerous. Nevertheless, he said, separation at this point in time was unwarranted.[49] Samuel Latham Mitchill, a well-known New York physician and former U.S. congressman, posited that a canal existed in the band and strongly argued that separation would put the brothers' lives at risk. Using the findings from his coughing experiments, he argued that cutting the band would clear "a large opening . . . into the belly of each, that would ex-pose them to enormous hernial protrusions, and inflammations that would certainly prove fatal."[50]

Another New York physician, who represented himself as the "Special Correspondent of the Medical Society of Paris," used these findings to try to undermine the conclusions of Mitchill. In short, Felix Pascalis argued that, if there was an open canal between the twins as Mitchill suggested, the weight and pressure produced by two abdomens on the one channel would already have produced the very type of debilitating hernia that was feared, that in such a case the common band would show signs of distress and the twins would suffer physical ailments—flatulency, pain when touched, ir-regular bowel movements, vomiting—which they did not and never had. Pascalis was arguing, in effect, that the twins' physical well-being was evi-dence that the twins could be separated and that, to preserve this strong health, it was necessary at the least to prepare both the twins and the care-takers for such a separation, if only to be undertaken upon the death of one. In reaching these conclusions, Pascalis drew not only on the initial report of Warren and the observations of Mitchill but also on a litany of anatomical studies done by earlier physicians and surgeons. To explain the presence of the connective band, the bodies' relations with this band, and the produc-tion of Mitchill's "mistaken" hernial tumor, what Pascalis called simply an "increase of bulk and hardness," Pascalis turned to published studies on dissection, anatomy, and mycology. Mitchill and fellow New York physi-cian William Anderson responded in a letter to the French academy that was published in exhibition pamphlets on the English tour, and in their response they, too, used medical literature to defend their position that the risk of an umbilical hernia was too great.[51]

In London, the twins again came under a battery of medical exams from a small army of medical specialists—thirteen named, with the acknowledgment that there were others. In the lead was Sir Astley Cooper, the "Great Lion of British Surgery," whose research Mitchill had used in his exploration of the dangers of umbilical hernias and who, in fact, had trained Mitchill; Sir Henry Halford, physician to the king; and Mr. Thomas, the president of the Royal College of Physicians. To some observers, the litany of medical prognoses had become comical. The "most amusing (often ludicrous) questions and observations of the physicians and metaphysicians, who thought themselves entitled to take a lead in the investigation," served more to distract attention away from larger, philosophical questions: "Some really supposed, that although each has a brain, there is only one sensorium; that there is a vascular connection between the two hearts by means of the band; that nutrition is conveyed from one to the other, and consequently that it is only necessary for one to take food. Some were of opinion that a division of the cord in the centre would be attended with no risk; while others considered the band in the light of an umbilical hernia, and consequently that a division would necessarily prove fatal."[52]

In short, these "experts" engaged in whimsical speculations only to reach contradictory conclusions. Nevertheless, their proclamations received wide play in American newspapers. Cooper, for one, declared that it was ill-advised to attempt to separate the two. He posited this based on his belief that a separation could prove fatal, on the good health that the twins shared, and, wryly, on the business concerns of Abel Coffin: "'Depend on it,' continued Sir Astley in his playful manner, 'those boys will fetch a vast deal more money while they are together than when they are separate.'"[53]

The twins had become part of a heated medical debate, one that borrowed from earlier medical cases to articulate the nature of the twins' physical attachment and on which medical specialists were staking their reputations. Alas, for them, redemption could occur only upon the death of the twins, which would not happen for more than forty years. So, in the meantime, they fulfilled the roles entrusted to them by Abel Coffin.

Their Souls

Cooper offered another reason to keep the twins together, one that reflected not so much physical concerns but psychological or philosophical: "Why separate them—the boys seem perfectly happy as they are."[54] The medical debate was also a philosophical debate; the physiological, psychological; the physical, metaphysical. And while the medical debate necessarily had relied on medical expertise for its grist, the philosophical debate at times became an unruly free-for-all.

Of course, physicians had their say. Felix Pascalis, the most vocal proponent of surgically separating the twins, said the twins' state caused him anguish. "Among the subjects of natural curiosity which are derived from the animated creation," he wrote, "none could excite more really painful feelings of pity than the contemplation of these ill-fated fellow creatures." Though he recognized their shared humanity, he counted them among the most unfortunate, deprived of experience of individual humans. Mitchill felt differently. "They are so perfectly satisfied with their condition, that nothing renders them so unhappy as the fear of a separation by any surgical operation; the very mention of it causes immediate weeping." Whereas Pascalis believed that the twins' condition imprisoned them, Mitchill thought that separating them, while extremely hazardous to their physical well-being, would also deny them free will. "It has been urged by many that they ought to be disconnected," he wrote. "We think such an opinion is incorrect. It cannot . . . be done without their consent. To this they are totally opposed."[55]

Some of the questions that the existence of the twins appeared ready to answer were specific to the twins. Were they of one mind or two? A single soul or separate? In these inquiries, examiners read the mind almost invariably through the body. To a large extent, a language barrier existed. On more than one occasion, a medical examiner lamented the fact that the twins did not (yet) speak English (or Latin or Greek). When questions were asked of the twins, they communicated through the Siamese interpreter who had traveled with them, or one of their managers—Coffin, Hunter, or Hale—spoke for them.[56] Instead, most observers drew conclusions about the twins' minds and characters through the twins' actions.

In those instances that an author emphasized the oneness of the two, there were plenty of anecdotes about one twin reacting when the other was touched or otherwise engaged. Tickling one of them resulted in the other demanding a stop to it; the toothache of one kept the other awake; one would not eat food that the other disliked.[57] But for those authors who wanted to emphasize difference, there were just as many anecdotes to offer. A whisper in one's ear was not heard by the other; smelling salts placed under the nose of one aroused only curiosity in the brother; one did not feel when the other's arm was pinched.[58]

More often, reports highlighted the twins' grace of movement to suggest some element of single-mindedness. This grace was an important part of their earliest shows, during which they performed somersaults and back-flips. "I expected to see them pull on the cord in different directions, as their attention was attracted by different objects," an early visitor wrote. Instead their movements were harmonious, apparently "influenced by the same wish." They moved about "with great facility," eating, drinking, and sleeping at the same time, seemingly "actuated . . . by one mind." They learned to play chess quickly—this, too, became a part of their show, as they invited volunteers from the audience to play against them—and sometimes, when playing a third person, they completed each other's moves without discussion, appearing to have the same plans. But when they played against each other, "so strong is their habit of co-acting, that such games go on with less freedom." They frequently spoke at the same moment, saying the same thing, but they rarely spoke to each other; "it seems as if they could almost read each other's thoughts, without the use of words." Another writer said the twins' "perfect concert of action was as if they possessed one volition, and one soul. Whatever the one wished to perform seemed strangely to originate contemporaneously in the purpose of the other."[59]

Yet, perhaps because their actions seemed almost always to be in concert, the occasional slips, when one body went one way and the other went another way, spoke loudest to observers that these young men were of separate minds. In such instances, "the total independence of the volition of the one brother upon that of the other could not be more strikingly exemplified."[60]

This proof of each brother's individuality seemed to relieve the various observers, for it confirmed something that they believed they saw in the brothers' faces and eyes. "They have volitions, as independent and distinct, as any two other individuals," one observer wrote. "To look in their faces is to be convinced of this." Many observers made similar remarks. One of the faces appeared stronger and healthier, the other gloomier. Most reports did not identify which of the two went with which description; indeed, the twins remained largely nameless in these early months and years. Only the report of Bolton in London made clear that Chang was favored with stronger physical health, even though Chang's spine was considerably curved because his arm was constantly flung over Eng's shoulder. Bolton said their intellectual abilities were equal, citing their shared skill at chess. Others said the more robust twin appeared intellectually superior to his brother, in large part because he generally did the speaking for the pair. So it caused great interest when the "superior brother" acquiesced to the impulses of the "inferior brother," as if patronizing him. The weaker of the two "then playfully leans against his mate for support, or the one pats the cheek or presses the forehead, or adjusts the shirt collar of the other, in such a way as betrays the kindliest feelings in each, and the tenderest affection for each other."[61] Not only were the two brothers distinct individuals, but a clear hierarchy also existed between them, and observers placed the actions of each into a relationship of superior and subordinate that made sense in a paternalistic society. The superior twin engaged with the world, offered support to his brother, and tolerated his whims. The inferior brother did not speak out of turn and made appropriate gestures of affection and gratitude.

Nevertheless, the general acceptance that these were two individuals made it all the more necessary to explain how they could be so similar, how they came to share such a keen understanding of each other's will. Warren argued that their united actions were "a habit formed by necessity." At one point, he said, their wills and corresponding actions probably did clash, but through years of the most intimate contact, they had simply learned to read each other. This was at once a confirmation of the individual but also of the role that environment played, a reminder that the human will, and a human's life, was very much bound to one's circumstances.[62]

These questions of self and soul were no longer contained solely to the twins. Instead, the issues at stake had a larger relevance for general society. Nature had given them different temperaments, but circumstances compelled that every aspect of their experience was the same. "The consequence is, that two minds are produced in the perpetual equipoise of similar motives and circumstances," wrote one observer. "They become physically and morally the same, with volitions similar and consentaneous."[63] The existence of the twins raised questions that came out of philosophical debates about the human experience.

Their circumstances also raised questions about how their minds and souls might be improved, in what way, and by whom. Most observers noted favorably that the handlers, sometimes anonymous, sometimes identified as Coffin, Hunter, or Hale, offered instruction in the English language and in other facets of Anglo-American customs and culture.[64] But what about religion? After all, Coffin had brought not only the twins but also a call for Christian missionaries to descend upon Siam. Were the twins receiving religious instruction in Protestant America and England? Newspaper reports acknowledged that some people felt the twins' religious education was lacking, but they often made light of attempts to convert the twins. For example, American papers reprinted widely a British report about a visitor to the twins who believed more should be done to instruct the twins about religion: "In his investigation of their condition, he asked, 'Do you know where you would go if you were to die?' To which they replied quickly, pointing up with their fingers, 'Yes, yes, up dere.' Their saintly friend, unluckily for himself, persevered in catechizing; and questioned them: 'Do you know where I should go, if I were to die?' to which they as promptly answered, pointing downwards, 'Yes, yes, down dere.' We are afraid that the laugh which followed was likely to efface the memory of the well-meant attempt to imbue their minds with Christian knowledge."[65]

There are multiple avenues of intended humor in the passage. First, there is the representation of the twins' speech; yes, they were learning English, but the result was not quite proper. Second, there is the possibility of confusion on the part of the twins, with their having who goes where all mixed up. Of course, the "saintly friend" should go "up dere"—to heaven—upon death, and the unconverted heathen should go "down dere"—to hell. If the twins were confused, though, and their guest did not know it, then he might take offense, in which case he also became a butt of the joke. But there is also the possibility within this avenue of humor that the twins were *not* confused, that they actually meant that they would go to heaven and their visitor to hell, thus suggesting an underlying tension that the twins meant to insult the man. (The preceding passage in the article had the twins getting cheeky with their English instructor.) Any of these possibilities relied on the contested space between heaven and hell. Third, there was a possible cross-cultural misunderstanding of which the reporter might have been making light. As much of the travel writing about Siam made clear, death rites there included cremation (even among most Chinese), which released the soul from the dead body to go "up dere"; in Britain (and America), the dead were buried "down dere." All of these intended avenues of humor pervaded the passage and provided a laugh for the reader. They also suggested, however, the limitations and perhaps the futility of meaningful communication and conversion, of translation and transformation, across cultural lines.

Nevertheless, some Christians expressed concern for the state of the twins' souls and for what the failure to convert them might say about Americans. "What real benefit [have] these immortal souls acquired" from their visit to "this Christian land" of America, a correspondent of the *Christian Watchman* asked. Did the "all-wise God [who] so formed these heathen" cause them to come to America only to gratify the idle curiosity of onlookers and bring profits to those who handled them? Looking ahead to the day when the twins would surely return to Siam, the writer argued that this was the time to imbue them with a love and understanding of Christianity that they could then pass on to others back home. The obstacle, in the writer's eyes, was not the incapability of the twins to accept such teaching. Rather, the obstacles were the Christians and missionary boards who did not accept such a responsibility and the anticipated "reproach and persecution from the idlers whose curiosity leads them to lounge around these youths." The presence of the twins in America and England had brought out the worst in some, but this was not inevitable, and it could be stopped. The reward would be "the satisfaction of seeing two of His spiritual children go forth as able and faithful apostles to Siam."[66] This did not happen, but the author's embrace of the twins' souls as being open to understanding and exchange with the West bore similarities to views expressed by some journalists, doctors, and philosophers who also were trying to find meaning in the twins' presence.

Just three weeks after the twins arrived in Massachusetts, the *Boston Galaxy* printed an irreverent meditation on the twins and their impact on American society. The twins, "condemned" to a lifetime stuck together, to "live in a manner alone in the community without the benefits of individuality or the prerogatives of single gentlemen," posed three "knotty questions" that vexed theologians, metaphysicians, and lawyers. What would happen, the article asked, if one twin converted to Christianity, whereas the other remained Buddhist? What would happen if one twin were indicted for a crime but the other brother was innocent? And how did the twins complicate the great philosophical questions of what's what and who's who? "If Chang and his brother were cut assunder would ye dare even assert that idem est idem?"[67]

It is necessary to note that this article was over the top and not to be taken without several grains of salt. It was trying to have fun, at the expense of philosophers, theologians, lawyers, and the twins. The article's main points deserve serious consideration, however, for two related reasons. First, this article raised these concerns for the first time and as such was a creative act, an original attempt to come to terms with the twins' circumstances. Second, these concerns, however lighthearted, reflected the questions of many people who went to see the twins, which was evidenced by the volume of imitators who asked these very questions and similar others again and again over the next forty-plus years: What would happen if one twin killed a man and the other remained wholly innocent? What would a train conductor do if only one twin paid his fare and the other refused? And what if one twin tried to join the Union army and the other the Confederate? In short, what weight did the position of the individual, a person's free will, carry when that individual was irrevocably bound to another? And, in a society marked by the institutions of slavery, coverture, and federalism and one increasingly racked by sectional differences and occupied with debates over states' rights versus national power, the twins offered a metaphor through which to explore these issues.[68]

Thinking not in terms of metaphors but rather with the aim to advance human knowledge through empirical means, philosopher George Tucker laid out a very clear research proposal to interrogate the opposition between external influences and inherent natural sensibilities. Writing under the pen name "Q" in the *Virginia Literary Museum*, Tucker hoped to demonstrate that men were born with innate differences, that humans were not solely a product of their education or their environment. He proposed a study that placed examiners on either side of the twins, whispering into each twin's ears identical questions that tested their memories, the associations they drew with certain words, and their reasoning faculties. Scholars could analyze the answers to see whether these two men, whose upbringing and experiences had been virtually identical, exhibited stark differences in mental powers. Similarly, hoping to strike a blow against phrenologists, he suggested that further experiments might reveal significant differences in character and personality despite relatively identical features of the head. In essence, Tucker hoped to show that nature played a greater role than nurture in determining a person's inner world but that these natural characteristics were not restricted to specific racial or national groups. Rather, within each group—indeed, between two conjoined twins—individuals could exhibit starkly different personalities and sensibilities. In short, Tucker saw potential in the twins to draw conclusions about humankind.[69] Such grandiose designs were, of course, at the heart of the enterprise of discovery and conquest that drove the expansion of Western imperialism, science, and knowledge in the early nineteenth century; the West depended upon the Orient for self-definition.

In the exuberance to find significance in the twins, journalists, missionaries, and scientists no doubt romanticized the brothers and the paths to enlightenment they offered. By divorcing the twins' inner worlds—their minds, their sensibilities, and their souls—from the physical constraints of race and deformity, commentators hoped to gain insights into the challenges and obstacles that they faced themselves. There appeared in much of the literature surrounding the twins' arrival in the United States and in England an overwhelming sense that their happiness, their innocence, and their harmony represented something larger. Certainly, on the one hand, they were the docile native, eager to adopt a new language, learn new games, submit themselves trustingly into the hands of their keeper. They signified to their Anglo-American audience that the West was best. But on the other hand, there was a compelling desire among many observers to find significance for their own lives, not validation but insight: "You feel at the sight, as if you contemplated a new tenure of existence, which might, perhaps, [throw] light on the master secret of our being; and the mind of the beholder teems with impressions, that light will somehow be elicited from their case, in relation to the mysterious tenure of that union of vital and intellectual action, which we call life. It seems as if, were they possessed of our combinations of thought, and our modes of explaining them, they could tell something, the one of what consciousness is in the other. But the more we examine, the more we are convinced, that shadows and darkness still envelop this subject."[70] In many respects, the twins proved to be a blank slate on which various interests inscribed their causes. In other respects, the twins seemed a dark unknowable.

Our Worlds

One month after the twins arrived in the United States, someone going by the name "David B. Slack" penned a stinging criticism of those hoping to find greater meaning in the twins. "The world has profited but little by wonders of any kind, either in story or in fact," he wrote. "Our feelings, perhaps, properly enough, impel us to see and hear such things at almost any price; but what reason deduces from them, is so inapplicable to the ordinary course of nature, that they are unprofitable objects of study." The brothers, he wrote, were *lusus naturae*, tricks of nature, anomalies, deviations, sources of amusement that depressed and weakened the mind, not models for enlightenment. Embedded in Slack's criticism was the same logic that privileged stark divisions among humans and understood difference as a wall to be breached at our own peril; bringing assorted varieties of people together—even if only to study them—held the potential not for progress but for degeneracy. Slack also invoked race to bolster his argument. The twins' countenances successfully hid their true feelings, and their color prevented "us from observing a thousand differences we should see if they were English." The twins were unknowable, unreadable, and unimportant. Indeed, he concluded, these "Siamese boys" held no more significance for human society than did a double-yolked egg.[71]

In some respects, David B. Slack was not wrong. These were two young men, far from home, with no ties to America and minimal English language skills. Physicians studied the deformity hoping to learn about the human body. Philosophers pondered the insights into human nature the brothers provided. How could these brothers tell us anything about our own world, our own bodies, or our own minds? And yet, a double-yolked egg never inspired thousands of observers, hundreds of newspaper articles, or a dozen medical reports, whereas the Siamese twins did in their first year away from home alone.

The preponderance of the written documentation that exists from that first year abroad show attempts in one way or another to name the discursive and material worlds of the twins. The meditations gave shape to the land from which the twins came, colored in the race to which the twins belonged, and set the features of their faces, their hair, and their bodies. They adorned the bodies with specific clothing, articulated certain mannerisms, and attributed an array of characteristics—physical and metaphysical—to the twins. In so doing, the authors of these documents were naming their own worlds, identifying those attributes and sensibilities that were important to them, that served to define their interests and motivations and to make others—outsiders—intelligible.

Naming the twins—articulating and attaching meaning to perceived racial, national, and anomalous characteristics of their physical appearance, their habitual behaviors, and their inner thoughts—provided specialists and laypeople with coordinates to address ambivalent spaces that lay between dichotomous categories such as self and other, nature and nurture, civilized and savage. And unlike my discussion here, naming the twins' worlds did not occur in neat, discrete divisions between origins, bodies, and souls. All three were closely related; the constitution of one served indelibly to constitute the others. And the act of naming these worlds fell to broad swathes of a transatlantic Anglo-American society, to merchants and sea captains, doctors and missionaries, wordsmiths and artists.

The impact of the twins on the way Anglo-Americans articulated their own worlds was widely felt. The physical anomaly provided a symbol that could be put to immediate use. As we have already seen, the twins were used as shorthand to describe other people similarly conjoined. Additionally, the twins became a metaphor to describe the lingering effects of marriages of convenience, suggesting a close relationship that was useful if not entirely favorable but that, if it fell apart, would prove fatal to an important cause held dear.[72] Meanwhile, the twins were often invoked as part of U.S. relations with Siam. They became a useful point of reference between Siamese and American visitors and also provided American visitors to Siam with a chance to articulate the experience of being a lone white body among a village full of Chinese or Siamese. An American missionary invoked the twins to relate a trip he took to a village along Siam's eastern seaboard in 1835, just six years after the pair had entered the American arena. "We had not been in the place ten minutes before we had attracted around us hundreds of men, women, and children, who were more eager to examine us than Americans were to examine the Siamese twins," Dan Beach Bradley wrote. "Probably the face of a white man has never been seen in this village before."[73]

While the twins themselves may not have offered insights into human nature, they nevertheless shaped the world. They provided different ways for people to think about and to speak about the body and the mind, relationships and experiences, ideas and feelings. Where they went, the ripples remained long after. But the ways in which observers named the worlds of the Siamese twins also had a significant impact on the twins themselves. Despite Edward W. Said's contention that "texts can *create* . . . the very reality they appear to describe," the passivity, servility, and helplessness often ascribed to In and Chun, or Chang and Eng, as part of a racial, paternalistic discourse of imperialism had a discernible impact on the twins as they struggled to name their own worlds.[74]

CHAPTER TWO

Under Their Own Direction

Traveling in Virginia in March 1832, Chang and Eng found themselves at the center of a public debate. The twins and their manager, Charles Harris, petitioned the state's General Assembly to exempt them from an exhibition tax that they claimed would erase any profits they might earn. The finance committee reported favorably on the request, but when the house at large took up the matter, discussion quickly turned to consideration of the twins' status. "One member got up, stating that if the House considered themselves doing any thing to favor the Twins by [lifting] the tax, they [would] be mistaken for it would only do good to some fellow in one of the Eastern States who had bought them of their Mother," Harris wrote of the affair.[1] A similar experience occurred a few days later in Norfolk, when a newspaper reported that the twins' mother had sold them to Robert Hunter and Abel Coffin, the men responsible for taking them from Siam to the United States.

The episodes left the twins shaken. Their trip to the Old Dominion, it seemed, had thrown them squarely into an inverted sectional debate over slavery: If Virginia complied with the twins' request, would it be enriching a northern slaveholder at the expense of its own citizens? The twins occupied an ambiguous position. Their life on the road, performing in exhibitions designed to show off their exoticness in a parlor setting that embodied familiarity, necessitated a certain script they had to follow, a specific type of interaction they could enter into with other people, and an acceptance of laws and customs that governed the ways in which they could act. In a very real sense, the twins had become objectified. The volume of representations about them—about their origins, their bodies, and their inner minds and souls—while serving to define Anglo-American society against this "other," had also constructed material obstacles, boundaries that appeared to constrain the ability of the twins to name their own worlds. Episodes in Virginia, Massachusetts, Ohio, and Alabama and with their "owner," Abel Coffin, showed the twins engaging in a series of battles—discursive, legal, and physical—to define the social and cultural spaces they occupied, or at least to shape them in ways that gave them greater mobility and opportunities.

Chang, Eng, and Harris, for example, saw Virginia's exhibition tax as a challenge both to their ability to travel around the state to earn a living and to their vision of what their performances—and the twins, themselves— were and were not. The tax—a licensing fee of thirty dollars to be paid by "every exhibitor of a show" in every county, city, or borough where the exhibition took place—was a single item in a general "Act imposing taxes for the support of government" that ran several pages and included a wide variety of taxes on property, businesses, transactions, and so on. The General Assembly approved the tax act annually—the 1832 version was passed on March 21, coincidentally just one week after the twins' petition—and an item taxing exhibitions had been part of tax acts since 1813.[2]

For the twins, the tax made much of Virginia off-limits. Their performances took two forms. In large cities that could support extended showings, the twins set up shop at a local hotel and received audiences in the hotel parlor for several days, at times a week or longer. In small towns and villages, Harris sent ahead fliers to advertise their pending arrival, and the twins exhibited at a lodging house or inn for one or two nights before moving on to the next small town. In most cases, audiences had to pay a twenty-five-cent admission fee. (Sometimes, the fee was fifty cents.) Having to pay the thirty-dollar exhibition tax at every location was "prohibitory," Harris argued in a memorial to the General Assembly that was signed by "Chang-Eng." While extended showings at a large city might reap a profit of several hundred dollars, lessening the impact of the tax, the income taken at small villages could be as low as single digits and often ranged from ten dollars to thirty dollars. The exhibition tax meant that they might lose money.[3]

Furthermore, they argued, this "Prohibitory Tax" was aimed at "Exhibitions of Jugglers, Sleight-of-hand men & others who might corrupt the public morals of the Community," as well as other exhibitions "of the same class" that brought together "large masses of People in the open Air, and thereby endanger the public peace." In this, Harris perhaps drew on a recent surge in public exhibitions that challenged an emerging bourgeois culture that disparaged public masses and common sensibilities. Harris and the twins took great pains to separate themselves from such riffraff, from exhibitions of dubious value to society. "No injury can possibly arise either to the morals or peace of the Community" from the "assemblage" of such fine people as would visit the room of the twins, they wrote. These united Siamese brothers, after all, afforded people a chance to learn about the wonders of the world, to become educated in the latest knowledge about the human race and the human body. Their presence also provided the opportunity to support these "strangers in the land, far from their own home & laboring under an awful disfiguration of the Supreme Being." The appeal to the state house covered an array of reasons why the twins should receive relief from this tax.[4]

Harris's appeal, in other words, was an attempt to situate the twins favorably alongside a refined way of life based on the form that their entertainment took—forthright and urbane, domesticated to a degree that no one could think it undermined the community's moral standards. The rejection of their appeal, however, was made squarely in terms of the twins' status and race. Were they slaves or not? The assembly's response, that it was not the twins who would suffer but their "Eastern" owner, as well as the treatment they received in the Norfolk newspaper, positioned them in a way not relevant to their conjoinedness but instead to the actions of their mother and, implicitly, the color of their skin.

The problem facing the twins was that the United States of 1832, and of the 1830s generally, was in turmoil, much of it revolving around slavery and ideas of racial equality. Three years before, a free black named David Walker issued his *Appeal to the Colored Citizens of the World*. Underlying his call for blacks to rise up for their lives and liberty was a revolutionary message: Blacks were the intellectual and moral equals of whites. White people had to accept the capacities of black people, and blacks had to convince them of their abilities, first by recognizing that the supposed naturalness of white supremacy was a fallacy and then by becoming educated and skilled. "You have to prove . . . that we are MEN, and not *brutes*," Walker instructed his literate black audience. "Let the aim of your labours . . . be the dissemination of education and religion." This message of racial equality was coming to be embraced by some northern abolitionists, especially those who worked alongside educated intellectuals of color. In January 1831, one of these white reformers, William Lloyd Garrison, published the first issue of the *Liberator* newspaper in Boston, becoming one of the most visible voices for immediate emancipation.[5]

Seven months before the twins made their own claims to moral uprightness, Virginia had been rocked by Nat Turner's slave rebellion, which cost fifty-five white lives and put much of the South on guard. Two months before the twins' appeal to the state assembly, that body had closed the books on a rancorous debate over slavery and emancipation. Unlike arguments coming out of Boston about moral rights and earlier Jeffersonian rhetoric about the humanitarian shortcomings of human bondage, the Virginia slavery debate of 1831–32 considered the question of slavery and emancipation in the context of the economic interests of whites, following in the footsteps of that state's constitutional convention a year before. The debate pitted the interests of nonslaveholding whites in western Virginia, who resented the political might of eastern slaveholders and feared the expansion of slavery through the state, against those of aristocratic planters, who worried that any policy of gradual emancipation and colonization—and that, not immediate emancipation, was the issue at stake—would violate their property rights and their wealth. Unable to reach a compromise, the two sides tabled the discussion in January 1832. The twins' entreaty in March held the potential to aggravate still-fresh wounds, and it, too, was dismissed, notably on grounds that related to the economic welfare of their "owner."[6]

Most likely unaware of the local context—and even if aware of the slavery debate, they and Harris probably did not see its relevance to them—the twins unexpectedly opened up a can of worms with their appeal to the assembly, though the charge itself did not catch them entirely off guard. By the middle of 1832, they had heard for three years the rumors that surrounded their leaving Siam and coming to the West. They knew that some people believed their mother had sold them. But statements on the floor of a government assembly and in the pages of a newspaper for all to read gave such rumors legitimacy in the eyes of the public, which proved too much. "These two incidents have had a very unpleasant effect on Chang-Eng," Harris wrote, "as they feel themselves aggrieved in being made . . . liable to be spoken of as 'slaves' bought and sold."[7]

In Norfolk, the twins confronted a reporter about the article. Surprised at their reaction, the reporter told them the article was the reprint of a medical report by John Collins Warren that had been widely published a couple of years before. This news, again, shook the twins. Was it possible that a doctor they trusted had spread such lies (as they saw it)? From whom had he gotten this information? Abel Coffin? An agitated inquiry to Mrs. Coffin written by Harris on behalf of the twins received in reply a copy of the Warren report. Judging from the impact of this on the twins—it calmed them down—this copy was of the 1829 broadsheet that was released immediately upon their arrival. Unlike a later report published in the *American Journal of the Medical Sciences*, the earlier publication said nothing about the twins having been sold by their mother.[8]

Nevertheless, the sudden recognition of an unflattering discursive representation of themselves and their mother that reportedly came from respected men of science served as a wake-up call to the twins. The incidents in Virginia, building as they did on an accumulation of public articulations of the twins and on their continued touring of an ever-growing list of places, served to galvanize a conflict with the Coffins that would ultimately lead the twins to declare their independence from the man who brought them to the United States. The turn that the battle took—an unanticipated tarring of their reputations and that of their mother—suggests the imposition of certain normative ideas of race that served to constrain or deny their agency; yet it also served as a motivation for the twins to make a greater effort to shape their own worlds, to name their own terms.

Speaking

The twins had left London in the middle of January 1831 and reached New York in early March. They returned from England changed men, in body, mind, and pocketbook. Their appearance was "very much improved"— they had gained weight during the year abroad—and they had learned to read, write, and speak some English. Newspapers reported, without going into specifics, that the "firm" of "Chang Eng & Co." had realized tremendous profits while abroad. Advertisements for their exhibition also used the experience in London to bolster the twins' credibility, and early reports of their return complimented the type of American visitor that the twins attracted. After having been admired by the "honorable," "renowned," and "first classes" of Britain, the twins' receptions or "levees" now drew America's "republican citizens," its "learned," "intelligent," "distinguished," and "venerable" gentlemen, and they were safe for consumption by the nation's ladies.[9]

Such positive imagery was good marketing on the part of Captain Coffin, his wife, Susan, and family friend Captain William Davis, a group the twins called the "Concern."[10] Praising their customers as upstanding citizens reassured other potential visitors that it was acceptable to show interest in these oddities. After all, the act of paying money to stare at someone's physical anomaly might have been regarded by some as a guilty pleasure rather than an honorable practice. Earlier critics made this point clear, criticizing those who called on the twins as giving in to base and idle curiosity. But most reports were not so critical. "They are indeed objects of powerful interest," the *Baltimore Patriot* opined, "and that curiosity is exceedingly pardonable, which profits by the opportunity, and seeks a gratification, in viewing a variety of the works of nature."[11] Furthermore, aiming the marketing campaign at the respectable citizens in society made sense economically; it was these people who would most likely have the means to bring the family at an admission price of twenty-five cents per person and to purchase memorabilia such as exhibition pamphlets and illustrations.

An accumulation of data reveals also that the twins used symbols of class and dignity, of which they became aware during their time in London, to stake out a place in the United States that demanded respect for the brothers as individuals of a certain bearing. The first such example of this representation of self to the world appeared in an interview published in the *New York Constellation* shortly after their return from England. The extended "dialogue" between the twins and a visitor in New York City's American Hotel covered such topics as appropriate terms of address, the prestige that came with charity, and proper ways to exhibit one's body, among other things.[12]

After exhibiting some clever wordplay, something for which the twins became famous, Chang and Eng made their first request in their struggle for respect. After seven exchanges with the visitor, in which the visitor referred to the twins as "boys" five times, Chang asked him to call them the "Siamese youths," and Eng told him not to call them the "Siamese boys":

vis: I beg pardon, gentlemen, for calling you *boys*—but really that is the title by which you are generally addressed is it not?

ch. eng: Never in England—in this country sometimes.

vis: But why not England?

ch: Boy is a boy there—a servant boy—cook boy—school boy—

eng: And a young gentleman is a young gentleman.

vis: Well, I am glad you have set me right in this matter—my mistake was of the head, not of the heart.

ch: Oh yes, I dare say—people don't think when they speak of the Siamese twins that they are young men twenty years of age.

eng: Suppose you call a young gentleman of your acquaintance, boy—won't he resent the insult?

vis: True—true—and why should not the Siamese young gentlemen resent such an epithet?

During their first weeks in the United States almost two years earlier, some reports had infantilized the twins as young children who had been taken from their loving mother by Abel Coffin and placed under his paternalistic care, who ran around ships as if on a playground, and who sassed their teachers as fun-loving schoolboys were wont to do. Illustrations of the twins, furthermore, often featured two young boys.[13] In this interview, the twins strongly protested against these representations on two grounds. First, they made the obvious point that they were twenty years of age. In another year, they would attain their majority, which meant that, legally, they would be adults. Second, and more astutely, they recognized that the term "boy" signaled a power relationship and that being identified as a "boy" placed them on the short end of that stick. Equally significant, however, is the realization that the twins objected to their own subordination, not to the hierarchy itself. In the passages leading up to the one reproduced above, the twins accept without comment the waiter calling them "gentlemen," then they turn around and suggest that their visitor give money to "the first poor boy you meet." Through these exchanges, the twins worked to position themselves among a more privileged group of people. They used the poor and unfortunate as the pivot on which to leverage themselves into a leisured gentlemanly position.

To emphasize their belonging to a higher class, the twins referred to giving money to the less fortunate, each flinging coins to a one-legged man begging for alms on the street. The "cripple," as he was identified by the newspaper, shouted to the twins, "Heaven bless you! kind young gentlemen." "That blessing is certainly worth more than the money I gave the old man," Chang said, while Eng added, "I hope it may make him as happy in receiving as me in giving it." The exchange also highlighted the difference between those unfortunate people who exhibited their bodies on the street for change and the twins, who had commoditized their bodies for a higher rate of return. During the interview, the twins sat by a window covered by blinds that allowed them to see the street outside but kept them hidden from view. "The Siamese youth don't exhibit himself at the window," Eng told the visitor, "he wouldn't make much so."

Yet this passage and the rest of the interview also revealed that their speech and actions continued to betray their difference, despite the extraordinary amount of adaptation to an American society that was foreign to them—and to which they were foreign. To the vast majority of Americans, the twins were mediated through newspapers, which could act to smooth some rough edges the twins still possessed, perhaps through cleaning up difficulties the brothers still had with English, in terms of both grammar and pronunciation. Conversely, the papers could draw attention to these imperfections simply by printing an odd statement or an occasional mistake with the language. The media had the power to give the twins voice but also to poke fun at them. The common theme throughout this dialogue, however, was that substance trumped form. The twins, a physical monstrosity but with good hearts, demanded respect from others and paid respect to those less fortunate than even themselves. The visitor, apparently a gentleman, begged forgiveness for offending the twins and received it with no hard feelings. "I look at a man's heart," Chang and Eng told him, "not his words."

This analysis presumes, of course, that the dialogue bears any relation to reality—to a real conversation that occurred between the twins and some visitor. The article's authors made this claim explicitly: "The foregoing dialogue is not a mere fancy sketch. Many of the remarks, sentiments and repartees contained in it, have been actually elicited from the Twins, in conversation with them by ourselves." The authors asserted that their motivation in this dialogue was to reveal the twins' true character, which was "not so generally known as it ought to be." In so doing, however, these sentiments mirrored earlier attempts to "name" the twins and their characteristics and, thereby, to describe the American character. So the dialogue featured Chang and Eng offering sharp criticism of Americans, who paid attention only to outward appearances in determining who belonged where in a social hierarchy, and who failed to take care of their society's less fortunate. (The twins also criticized as vain the attempts of Americans to attain beauty through clothes and adornments.) To drive home this assessment of American society, the authors wrote approvingly of the twins' critical eye. "We hazard the assertion that there will be found in the Siamese Twins an observance of the laws of politeness, more scrupulous and exact than in thousands who boast of their superior advantages," they concluded. Certainly, the authors were using the twins to make a point about society at large, a sort of ventriloquism at play. Yet reading the interview in conjunction with other sources that gave (some) voice to the twins suggests that the sentiments expressed here did not stray far from their true feelings. Constantly the twins nudged the discursive boundaries that hemmed them into certain convenient tropes that made it easy for Americans to "understand" them. In nudging, the twins were able to create space to maneuver better, to claim greater liberties. But in so doing, they also created resentment among many Americans around them.

Fighting

Not everyone in society was "distinguished," "learned," or otherwise worthy of admiration, and so there were people who came into contact with Chang and Eng who received respect from neither newspapers nor the twins. Some papers used the occasion of the twins' levees to ridicule certain groups in society. These jokes often exhibited characteristics that reinforced racial stereotypes. At one levee, a "countryman we presume of Irish descent" remarked that the twins looked "amazingly alike, especially the right-hand one!" On another occasion, the twins confronted a "coloured man" who had snuck into the levee without paying. When the twins marched up to him and flung their accusations, it "so frightened the poor fellow that he fainted." Each of these articles reinforced images of the stupid Irish and the dishonest African American. Similarly, the twins faced criticism, often framed as humor. Their shrewd business acumen seemed to some observers designed simply to come to town, take the money of the curious, and leave.[14]

A sense of unease greeted the representation of the twins as model citizens, especially as jokes about them served to racialize some groups and to insinuate that the twins were becoming rich at the public's expense. During a two-year period from 1831 to 1833, the twins became embroiled in a number of altercations. Several were physical, pitting the twins against observers who they believed had in some way caused offense. A couple, such as the incident in Virginia, were verbal, calling into question the twins' status, especially in relation to the Coffins. Some were public, unfurled in competing newspaper accounts, and others were private, escalating in a series of combative personal letters. One of these incidents, occurring in the summer of 1831 in Lynnfield, Massachusetts, illustrates three interconnected themes that ran through all their altercations: first, the balancing act between being public figures and living private lives; second, the struggle to stake claims to honor and integrity; and third, being a racial or foreign "other" whose ability to speak was in question. Each of these themes offers insight into the twins' attempts at social positioning.

PUBLIC AND PRIVATE

The Lynnfield incident received the most publicity in newspapers and in many ways set the stage for a discussion of all three themes. In July 1831, the twins, exhausted after a month of performing in the debilitating heat of Boston, wanted to rest before continuing on to smaller towns in the Northeast. James Hale, their manager, picked as their retreat Lynnfield, "recommended as a very quiet & retired place, and a healthy one too."[15] At this "quiet & retired" community, Chang and Eng encountered such excitement that newspapers reported about it for a month afterward.

Initial reports offered the general facts of the case, framing the twins as sympathetic figures trying to escape the public eye who were, nonetheless, hounded and pushed into an open confrontation. The two brothers, together with an attendant named William, were hunting fowl in fields near Lynnfield. Shooting game for sport was an activity associated with men of means, signifying both masculinity and class. For these two men of color and ambiguous status to have engaged in the activity, in the process likely ranging widely across public and private property, was to attract attention both from those men who did not have the wherewithal to engage in such activities and thus resented the twins their opportunity and from those men who did have the means and resented the twins' intrusion on their turf. Additionally, it was perhaps only natural that residents would be curious to catch a glimpse of these natural wonders, and over the course of the day a crowd of some fifteen to twenty "idle" men and boys became "troublesomely obtrusive" to the twins, "harassing and irritating them." After a time, two men from the crowd—identified as Col. Elbridge Gerry and Mr. Prescott of Stoneham—approached the twins, whose attendant requested that the men keep away, adding "by way of bravado" that if they did not, the twins would shoot them. The two men did not back off, instead daring them to fire. The twins did not, and "the Colonel then indiscreetly accused them" of being liars. The twins reacted indignantly—"He accuse us of lying!" they reportedly exclaimed—and one of them struck the colonel with the butt of his gun.[16]

The colonel picked up a heavy stone and flung it at the twins, striking one of them in the head and drawing blood. The twins then "wheeled round and fired by platoon" at the man, who was "horribly frightened as most other people would have been," even though, the story reported, the gun turned out to be charged only with powder. The crowd quickly dispersed, and the twins returned to the hotel intending to load their gun with ball. Prescott, the reports claimed, ran and hid in a hayloft, while Gerry ran to alert authorities. Outside parties stepped in at this moment to defuse the situation, and Gerry agreed not to press charges. The next day, however, Prescott did file charges. A magistrate came from the Essex County seat of Salem to convene a special court, at which the twins were arrested for disturbing the peace and forced to pay a bond of $200 guaranteeing their good behavior. "Many timorous people in that neighborhood had got into a great fright," one report concluded. "The truth, however, is that they [the twins] are as harmless as kids, if unmolested. There's no danger from them, if they are not attacked by *Stone'em* people."[17]

These initial reports took their material from the *Salem Mercury*. Some papers simply reprinted the *Mercury* story, whereas others rewrote it, slightly modifying its language and adding their own reflections. Of these, most portrayed the twins as the injured party, despite the fact that in the end they were brought before a magistrate. "The Siamese twins have had a fashionable quarrel with some unwelcome visitors," one reported, apparently unaware that the twins were actually *not* accepting visitors, indeed were not even on show. Another report, calling the twins "inoffensive," minimized their culpability and turned attention to the two men from Stoneham who had "obtruded on their retirement" and "provoked hard words and blows."[18]

Together, these initial reports of the Lynnfield incident revealed the implications of lives on display. This altercation was an unscripted moment in a narrative that had thus far been highly scripted, and it exposed the twins as emotive people with feelings that could be hurt and tempers that could flare and in so doing made them appear more sympathetic, perhaps more human. But the incident also suggested the existence of the Siamese twins as a facade, an act that necessarily masked the twins' human side. Just as the twins told the interviewer in New York that they could not afford to allow the public to freely view their bodies, the twins had to be careful about letting the public view their private selves.

Their attempt to mark off a private space away from the public eye signaled an exercise in self-expression, for privacy was not something that came without a struggle. Indeed, the very fact of this vacation, demanded by the twins, illustrated a growing authority voiced by Chang and Eng in deciding the course of their lives. Their relative powerlessness to refuse to work when feeling ill or tired had been, and continued to be, a sore point between the brothers and the Coffins. Letters written to Newburyport by the twins' managers over the course of late 1831 and 1832 reveal the twins' resentment at being forced into public view for the sake of profit even when they were not well. They also bristled at an attempt by Mrs. Coffin to deprive them of their private transport—a horse and wagon—and subject them to the "inconveniences of public transportation" in an attempt to save money.[19]

The desire for privacy was at once practical and also symbolic. Offering the public the opportunity to see them undermined the twins' economic positioning; if people could gaze at them for free, why should anyone pay to visit them? Also, it was a great annoyance to the twins to have people staring at them all the time. Additionally, the market revolution was transforming society. As a middle class emerged that placed greater emphasis on maintaining a domestic haven separate from the noisy commotion surrounding the workplace and public areas shared with a working class, the ability to withdraw into a private sphere suggested a status reserved only for a certain type of person. The conceit of the parlor in which the twins received visitors was a function of this symbolic relationship between privilege and privacy, which would be undermined by riding public transportation.

More than just a physical space to call their own, however, the twins yearned for privacy in which certain details of their lives and their bodies would be kept from public consumption and discussion. This desire was apparent in the aftermath of the Virginia debate over their status. The allegation that their mother had sold them proved just as devastating to them as the claim of their being slaves. "These incidents in the state of Virginia are made the subject of almost daily conversation," Harris wrote on the twins' behalf, "and the idea of persons looking on them as children who had so hard-hearted a mother has sunk but too deeply in their minds." The twins had come to the United States as part of a contract, dated April 1, 1829, between them and Captain Coffin in Siam. Chang and Eng, signing their names with Chinese characters, acknowledged that they had agreed to go with Coffin to the United States and Europe with their "free will and consent" and that of their parents and the king of Siam. They would remain with Coffin "until the expiration of the time agreed upon"; Coffin would pay all expenses for the twins in the course of their travel; and Coffin would return the twins to their homeland within five years.[20]

While the contract did not specify compensation to the twins' mother, Hunter and Coffin later said that they gave her $3,000 cash; the twins said that the sum was $500. The concurrence between the parties that some sum was paid in exchange for the twins' agreement to exhibit their bodies notwithstanding, the common belief that their mother had sold them was intolerable. Virginia "excited the bitterest feelings in their minds," Harris wrote, "to think that their private affairs should have been made the subject of conversation so much as to have caused such a speech in a legislative assembly whose proceedings are listened to by so many."[21]

In spite of these sentiments, or perhaps because of them, the twins apparently felt it necessary to display public signs of affection between them and their family back home. In part, this was a response to the repeated queries about their mother. "How often am I provoked and almost incensed to blows by the foolish questions asked me by the people in this country," began an open letter purported to be from Chang and Eng to their "Mother and Little Siss," which the *New York Constellation* published in February 1832. "'Chang Eng,' say they, 'have you a father, a mother, or a sister at home?' Then I say, 'Chang Eng has no father, for he is dead—he has a mother and a little sister.' 'Oh!' they say then, 'and do you love that mother and little sister?' Love them! Oh what a vile and senseless question to put to Chang Eng, as if he were a wild beast or a monkey, destitute of natural affection. But I do not reply to such boyish questions. They who ask them are too far beneath the notice of Chang Eng for him to deign to converse with them."[22]

There are obvious issues about authorship. It is certain that the twins did not pen the letter themselves. (There are very, very few extant samples in which the twins—or, more precisely, one of the twins—actually put pen to paper, and those that do exist show an entirely different style of using English to communicate ideas.) It is problematic that a letter in English to their mother (who could not read English) appeared in a New York newspaper. And it is surprising that the letter attacked their guests—their customers—so aggressively. Yet, as we will see, the twins often dictated letters through their managers, especially Charles Harris, and these letters always brought the twins' language into more widely accepted syntactical and grammatical forms. Communications from America to Siam, or from Siam to America, had to be translated in Bangkok by American missionaries. And it was in no way unprecedented for the twins or their managers to express frustration with the types of questions they faced. It is likely that the letter home, authorized by the twins or not, expressed sentiments that could have originated from them. And clearly it invoked the private—the conceit of a personal letter to a beloved mother—precisely to satisfy public curiosity about the status of the twins' family relations and to foreclose any further inquiries or attacks along these lines.

Evident also in the circumstances described by the twins' letter was, on the one hand, the failure of their visitors to see them as people with the capacity to experience the same emotions and sentiments felt by others and, on the other hand, the similar failure of the twins to empathize with their guests, people who, if we take the rhetoric of the twins' advertisements at face value, were there not to gaze at freaks of nature but to learn about natural wonders, to engage in an educational experience, by definition an encounter with the unknown but knowable. Yet between these two parties there was evident hostility. The position the twins occupied was contested; the positioning the twins engaged in was challenged. Audience members, coming to gaze at these freaks of nature, were in one sense positioning themselves as superior to the brothers. The twins, in turn, attempted to place themselves higher by calling out those "too far beneath" them, but they also used the negative example of such interrogators to lift up those who did not ask them such questions.

Within the viewing room, there was a set of expectations that each side followed, which allowed all to act in predictable ways. Outside this room, the twins wanted privacy, something, it turned out, that they could not demand or receive; it was something to which they had no claim. The "battle at Lynnfield," as James Hale later called it, occurred outside the exhibition hall, in a public space and yet a place where the twins tried to act as private, or at least nonpublic, individuals. Because the encounter occurred outside the normal bounds of observation, there were no rules to guide interaction, and because there was no respect for the honor or integrity of the other party, conflict resulted.

DECEIT AND INTEGRITY

Two weeks after the first reports of the Lynnfield incident, newspapers published a response from Colonel Gerry intended to set the record straight. With *"witticisms"* and "misrepresentations having been published in relation to my conduct and treatment of the persons called *Siamese Twins*," he wrote in a letter titled "To the Public," "I feel it to be a duty I owe to myself and the public, to state the *facts* as they were, that those who will examine them may judge who was in the wrong." Indeed, the aftermath of Lynnfield left Gerry, paired with Prescott, as the recipient of much snickering. A colonel had been "horribly frightened" by a shot from a gun that was not even loaded, while his partner became "demented with fear" and fled from these "gentle" and "unoffending" Siamese brothers. For months after, jokes sprinkled the newspapers. Within the twins' circle, Gerry had also made a comical impression. Hale wrote to a friend that he would like to make a re-creation of the incident an annual event, "to hang out the bloody flag near the battleground in Lynnfield 'fam'd for deeds of arms'—and I think for a device [we] shall have the valiant Colonel in battle array." Apparently, the focus on the "Elbridge Gerry" name became so intense that notices ran dispelling any ties to a more famous Elbridge Gerry. "We are requested to say," one newspaper reported, "that Col. Elbridge Gerry, who has lately been in collision with the 'Siamese Twins,' is not the Son of the late Vice-President, and in no way connected with his family." Seen as a bully by some, a coward by others, an object of ridicule and derision, the good colonel felt it necessary to speak out in a public forum.[23]

Colonel Elbridge Gerry was born in Stoneham in 1793, almost certainly named by his parents after the revolutionary hero and Massachusetts political leader. He had matured into an officer in the state militia, a gentleman, and a sportsman of some renown. In almost every respect, Gerry's version of the Lynnfield events differed from the initial reports. Gerry had just arrived at the Lynnfield Hotel in late afternoon, on his way home from Ipswich, traveling with a pair of gentlemen, whom he named to provide character witnesses if necessary. Someone unknown to him shouted that "the twins" were behind the hotel. "It did not then occur to me that they were the persons spoken of as 'the Siamese Twins,'" he said, but he nevertheless followed a group of eight to ten men to have a look. They approached to within twelve rods of the "persons with guns," who then moved toward the crowd, cutting the distance in half. The hunters' attendant, a "young Englishman" named William, accused the men of having followed the twins—by now, it was clear who these sportsmen were—all afternoon. Gerry, having just arrived and thus wholly innocent of any such deed, took no notice of the charge. Despite protests of innocence from the other men, the young attendant then threatened that if they continued to follow the twins he would "blow us through," pointing his gun at them in a "most provoking and insolent manner." At this, Gerry remarked, "Such conduct ought not to pass unnoticed," and he told the attendant to put down the weapon. Instead, the young man "advanced near me and said if I spoke or opened my head, he would blow my brains out. I replied to him that if blowing is what you want, blow my heart out, and at the same time unbuttoned my waistcoat, to indicate that I was ready for his fire, if he wished to make it." All the while, Gerry reported, the twins egged on William and made similar threats of their own.[24] The thirty-eight-year-old colonel appeared neither a coward nor a hothead with an overkeen sense of bravado, as earlier reports portrayed; rather, he was acting to put insolence in its place, to restore a sense of order to an encounter that appeared to be spiraling out of control. He was a man of integrity.

Before continuing with this account, it might serve us well to take a moment to reflect: Speaking up, stepping forward, unbuttoning his coat—none of these were the only paths that Gerry could have taken. He might have remained silent, anonymous, and one of the group, following their lead. He might have listened to his initial belief that this confrontation had nothing to do with him and gone away, as the attendant demanded. But this was a man who was colonel of his regiment in the state militia, "a noted sportsman, a citizen of wealth and distinction . . . and prominent in town affairs."[25] And these three were strangers, outsiders, foreigners, a young Englishman and two Siamese brothers, challenging him with mortal threats. Staying silent, walking away, or backing down would not be actions suiting a man of such rank. The choices he had already made, and those he was about to make, fit neatly into a logic of social relations that called for public recognitions of status to guide ambiguous public encounters.

And so, he told them they dare not fire, and indeed, the attendant turned around and walked back to the twins. While his back was turned, Gerry picked up a stone—"weighing about a pound"—to use if necessary. Still muttering among themselves, the twins and their attendant "passed near the fence." Were they approaching the group? Walking away? Approaching the group but with the intention of walking away? Gerry's letter does not make this clear, but his response indicates that he felt the twins had not acted, and were not acting, appropriately in this encounter, and he was not going to let them get away with it. "I remarked to them that they were liars"—a terrible thing to call someone—"and that I should not put up with such treatment." The twins asked their attendant what Gerry had said, then replied that "if any one called them liars they would shoot him." At this moment, the attendant struck Gerry with the butt of his gun, and the twins, now within ten feet of the colonel, both fired guns at the same time. In immediate response, Gerry threw his stone and struck a twin in the head—"as I intended"—then proceeded to look for another stone as the twins, not he, ran away. Were the guns loaded? "I cannot say," but "those in company with me said they heard the whistling." Upon returning to the hotel, he learned that the twins had reloaded and were looking for him, but a townsman intervened and took their guns away. "I thought the conduct of the three highly improper, and that they deserved to be punished," yet, reasonable man that he was, he agreed not to pursue legal action upon the assurance of "Mr. Hale, their keeper," that he, too, did not approve of their conduct and that they would not engage in such behavior in the future. Gerry thus distanced himself from Prescott, who did press charges—"I had no previous knowledge or acquaintance [with him], and was not in his company at the time"—and Prescott's alleged cowardice. "I pledge myself to prove, if necessary, that the foregoing statement is true," he concluded.[26]

Gerry's self-proclaimed commitment to honor and integrity was not universally shared in his northern society—after all, he received much ribbing from other members of the public for it—but he also was not alone; indeed, many examples can be found just by following the twins. In May 1831, for instance, while exhibiting the twins in New York City, James Hale found his character under attack by an anonymous correspondent to the *New-York Commercial Advertiser*. The unsigned letter to the editor asked the newspaper to defend the public against the humbuggery surrounding the twins, "who are *not being exhibited* in this city." By this, the writer meant that Hale—"a most uncourteous keeper"—dominated the show, "prating to the visitors about the boys, and preventing anyone from examining them ... or ascertaining in any way the truth of the wonderful stories which he (their keeper) forces the public to swallow." Hale responded with bluster, appealing to the paper for the name of the writer, and getting it, then publishing his own intention to take the man to court. "It is the first time I have ever been thus assailed, and as I have generally received the good opinion of the public, they will, no doubt, give the writer of the aforesaid article all the credit he deserves," Hale wrote, signing himself "the *Keeper*." Hale did file suit for libel (although the jury found for the defendant a year later) and apparently pressured the *Commercial Advertiser* to give the twins some positive press, which it did the next day, writing a review of the twins' show that concluded with the hope that no one would miss this opportunity to see "this wonderful phenomenon."[27]

As a businessman, Hale believed it was crucial to maintain a public facade of honor and integrity. In part, this meant protecting his own image as a gentleman, a trustworthy caretaker for the young men under his watch. If the glowing reports about him—with the one notable exception—were any indication, in this endeavor he succeeded. Sometimes, however, protecting his image had nothing to do with the twins or responding to newspaper reports and instead concerned monitoring the whispers and gossip he heard in public circles and managing his business affairs with Susan Coffin. He bristled at what he perceived as her micromanagement, not only with what he portrayed as her obsession with keeping track of their movement and earnings but also at times with her strong desire to travel with the twins and Hale, to keep a close eye on things. Hale detected "many reports in circulation" that were "injurious to her character and to mine too." He dismissed the stories as foolish; "still I should hardly think she should wish to brave public opinion, but she says she cares not a cent for the opinion of the world." Hale called this "*independent*" but imprudent for someone "who wishes to sustain an honorable situation in society."[28] Hale recognized that working effectively in society required maintaining a degree of artifice, a public face that met public norms of acceptable behavior. Ironically, only by meeting these standards—by donning a mask—could one make a claim to integrity.

In the end, he could not work for someone who he believed undermined his authority, and he resigned his position in September 1831, to be replaced by his friend Charles Harris. Harris was more forthright than Hale, but the two exchanged letters regularly, with Hale giving Harris advice on maintaining a facade. In counseling Harris on how to frame the twins' shows so that they would not be susceptible to exhibition taxes as they were in Virginia, he said: "I was always very particular to abstain in my announcements from the words 'exhibition,' 'being exhibited,' or anything of like import. In fact no notice is given but simply that our young friends will be happy to receive company." He assured Harris—incorrectly, as it turned out—that the Virginia assembly would side with the twins, attesting that judges had always told him that their "business" was not "a *show* in the strictest legal sense."[29] As we have seen, though, sometimes political concerns, with social or cultural underpinnings, took precedence. The twins themselves were coming to learn this same lesson.

Initially, the twins had adhered to a trust in the people who said they were acting with the twins' best interests in mind and in the law and reason that were the supposed underpinnings of this new civilization in which they found themselves. Since 1829, newspapers had emphasized the paternal affection they believed Abel Coffin felt for the twins. This certainly had been an exhibition strategy of the Concern, and it played a number of functions. At once it placed Coffin and the white American (and Christian) civilization that he represented in a position of benevolent authority over the infantilized twins and the Asian (and heathen) people that they represented. The knowledge that this good man looked after these "boys" addressed concerns that they had been taken from their mother. And it also addressed fears of a deformed, foreign freak of nature being brought to the country and spreading disorder—perhaps contagion—of one type or another. On the twins' return from England in 1831, papers continued to substantiate the image of a paternal Captain Coffin.[30]

At one level, Coffin also saw himself as the loving father figure. After parting from his wife and the twins in England in January 1831 and making his way back to Southeast Asia, Coffin wrote fondly of the twins in a series of letters. "Give . . . my love to Chang Eng," "God Bless Them," and "I long to see my dear children and Chang Eng," he wrote. Certainly it was necessary to provide firm discipline, to ensure that the twins—children, really, in Coffin's mind—did not stray from an appropriate path. At times that discipline may have caused hard feelings, but it was all for their own good. "Tell them although they might think I was hard with them, I think their own good sense will convince them that I have never done anything but what is for their good, . . . and that I feel that I shall always do by them as by my own children."[31]

At another level, Coffin clearly saw the twins as a business investment. In the first letter to his wife in January, he told her to be sure not to allow the twins to demand too much by way of overhead, and this direction likely led to Mrs. Coffin's firm hold of the purse strings—and the bitter resentment the twins began to feel toward her as a result. To protect his investment, Coffin had taken out insurance on the lives of the twins. To keep down costs on the trip to England, he booked the twins into steerage, at $50 each, while he, his wife, and Hale enjoyed full cabin passage for $150 each. Chang and Eng, perplexed at the time by the ill treatment they were receiving—an "altogether . . . different manner to that in which the rest of the cabin passengers were treated"—complained to Coffin. To preserve a bond of goodwill, a fiction of paternal care, which he thought necessary to maintain his control over the twins, or at least to smooth any rough edges that his authority might create, Coffin told them that he had paid the full fare and that the discrepancy in passage lay with the ship's captain, and he urged them to "never mind." In other words, he lied to them.[32]

But what brought these specific tensions into the open was the twins' refusal to play the role of unquestioning subordinate, of obedient child. Instead, in a land that celebrated the rule of law and reason, the twins continually served to reveal the illogical sentimentality of custom that informed everyday life in the United States. Early on, they complained to Coffin of their treatment on the ship. In newspaper interviews, they commented on the discordance between women who apparently disdained public attention yet wore fashionable dresses and made up their faces. In public letters, they commented on the discrepancies between how Christians professed their faith and how they acted. With their increased exposure to the contradictions between American words and deeds, with their growing fluency in American ways and the English tongue, came more frequent challenges to the people who visited them and the representations they made. In Virginia, they challenged a writer who said that they had been bought and sold—and learned that a doctor they had trusted had composed those very words. At a reception in New York State in 1832, they had the opportunity to challenge the very ship captain who had carried them across the Atlantic three years before, and from him they came to know that the man they had trusted, Abel Coffin, had lied to them.[33]

American practices of deception and integrity, the twins began to see more clearly, were useful primarily in keeping power—of influence, reputation, and treasure—out of their own hands. Again and again, the twins attempted to use the power of rational argument to explain the requests and decisions they made. And, repeatedly, their audience did not listen, instead viewing the twins as insolent, arrogant, and out of line. The twins' use of reason was an affront to their audiences, and the public order that deception and integrity helped maintain was infused with a sense of hierarchy. But on what categories was this hierarchy built? The implications of whether those who assailed the twins understood that people of color had strong identities built around integrity are unclear, as are the implications of men of color demanding respect from whites. This racial dynamic leads to a last question: To what extent were the twins performing as racialized actors? The question holds relevance not only for the ways in which people responded to them as they made their cases for respect but also in the way their cases were reported to the wider public. The content of their message was built on a quiet logic and common sense. Yet it was wrapped up in Orientalized speech and presented as humor; the silliness of the irrational representation undermined the serious rationality that pervaded their argument. Logic, coming from a person of color, became humorous or ridiculous or a threat worthy of a violent response.[34]

RACE AND REASON

Let us return to the initial reports of the Lynnfield incident. Some asked the familiar question of what would happen if one twin committed a crime of which the other was entirely innocent. The *Essex Register* printed a letter purported to be written by Eng to a London newspaper during the twins' visit to England the previous year. "I tremble lest the allurements of a great city should lead him astray," Eng allegedly wrote of Chang. If he incurred fines but was unable to pay, "must I go to prison with him?" If he should commit murder, "I being no *particeps criminis*, but having opposed his wicked design with all my might, am . . . I to be required to attend his execution at the old Bailey?" He continued: "I hope not. Your law, I am told, considers that two guilty persons had better escape merited punishment than one innocent person should suffer. Of that saving principle I claim the benefit and insist that whatever crime may be perpetrated by Chang, no one has any right to lay hands on him, so as to punish me."[35]

Two things jump out immediately about this quotation. First, the newspaper prefaced it by commenting that, in the Lynnfield case, the question was moot because it appeared that both twins acted equally. Second, it presents a rational, legal argument for why the pair's identities as two separate persons under the law ought to be taken into consideration in decisions to prosecute one or the other. And, this argument was written in perfect English, replete with Latin legal terms; it did not resemble in any way the initial quotation attributed to them, "He accuse us of lying!" The questions raised here are twofold, mirror images of each other. To what extent did these legal ideals extend to those people who likely were in no position to understand them fully, if at all? And to what extent did those people who claimed these legal ideals but were unable to articulate them properly truly understand them, and how legitimate was their claim? A third report of the battle at Lynnfield shed light on these questions, introducing to this discussion in explicit fashion the presence of race and class.

On August 17, 1831, just two days after Elbridge Gerry's letter first appeared, the Boston *Columbian Centinel* published eyewitness testimony of the court hearing. The article, authored by someone calling himself "Carlo," confirmed parts of the earlier accounts. It repeated the first report's claim that a group of idle men, some twenty to thirty strong, followed the twins throughout the afternoon. It reiterated that Gerry and Prescott came only in the late afternoon, as the twins were returning to the hotel, and that Gerry had not harassed the brothers, although he did call them liars. The report also distanced Gerry and Prescott from each other; they were not traveling companions or partners in cowardice. At every instance, however, the *Centinel* piece provided a wealth of detail that served to fill in blank spots and to amplify what was already known.[36]

As they were pursued through fields and woods, the twins and their attendant "repeatedly requested the people not to follow them," but no one listened; instead, "they were as zealous as if in pursuit of a wild beast." At nightfall, just before Gerry appeared on the scene, the crowd began insulting the twins, "calling them '*damned niggers*' and using in a most foul and disgraceful manner opprobrious epithets in relation to their mother." When the twins protested, "Their pursuers cried out, 'Let's take away their guns and give 'em a thrashing.'" After Gerry called the brothers and their attendant "*all liars*" ("Eng asked, 'You say I'm a liar?' 'Yes,' was the reply"), Eng struck Gerry in the arm with the butt of his gun, Gerry threw a rock ("somewhat larger than a man's fist, surrounded with sharp corners"), which struck Eng in the head and cut through to the skull, causing profuse bleeding. The twins immediately fired, with powder only, although "a slight peppering with small shot would have taught the aggressors a salutary lesson in a practical way." The mob fled, Prescott took cover in a haymow, and the twins, "in a state of rage," loaded their guns and sought the man who threw the stone, only to be stopped by a town resident. Rumors circulated that the reason Gerry did not press charges was that he had been paid off—the sum varied from $100 to $400—although this was false. Nevertheless, the gossip prompted some greedy men—of whom Prescott was one—to consider filing a complaint in the hopes that they, too, would receive a settlement. In the end, the article claimed, the judge agreed that the twins had been provoked and "most outrageously abused," but to prevent further disruptions of the peace, that is, to ensure that the twins would not react violently to further provocations, he required of them a bond of $200, with which the twins "cheerily complied."[37]

"Carlo" presented these details "as nearly and truly" as he could, though he conceded he was not impartial, "for though I am not connected by any stronger tie than a friendly regard with the twins; yet I am most deeply prejudiced against the aggressors, and entertain no respect for their character or manners."[38] Indeed, while the narrative he offered marked the twins in ways unprecedented in public discourse, it also served to an even greater extent to malign those who harassed them.

The account offered greed as the primary motive in pressing charges against the twins. Additionally, the use of "nigger" and other "opprobrious epithets" against their mother—which, for those readers who had been paying attention most likely brought to mind the possibility of their having been sold—not only brought into public discourse a way of looking at the twins that rarely received ink but also cast those people who harassed them in a negative light. Similarly, such usage with respect to the brothers almost certainly meant to suggest that the twins were a racial other, but not that they were of African descent. Indeed, a wide variety of racialized cultural attributes were appended to them during these years. Most publications had ceased offering physical descriptions—with respect to both their national origins and their anomalous ligature. Now, references to these attributes came out in isolated blips. These ranged from Abel Coffin speculating from afar that they must be "almost white[, with] so many ladies kissing them," to a journalist saying they "have very much the American Indian physiognomy and complexion," to a New England mob calling them "damn'd niggers." As we will see, it manifested also in relational anecdotes in which the twins were disparaged for being lazy like free people of color or were placed side by side with Native Americans on exhibit or when their status as owned men was debated in the Virginia assembly.[39]

Yet, despite Carlo's tone, perhaps even this last report did little to disparage the men who antagonized the twins. The mob action against the twins in July 1831 might be viewed productively as a precursor to the Jacksonian riots that swept the nation—South and North, including Massachusetts—later in the decade. These riots were antiabolitionist and anticriminal, antiblack and anti-immigrant, and anti-Catholic and anti-Mormon. They were peopled by native-born white Americans—laborers, merchants, and propertied gentlemen—who feared losing their identity and social position amid changes promised by immigration and, especially in the 1830s, the abolitionist movement. A long-standing "Negrophobia," to borrow the phrase of one historian, united this diverse group of men who felt threatened by the specter of amalgamation or interracial sex. In the early 1830s, however, Massachusetts whites felt increasing hostility against blacks, in part because gradual emancipation resulted in a growing free black population, in part because of the increasingly vocal abolition movement right down the road in Boston.[40]

But the use of "nigger" meant to suggest that the twins were a racial other, not that they were of African descent. Indeed, New Englanders would soon be talking about *Irish* "niggers." And in just three years—1834—another mob would burn down a Catholic convent in nearby Charlestown as part of what some said was a larger effort to destroy Catholic churches and "disperse the Irish."[41] It is worth noting that our Elbridge Gerry of Stoneham showed up again as a witness in the Charlestown convent trial. Again, he said he was just passing by—this time on a walk after supper—when the commotion attracted his attention. This time, however, he appeared to have remained a bystander, or at least he claimed to have done. Authorities questioned the man he was with as to whether they participated actively in breaking down the convent's gates, but the answer, naturally, was negative.[42] Gerry's presence at both incidents may have been sheer coincidence, or it may have been an example of the sentiments of at least one "gentleman of property and standing" with respect to challenges posed to the existing social order by racial outsiders. Regardless, his presence and that of countless other bystanders, if not participants, reflects what one historian has called the "secret satisfaction" of most residents of Massachusetts at such mob actions.[43]

This tacit approval is shown by the fact that very few newspapers reprinted the sensational account of the mob eager to thrash "niggers"—at least the part of the article that I have shared thus far, which comprised all but one final paragraph.[44] Gerry's presentation of the events at Lynnfield served to distance him from any accusations that his quarrel had anything to do with the race or anomaly of the twins, that he had assaulted anybody without provocation, and, conversely, that he had been bested by a nonwhite person. Much of the *Centinel* narrative, though, could be interpreted as a condemnation of a group of Massachusetts men, neighbors, really, which newspapers apparently were unwilling to do in explicit terms. And so, while conceding that the particulars in the *Centinel*, "if true," were "equally disgraceful to the Lynnfield people," but leaving out the racial epithets attributed to them, the only part that newspapers reprinted was the concluding paragraph, which quoted "one of the Twins" expressing his dismay at the complainant and which "afforded much amusement to the Court": "'You swear you fraid o' me; you fraid I kill you, shoot you—at same time you know I have guns—you see I shoot you if I choose—and you keep round me—you wont let me go away—you call me and my mother hard name—and yet you swear you fraid I kill you. Now, suppose I see a man in my country, in Siam—he goes out into woods, and sees a lion asleep—he say, "Oh! I fraid that lion kill me"—what I think of that man if he go up and give that lion a kick and say get out you ugly beast? I wish you'd answer me that.'"[45]

There is something devastating to the recipient of the criticism offered here; what kind of fool kicks a lion despite being fully aware of the potential consequences? How could one quarrel with that argument? One could not, and that was the point. And yet, framed in a particular context foreign to an American audience, articulated in broken English that amused the court, and voiced by an infantilized Asian whose "keeper" at the time of the altercation was not present, the performance served also to distance the twins from an American context; their argument was antithetical to the universal principles that underlay arguments of reason. Just as the Virginia assembly refused to consider the twins' petition on equal footing but instead considered them only to be someone else's slaves, the battle of Lynnfield marked them as irrational foreigners. To further drive home the belief that the twins' argument was a function of race, not reason, some papers labeled it "Siamese Logic."[46]

And as the twins attempted to voice a shared humanity—or, depending on one's point of view, mouthed off—they came to be seen as ever less humorous and increasingly insolent. Their disrespect, some papers claimed, represented an obstacle to scientific progress, which required pliant subjects, not petulant brats. When a physician in Exeter, New Hampshire, "who was doubtless prompted by a due regard to the advancement of science," asked what would be the effect on Eng if he stuck a pin in Chang's shoulder, Chang reportedly replied, "If you stick a pin into me, my brother Eng will knock you down." This response led newspapers to label the twins as "spoilt children" who "use[d] their own whims and freaks a little too much."[47] When newspapers reported that an Ohio court had found the twins guilty of assault and battery "on an old and respectable citizen," a poet commented, "Gentle ye seemed when ye were here, a show, / And found us ever willing / To pay our shilling; / What miracle has changed your nature so, / That for her twins, sad Siam's doomed to sigh, / And Ohio cries O!"[48] And when another man of medicine, this time in Alabama, proposed to examine their connective band, the twins "objected . . . in rather a rude and insulting manner," after which someone called them impostors, and as a result "the Twins made battle."[49] None of these accounts mentioned any attempt to negotiate a common ground. Nothing hinted that the twins might have first responded with anything other than belligerence. These reports did not recognize even the possibility that attempts at rational argument were made; it was natural that these "changed" Siamese twins reacted immediately to any reasonable request with violence.

Evidence suggests, however, that while the final resort to violence was an accurate reflection of the twins' growing frustration at their treatment, the breakdown typically occurred only after attempts to engage in a rational discussion failed. By this time, their public performance had changed from their early days. Rather than dress up in "Oriental" garb and perform somersaults and other physical feats, the twins dressed in suits and ties and performed more mundane tasks, such as answering questions from the audience in a parlor setting. And, while in their first years on tour they had submitted to poking and prodding, they now objected to such invasive physical contact. Their act had become, in a way, a model of rational, refined behavior. But this facade was sometimes broken.

In Alabama, for instance, when the doctor requested to examine the twins' connection, Chang and Eng responded that he had the same chance to see it as everyone else. This was not enough, the physician said; he wanted the same opportunity that other medical experts had had to perform a thorough examination of the ligature. The twins refused. They had not submitted to any such examination for more than two years. Indeed, one purpose of the exhibition pamphlets was to publish the medical reports of many distinguished surgeons with respect to their physical anomaly. This was, in other words, a medical mystery that needed no further explanation and could not benefit from any further exploration until the twins died. The twins had first responded with equanimity and then, when the doctor objected the first time, with the backing of scientific studies. It was not the twins who were behaving irrationally. "After sitting quietly for a moment," their manager wrote after the fact, "the Doctor rose from his seat in a state of very great excitement, and approaching the Twins, he said, in an angry tone, 'you are all a set of impostors and pickpockets.'"[50]

What had he said? the twins asked, providing the doctor an opportunity to back down, to embrace civility rather than crudity.

"You are," the doctor replied, "a set of grand rascals."

And then all hell broke loose.

The weapons used offer some idea of the domestic amenities on hand in the parlor setting. A cudgel was swung and a dagger was thrown, but also a chair flew across the room, as did an andiron and a coffeepot full of hot water. Until the doctor spoke up, their guests had been orderly and pleased; once the affray began, "there did not seem to be any of those present desirous to keep the peace, but all sided with the Doctor." The twins, Charles Harris wrote, were lucky to escape with their lives.[51]

Chang and Eng were made to pay for the unrest. They returned the admission money of those who had been in the room, and they went before the magistrate and put up a bond of $350 to guarantee their future good behavior. And yet, with Harris as their mediator, they made a final appeal to rational thought and a defense of violence when reason fails. "The Twins regret exceedingly that anything of the kind should have occurred in their room," Harris wrote in a letter to the public that was published in the local newspaper, "but at the same time, they feel that there is a point at which forbearance must cease, and they do not consider the terms 'impostors, pickpockets, or grand rascals,' as language which ought, under any circumstances, to come from the lips of a gentleman."[52]

Harris did not say who struck the first blow, though the expression of regret, coupled with earlier incidents, suggests it would have been entirely in character for the twins to have struck out against the insult. Calling the twins liars, spoilt children, or impostors served effectively to cut off lines of dialogue, not only to question their good faith or their facility for rational discussion but also to deny any common ground, in a sense to deny their humanity. Yet the twins did not face the structural forms of oppression or abstract expressions of racism that plagued African Americans and Native Americans. Take, for instance, the very fact of their participation in a southern culture of violence. In the American South, especially, men easily resorted to violence—duels, certainly, but also less formal fisticuffs—to settle affairs of honor or any other dispute.[53] Such violence, however, was limited to white combatants. Blacks who crossed whites would be whipped, beaten, or perhaps killed, but they could not fight back. The twins, however, *did* fight back and lived to tell about it, suggesting that they *could* fight back. The only recourse that their white antagonists took was legal—they pressed charges against the twins in a court of law. For them there was still room to negotiate their way between the bars of an iron cage descending on racialized others. Chang and Eng were a very particular—and public—case, and not a looming threat. As a result, their altercations, verbal and physical, resulted in bruised egos, not battered bodies, and certainly not death. Indeed, they emerged as winners from the most important battle they fought, the battle against the Coffins for their independence, which was most fraught with racializing implications.

SLAVERY AND FREEDOM

Well before the Virginia incidents in March 1832, the twins were anxious about their status in relation to the Coffins, with respect to both the public perception and the private arrangement. In January 1831, during the England tour, a rift emerged between the twins and Mrs. Coffin. This turned into a simmering conflict upon return to the United States, when the captain's wife undertook a series of measures designed to forestall any future clashes. She first ignored requests from the twins, then used delaying tactics, telling them to wait for her husband to return from his Asian voyage. Finally, she lashed out at the twins, who, already suspicious that Mrs. Coffin was not dealing with them in good faith, responded in a series of lengthy letters dictated to Charles Harris that laid out the case for a permanent break from the Coffins.[54] In a very real sense, the Coffins' failure to negotiate with the twins over a series of pressing issues, trying instead to maintain what they saw as a master-subordinate relationship, cost them all claims to the pair.

By late 1831, after Harris had already replaced Hale as their manager, the twins engaged in their first epistolary battle with the Concern. Initially, in a letter written in their voice and signed by them that was directed to Susan Coffin, the twins cut past extended social pleasantries and argued simply and straightforwardly for an additional three dollars every week to help feed their horse and maintain their wagon, this in addition to the fifty dollars they received monthly to pay for their expenses. "I should like very much to have an immediate answer to this," they concluded, before sending their best to her and her children. After receiving an unsatisfactory response in which Mrs. Coffin neither agreed to nor rejected their appeal, the twins asked Harris to run the figures to show the advantages of their position. Claiming he did not want to be caught in the middle of a fight, Harris concluded the extra money would be "a *decided saving of expence*" over the alternative, taking public transportation. To this, Mrs. Coffin responded that the twins could do as they please; they could keep the horse and wagon or sell it, but they could not have the extra money. This confounded Chang and Eng: "The twins thought . . . it was like taking a bird, clipping off his wings, and then holding it up on one's hand & saying 'Now you may fly if you wish.' (*This latter sentence is in their own words*)," Harris wrote.[55] The conflict with the Concern—with Mrs. Coffin, specifically—gave the twins the incentive to claim a voice of their own.

Well, sort of their own. Harris, after all, was putting the actual pen to paper, and we can only assume that he was forthright when he wrote, repeatedly, that these were the twins' words. Indeed, Harris often tried to distance himself from the twins, fearful that Mrs. Coffin would confuse their sentiments for his own. "I feel certain that you will perceive at a glance the very unpleasant position in which I am placed in being the writer of their letter," Harris wrote in the exchange about the horse and buggy. "If Chang-Eng could take up a pen & write a letter for themselves, then I would not be mixed up in the transaction. As the matter stands, I am very anxious that you should be guided against the idea that my feelings are enlisted at all in the matter." Just a week later, Harris made a stronger case for the twins' right to have a voice and for Coffin's and Davis's responsibility to listen to it. "You should understand the feelings of Chang-Eng concerning the subject, & likewise the grounds & causes of these feelings," he wrote, still in reference to the transportation issue. This "being a subject dictated entirely by Chang-Eng, they wish me to make a separation or division in the letter & have asked to sign their name to it. To this I can offer no objection." (Chang and Eng signed their own names "Chang Eng.") Eventually, Harris stopped reporting what the twins said and instead wrote from their point of view, although he also continued to write his own observations of business, their travels, and the twins' state of mind.[56]

The twins seemed increasingly anxious. Business in the winter of 1831–32 was bad, and at times, Harris said, the twins worried about making enough money to live on. They regularly asked when Captain Coffin would return. In part, Chang and Eng already were looking ahead to their twenty-first birthday—in May 1832—which would, as they understood it, give them greater control over their own labor. They also were anxious to speak with Coffin because Mrs. Coffin had started to answer their various requests— for more money, for more pamphlets, to forward belongings—by stating that they should wait until her husband returned from sea. In his letters, he had given her reason to believe that he would return by January 1832; as things turned out, he did not arrive until late summer. By then, relations between the twins and Mrs. Coffin had deteriorated beyond the point of reconciliation.[57]

The insinuation of their enslaved status that they encountered in Richmond and Norfolk aggravated anxieties about their position with respect to the Coffins. Harris told them he was surprised these incidents had affected them so, and they "made a most mortified reply 'that they were not at all surprised for it was not the 1st or 2nd time that they were questioned on the subject of matters which ought to have been kept private & never ought to have been made the subject of idle conversation.'" Also to Harris's surprise, the events increased the twins' anticipation of Captain Coffin's return. "The return of their friend Captn. Coffin . . . is so frequently & particularly mentioned that I cannot account for it," he wrote. Among themselves, they mulled over the possibility of asking Mrs. Coffin and Captain Davis to meet with them, though they decided against that idea.[58]

In any case, Mrs. Coffin did not listen to their feelings. Abel Coffin had directed her to make sure that the twins minded her, not the other way around. So, when the twins informed Mrs. Coffin that they would be leaving the captain's aegis at the end of May, she reproached them, through Davis, accusing them in one place of breaking their "promise . . . that they would stay under Mrs. Coffin until the return of the Captn to the U.S.," in another of not "keeping their word." Further, she said that everything done for the twins "had been for their own comfort." Captain Coffin was actually losing money "as it now stands," insinuating that the twins had not fulfilled their obligation to him, perhaps even that they had taken advantage of their situation.[59] Predictably, these accusations stoked the twins' tempers. But, unlike confrontations in their exhibit rooms, which degenerated into physical violence, this quarrel provided the twins the opportunity to unleash an unprecedented verbal barrage of recriminations, grounded in reason, drawing upon cool economic calculations even while sprinkling the documents with double underlines and multiple exclamation points and accusing the Coffins themselves of lying.

To the charge that they were breaking their word, they first defended themselves, claiming that Captain Coffin had promised them that when they reached their twenty-first birthday, they would be "Their Own Men." They said they had asked for an affidavit to this effect, only to be told that "of course" they would be released. As for any assurances that they would wait until Captain Coffin returned, they pointed to the fact that five months had passed since Coffin said he would return. "According to that view of the case . . . if Captn Coffin should never return to the U.S., they would to the end of their lives remain as they *now are.*" They then turned the tables, saying that it was Mrs. Coffin who was deceitful and greedy. To her claims that she loved them and did all she could for their comfort, the twins replied that "they have no doubt that the number of thousand of hard shining Dollars which they have enabled her to spend have made her like them." In other letters, they claimed that Mrs. Coffin did not see them as living beings but as tools to make money. Time and again she had forced them to exhibit themselves in crowded rooms when they were fit to be in the hospital or in bed and had claimed that the payments they received were gifts and that the items they bought with their "hard earned" money belonged actually to the Coffins.[60]

To the charge that they were setting the Concern up for an economic loss, they replied that this was the Coffins' business, not their own. "As to myself, all I can do is to prove (which I can do very satisfactorily) that this over-expenditure has not been on my account." They included an extensive list of the expenses of the England trip that went well beyond what they saw as necessary. This included the large number of "persons & *animals*" hired to attend to the party's visit, including "one cook, one man servant, one chambermaid, . . . one coachman, a boy to clean the house, 4 or 5 men to carry boards, one doorkeeper, one cheque taker, a man employed every day to clean our room & in addition to all these, two living animals in the shape of horses." It also included Mrs. Coffin, who, rather than assist the outfit as a way of saving money, instead spent money shopping.[61]

They expressed similar contempt for her management of the business upon their return from England. Aside from the handling of the horse and wagon, the question of their attendant attracted the twins' criticism. Hale's choice of the "boy" William, whom the twins found "quiet, civil, & attentive," was met with disapproval by Mrs. Coffin, who liked instead the *"Gentleman from Newbury Port,"* Tom Dwyer. Wasn't twenty-five dollars a month too much to pay for William? she asked. But by studying the account books, the twins figured that the *"Gentleman from Newbury Port"* was making a base of thirty dollars per month, plus incentives that put his monthly fee at forty-six dollars. To this accounting, Chang and Eng attributed not incompetence but deceit. Mrs. Coffin "had misled me," they wrote. "[What] was the cause of Mrs Coffin misleading me in this matter? For it was no concern of mine & the money did not come out of my pocket." And yet, the twins concluded, she had lied.[62]

It was during this very period that the twins learned of Captain Coffin's deceit about their passage to England, and much of the anger they had aimed at his wife they now turned toward him. If Captain Sherburne's affidavit that Captain Coffin had paid only steerage for the twins and had listed them as servants was true, "then a most pitiful & contemptible piece of deception was played off on me—a deception the more contemptible & the more pitiful from my being at that time ignorant of the English & unable to make any complaint except through the medium of the Siamese language." What is more, they realized, he used their perception of substandard treatment at the hands of Captain Sherburne, as well as their ignorance of the true state of affairs, to bolster his own position in the public eye as a devoted guardian, asking the twins in public to discuss their experience on the ship.[63]

Any number of reasons exist for why the altercation with Susan Coffin and William Davis played out as it did. Most obvious was the distance involved; the twins at this point were in Upstate New York, and when they finally requested a meeting with Mrs. Coffin, she declined. There was the presence of Charles Harris to channel the twins' sentiments into forceful language. There were also clear legal implications. Some of the letters included sworn affidavits, and others laid out point by point the grievances that the twins had filed away mentally over the course of two years on the road, along with claims that their statements could easily be verified. Some letters reveal the agitation that the battle caused for the twins. In one, written at half past midnight, the twins said, "You may think this a queer time to sit up & write letters, but my feelings are so strongly worked upon & have been so excited . . . that I find it impossible to sleep & therefore have got up from my bed & as Mr. Harris sleeps in the same room . . . I have asked him to obtain a light & sit down to write to you."[64]

From late May to late July, the twins dictated a series of letters that laid out a sound rebuttal to Mrs. Coffin and a rational argument for their own independence. And, quietly, in short notes whose tone could not be more different from that of the twins, Harris did not negotiate so much as stipulate the terms of their freedom. Their freedom, after all, meant more responsibility for Harris but less oversight from an absentee employer. His salary remained the same, but he now controlled the books and was accountable only to the twins. So, after May, he forwarded to the Coffins the proceeds from shows already performed. He surveyed the market for horses and carriages, then declared the fair price to purchase that which they already used and paid it to the Coffins. And, last, he closed the books on the twins' dealings with the Concern and offered them up for inspection by Abel Coffin whenever he returned. Amid the rancor between the twins and the Coffins, he hoped to avoid any chance that his work as road manager would be undermined, and sending his books to one of the warring parties without documentation might do just that.[65]

When Coffin returned to Massachusetts, he met immediately with Hale to ascertain where the twins were. When Hale told the captain that the twins would not agree to reenter any working relationship, Coffin accused the former manager of "exciting *his subjects* to rebellion." While Hale never encouraged the twins to stay with Coffin, the evidence clearly shows that they had excited themselves into rebellion; they did not need anyone else to tell them how to feel. Coffin proceeded to pursue Chang and Eng across New York State—a "wild goose chase," he wrote to his wife, during which he "travelled night & day" until he was "almost beat out with the rough roads." After some false leads, he tracked them down in Bath, New York, a village some eighty miles south of Rochester.[66]

When Coffin returned to Boston after meeting with the twins, he embellished the story of the encounter to acquaintances, according to Hale. Coffin claimed that he found the twins indulging in "whoring, gaming, and drinking" and, as a result, "gave Chang Eng 'the damndest thrashing they ever had in their lives'—and that before he left them, they acknowledged he 'was perfectly right in beating them, as it was for their own good'!!" If Coffin did tell this story, it highlights Coffin's self-identified paternalistic role toward the twins. When he and his wife had control over them, Chang and Eng had been clean-living members of the family; once they broke away, they turned to vice. Only through a firm hand could the twins regain their footing and lead a proper lifestyle. Coffin provided that firm hand briefly, but with him out of the picture, the twins would fall again. And what about Hale? How did passing along this story serve his interests? It aligned him with the twins, against Coffin. While perhaps not stirring up trouble, as Coffin claimed, Hale did want to keep the lines of opportunity for future collaboration with the twins open, and in this, he would be successful.[67]

Coffin's report to his wife was much more sober and much more resigned. "We have had much talk," he said; "they seem to feel themselves quite free from me."[68]

And he was right. Chang and Eng were their own men.

Re-presenting

The change in status of the twins was not widely publicized. The first mention occurred almost a year later, noting that they had "attained their majority," "dissolved their connection with Capt. Coffin," and were "carrying on business for joint account."[69] In the immediate years before and after the parting of ways, there was no noticeable shift in public perception. The physical altercation in Massachusetts took place before their independence, whereas those in Ohio and Alabama occurred after. Published reports before June 1, 1832, criticized the twins for their "privilege of living without labor," and reports after this fateful date did the same. Throughout the 1830s, writers criticized what they perceived as the twins' lack of self-respect and esteem that attended the exhibition of their bodies.

This representational continuity suggested the ambiguity that surrounded the twins—their race, their status, their position. Were they Chinese or Siamese? Indians? "Niggers"? Enslaved? Free? Were they models of how to act, or how not to act? Were they a comedic device to poke fun at others, or were they the butt of the joke? Were they speaking for themselves, or were they ventriloquists' dummies? These questions remained for the rest of the 1830s (indeed, for the duration of their lives). Ironically, the twins, in trying to situate themselves in American society as favorably as possible, turned to racial and cultural representations to draw comparisons between themselves and mainstream society.

Robert Dale Owen, son of communitarian social reformer Robert Owen, got his first glimpse of the Siamese brothers in March 1832, during their exhibition in Petersburg, Virginia. The former resident of the failed New Harmony utopian community aimed the brunt of his commentary—his criticism—at questions of work and wealth, self-respect and greed. The twins or someone else was making a great deal of money off these exhibitions, he decided; despite their physical anomaly, they occupied the privileged position of being able to live without labor. "And, in truth, how many far greater sacrifices than any consequent on these twins' deformity, are voluntarily made every day—every hour—by those who hold," he wrote, "that the orthodox text regarding the inestimable value of the soul should rather read, 'what shall it profit a man if he gain respect, esteem, affection from others, the approbation of his own breast and the whole world of virtues and moral graces, yet lose—the chance of getting rich? Or what shall a man give in exchange for Gold?'" The twins, Owen thought, had exchanged too much—respect, esteem, or, in the language discussed earlier, honor and integrity—for money. Ironically, he juxtaposed the twins' "mercenary" sensibilities against the "refreshing" exceptions to be found in communities such as New Harmony. This is to say, he condemned Chang and Eng by placing them squarely in the capitalist market economy, where the accumulation of wealth was paramount.[70] Others, however, similarly criticized the twins' perceived accumulation of wealth through an emphasis on their race.

Although accounts no longer included lengthy descriptions of the twins' physical features, every story referred to them by what had become their stage name, the Siamese twins. This served to underline both their national and racial origins and their physical anomaly. And while the occasional interposition of racialized language provided dramatic exclamation points to the fact of their difference, private writings show that the "friends" who came to visit in levees always saw the twins in racial terms. "This astonishing freak of nature is exceedingly interesting, and the sight of it is not disagreeable," one man wrote in his diary. "But their faces are devoid of intelligence, and have that stupid expression which is characteristic of the natives of the East." Another remembered "their strange foreign features" and "harsh" accent. Owen and others turned to American Indians, explaining that the brothers had "somewhat the appearance of the aborigines . . . of a swarthy complexion [with] coarse black hair." Still others turned elsewhere: "They are a couple of ugly, tawny fellows, in features resembling the African quite as much as the European."[71]

As Americans in the early 1830s experienced economic depression and political crisis, crowded cities and disease epidemics, and an increasingly diverse workforce and vocal abolitionist movement, these two with their foreign faces and freakish bodies traveled from town to town, attracting crowds and taking money. Still widely publicized, the twins found that familiarity was breeding contempt. "Some work to gain a living, and some to spend their substance; some labor to improve their intellects, and some to destroy them; but we know of nobody in this nation who does not work, unless it be the Siamese twins, and the free people of color," the *Western Monthly Magazine* wrote in its New Year's message for 1834. Other newspapers wondered if it was time for the twins to return home.[72]

Coming out of their relationship with the Coffins, the twins understood their position in terms of freedom and slavery. And in the next phase of their presentation to the public, they hoped to make clear their free status. This would be done through the production of a new exhibition pamphlet, which Hale initially hoped to call "An Account of the Siamese United Brothers, by Themselves." Hale would write the pamphlet, a necessity because Captain Coffin retained the copyright for the old one, but he would do so in consideration of the twins' wishes. "I will venture to say there will be nothing in it which shall [be] contrary to your inclinations," he wrote to Chang and Eng. "It will be of no use for me to write and get printed any thing unless it meets your approbation."[73]

The twins' primary interest in this new publication was not only to dispel any thought that their mother had sold them into slavery but also to show that they had been treated like slaves by Coffin. The motives behind this framing were multiple. On the one hand, there was the opportunity to take the fight once more to Abel Coffin. Hale, whom the Coffins blamed for the twins' defection and who feared a lawsuit by the Coffins, embraced this sentiment most heartily. "If he [brings a lawsuit], by the gods, I'll write such a 'History of the Siamese Youths' and their *owner* Capt Abel Coffin, as shall make him curse the day he ever heard of Siam," he wrote. The twins also threatened to expose Coffin as a slaveholder rather than guardian. Such threats expressed more than the plaintive cry of aggrieved men; Hale and the twins believed that they would undermine the public standing of Coffin and his wife. "[I] have refrained from saying many things which I might have done," Hale wrote, "[but] I think I shall yet let him know that as large as he is I can bring him down pretty low between the leaves of a 50 page pamphlet."[74]

But, on the other hand, a full year after they had attained their majority, the twins were not so concerned with sullying Coffin's reputation as with redeeming their own. Hale's reassurance in May 1833 that "your request that the public should know you 'are no longer slaves' will of course be attended to" suggests that this issue still haunted them.[75] And as we have seen, their freedom alone did not garner them respect, as they continued to be contextualized alongside embattled free people of color and American Indians.

Ultimately, though, it took longer than they had imagined to produce the new pamphlet, and once it finally appeared in 1836, they turned to an entirely different racial order to position themselves favorably. The early pamphlet, published first in 1829, was also written by Hale, with substantial input from Coffin. It portrayed the twins as Orientalized youths, juxtaposing them against Western norms: "They continue to dress in their native costume, and their hair, which is about four feet in length, is braided in the Chinese style." Similarly, the advertising posters that attempted to attract visitors to the shows played up the exotic. One poster, printed in 1830, shows a pair of young boys, dark-skinned, with long queues, dressed in Chinese garb, standing amid a tropical landscape. Another image shows the twins as boys with playthings in their hands. In the earliest years, the twins also dressed in Chinese costume for shows, performing somersaults, lifting heavy men in the audience to demonstrate their strength, playing games such as chess, or mingling with the audience.[76]

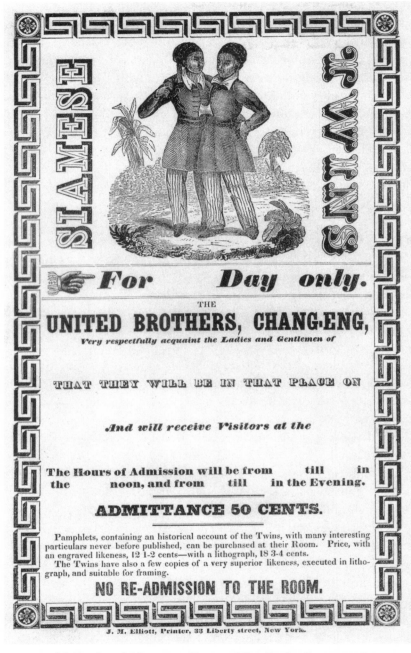

SIAMESE TWINS

👉 For Day only.

THE
UNITED BROTHERS, CHANG·ENG,
Very respectfully acquaint the Ladies and Gentlemen of

THAT THEY WILL BE IN THAT PLACE ON

And will receive Visitors at the

The Hours of Admission will be from   till   in the
the   noon, and from   till   in the Evening.

ADMITTANCE 50 CENTS.

Pamphlets, containing an historical account of the Twins, with many interesting particulars never before published, can be purchased at their Room. Price, with an engraved likeness, 12 1-2 cents—with a lithograph, 18 3-4 cents.

The Twins have also a few copies of a very superior likeness, executed in lithograph, and suitable for framing.

NO RE-ADMISSION TO THE ROOM.

J. M. Elliott, Printer, 33 Liberty street, New York.

Exhibition broadside, 1830s. Chang and Eng Bunker Papers #3761, Southern Historical Collection, Wilson Special Collections Library, University of North Carolina at Chapel Hill.

The 1836 publication showed the men growing in more ways than one. The pair had adopted an American style of dress—images from this period show them wearing Western-style suits, with coat and bowtie—with the notable exception of their hair, which remained long and braided. They were shown as young men, not boys, in dress and in their height in relation to other items in the illustrations. (Their illustrated facial features also began resembling what photographs later showed they actually looked like.) They had grown in terms of responsibility, as well. Whereas the earlier version of the pamphlet had been written when the twins could not yet speak adequate English or really know what was going on, this version had been written under their supervision, offering the chance "to correct any erroneous statements which may have occurred in previous publications." Instead of tumbling, swimming, checkers or parlor tricks, the twins now embraced hunting.[77] Whereas the earlier publication had assigned them to the "poorer class" in Siam and dismissed their claims to be merchants as "facetious," the twins now emphasized their Chinese origins, the privileged role that Chinese play in Siamese society—including their exclusion from corvée labor—and their family's experience in the duck and egg trade. In other words, their exceptional Chineseness was juxtaposed against the common Siameseness of the Siamese, and in so doing they positioned themselves at a level similar to the privileged white bourgeois against a racially ambiguous proletariat.

To combat rumors that their mother sold them into slavery, they said that neither they nor their mother had expected them to be gone from home for more than eighteen or twenty months. Furthermore, the pamphlet said, a trade representative of President Andrew Jackson had visited their mother recently, and she was glad to learn that the twins were in good health. Claims such as these served to erase doubts about their origins and about their mother and to establish certain class respectability for the twins. Royalty had come to see them on their tours of Europe, and representatives of the U.S. government were visiting their mother.[78]

The rest of the publication focused on the twins' sightseeing while on exhibit in Europe in 1835 and 1836. In Paris, they visited museums that boasted "a very extensive and well-arranged collection of living beasts." Traveling to Belgium, which was still feeling the aftereffects of the Belgian Revolution, they admired Flemish paintings, the churches of Antwerp, and attractive women. The book goes into detail relating how the twins braved the wartime border between Belgium and the Netherlands, winding their way through troops on patrol and bureaucratic red tape. At the museum at

"Eng-Chang" engraving, 1839. Chang and Eng Bunker Papers #3761, Southern Historical Collection, Wilson Special Collections Library, University of North Carolina at Chapel Hill.

The Hague, the twins admired the "very extensive collection of curiosities" on exhibit, and in Amsterdam they visited the king. Their trip to Holland allowed them "an opportunity of seeing Dutchmen in all their glory." In short, the narrative of their European tour allowed Chang and Eng to turn the gaze around. Rather than be the object of scrutiny, the twins did the scrutinizing. And coming into contact with the great museums and cathedrals of Europe and rubbing shoulders with royalty enabled the twins to make another claim to class respectability.[79]

In their dress, in their speech, and in their access to markers of class, the twins were beginning to position themselves as deserving of a certain American identity. In reporting to an American audience their experiences in Western Europe, a place that still represented in many circles high culture and civilization, the twins became mediators between ordinary Americans, on the one hand, and great arts and culture, on the other. At the same time, however, these exhibition booklets also served to point out examples of ignorant Americans—often rural or lower class. By sharing these stories with their visitors, the twins were in effect inviting their visitors to join with them and laugh at the ignorance of others, creating a sense of shared experience, while also letting their visitors know the high places and important people that they had met, thus lending an air of respectability about them.[80]

Nevertheless, an increasingly diverse—and complex—northern society offered fewer and fewer positions from which the twins could assert their own equality. Put another way, there were more and more marginalized positions into which the twins found themselves slotted. Some published reports took direct aim at their claims to be devoted children. In 1838, newspapers began excerpting a journal of an 1836 U.S. diplomatic mission to Siam that reported that the twins had the reputation in their homeland "of being dissipated and unfilial." William S. W. Ruschenberger, the surgeon to this mission, wrote that a man told him "their poor mother cry plenty about those boys. They say they make plenty money; no send never any to their poor mother."[81] Such reports played on earlier criticisms of the twins as "pickpockets," desirous only of capitalizing on their physical anomaly. Reports circulated in the late 1830s that the twins had accumulated a fortune of $100,000, "the proceeds of a voluntary tax paid to curiosity." Even those who did not lay the sin of greed at the feet of the twins nevertheless saw the position that they occupied as racialized exhibitors of singular bodies as a demeaning one in which an immoral capitalist society placed the twins. The brothers became a cautionary tale for the unfortunate paths that American society might encourage other exotic curiosities to follow. In 1839, when there was public discussion over what to do with the Amistad captives if they indeed won their freedom, some papers editorialized that "we trust . . . they will not be allowed by a Christian public, to be led about for show, like the Siamese twins, where the benign rays of Christianity can never reach them."[82]

Try as they might, Chang and Eng were unable to escape a racial and ethnic order that they themselves participated in constructing. The brothers had positioned themselves as free, but not necessarily as equal. After exhibiting their conjoined bodies around the United States and Europe for almost a decade, they began entertaining thoughts of retirement. In 1838, they explored briefly the possibility of return to Siam.[83] Ultimately, however, they decided instead on the American South.

CHAPTER THREE

The Connected Twins

In 1839, Chang and Eng retired to a small, rural community in northwestern North Carolina. In Wilkes County, the Piedmont ran out of real estate and the Blue Ridge rose in its place. Streams with their origins in the mountains that ringed Wilkes to the north, west, and south fed the county's major waterway, the Yadkin River, which in turn nourished a fertile landscape. On respectable farms, men of influence produced healthy quantities of tobacco, wheat, rye, oats, and, especially, corn. In the forests, early settlers of the state's western lands could hunt pheasant and venison, squirrels and bear. And at home, these men, pioneers of their state's expansion and veterans of their nation's struggle for independence, wished they could rest assured that their homes and their families would prosper, that the Upper Yadkin would continue to deserve the name "Happy Valley." Alas, they could not.[1]

Wilkes County was established with the birth of the nation and had been peopled in large part by veterans of wars with the British and Indians, attracted by the wild beauty and natural resources of the land, and their families. By the late 1830s, however, the residents of Wilkes County were experiencing an extended period of diminishing economic opportunities. In this, Wilkes was not unlike much of the Carolina Piedmont and indeed much of the southern seaboard, which saw thousands of young families migrate to the Old Southwest between 1810 and 1860. Even when compared with neighboring counties, however, opportunity for Wilkes County residents—in agriculture, manufacturing, education, and a host of other indicators—seemed to lie elsewhere.[2]

But for the Siamese brothers Chang and Eng—and for the Irish-born Charles Harris—Wilkes County offered opportunity. For much of the previous ten years, life for these three had consisted either of traveling from small town to small town, always strangers or outsiders, or of spending months in large cities, most regularly New York, trekking daily from boardinghouse to exhibition hall. The northern United States, gripped in the early years of industrial revolution, was in the 1830s in the midst of a social transformation. The North was increasingly urbanized, the population ever more dense; even the rural North was becoming functionally and sociologically "urbanized." Disparities in wealth grew, not only between the highest and lowest classes but also between bourgeois and working classes. Gradual emancipation engendered hostility to people of color and transients; a swell in the number of immigrants resulted in antagonism against foreigners, especially Irish. Spatial segmentation ensued, with clearly demarcated spaces for working and residing and for rich and poor. There was the lily-white order of the private sphere and the motley hue of public disorder. Claims to higher status rested often on the ability to create private spaces to which one could retreat, far from the rabble.[3] The twins' identities, and that of Charles Harris, were too closely linked to their public exhibition and their foreign origins; there was little room in the North for them to settle down to lives of quiet respectability. In the South, however, there was more space, physically and socially, in terms of class and race and sex, in which these itinerants could ground themselves. In Wilkes County, the twins made important connections among the community's commercial and professional class, took oaths of U.S. citizenship, and acquired property for themselves far from the public eye. In Wilkes County, Chang and Eng built relationships over time with people around them and, ultimately, found love.

Social Networks: Paths to Community Membership

The decision to settle in Wilkes County appears well orchestrated; it was not spur of the moment. On May 8, 1839, more than a month before the twins arrived in Wilkesboro, Charles Harris left the traveling party in Carnesville, Georgia, for New York City. As Chang and Eng made their way through northern Georgia into western North Carolina in late May and into early June, Harris fetched a trunk of the twins' belongings, bought new clothes, and repaired old accessories, including the twins' pistol.[4] On June 7, Peter Marsh, who scouted out locations and arranged for lodging and show venues, left the twins in Statesville and made his way to Wilkesboro to secure accommodations for the party. On that same day, Harris booked double passage from New York; the extra fare was for baggage. He arrived in Wilkesboro by stage on June 20 after traveling via Philadelphia; Baltimore; Portsmouth, Virginia; and Weldon, Henderson's Depot, Raleigh, Greensboro, Salisbury, and Statesville, North Carolina. The twins, meanwhile, had since June 11 settled in at the Wilkesboro inn operated by Abner

Carmichael. There was a final performance in Jefferson, Ashe County, on July 3 and 4, and that was that. After traveling and performing almost non-stop for ten years, the twins made their way back to Wilkes County, to Carmichael's inn, and took a long, long break.[5]

Wilkesboro, then, appears not to be a random spot at which the twins, as well as Harris, decided suddenly to settle down. Rather, it was a destination. So, the question: Why Wilkes County? Of course, the southern community offered a contrast to the urbanizing North, in ways already discussed and other ways still to be considered. For the twins, "attracted . . . by the purity of the air, the salubrity of the climate, and the rich and beautiful mountain scenery," this was a chance to enjoy a respite from their worldly weariness; here, on the hundreds of acres of farmland and woodland that they would buy, they could "be free from the scrutinizing gaze of the public eye," a contemporary wrote in the 1840s. It was a chance to "engage in chasing stag and catching trout, . . . to enjoy the recreation which they had desired to find far away from the hurrying crowds," a family friend wrote sometime after their deaths in 1874. But also, a North Carolina folk writer posited in the 1930s, it provided for the twins a "transition from the monotonous museum to the gay society of Wilkesboro [that] was about as great as if a tired slave, who expected nothing, had fallen asleep under his burden of work, and woke up in Heaven."[6] These observations by third parties who claimed to have known the twins express likely truths. The twins appreciated the reprieve from large crowds and the public gaze, the opportunity to hunt unmolested, to become part of a community rather than merely passing through. And these factors could explain why they chose country life over city life and South over North. But the decision to settle in Wilkes County grew not out of general attitudes but out of specific networks the twins developed while on the road and reinforced once they arrived in North Carolina.

More than anything else, the twins were social actors. Their job, their expertise, was to engage in conversation, to make their visitors feel at ease, through light banter or substantive dialogue, even as their physical anomaly made visitors discomfited—to make connections with others even as their connection to each other was the hook that at once attracted and repelled their audience. Similarly, Wilkes County, North Carolina, and the South generally were not isolated entities but part of complex commercial, educational, cultural, and social networks that made the United States figuratively smaller even as it was becoming literally larger. Wilkes County had commercial, political, and educational ties to the commercial hub of Salisbury, 60 miles south in Rowan County; to the college town of Salem,

50 miles to the east; to the state capital of Raleigh, 150 miles to the east; and to the nation's biggest cities, including Philadelphia, more than 500 miles to the north, and New York, 600 miles away. The twins and the community they now called home; North Carolina, the "Rip Van Winkle" state, so-called in the early nineteenth century because many people believed it seemed to have remained asleep while the rest of the country progressed; and the South: none of these were islands, and they cannot be fully understood unless their relationship in larger networks is taken into account.[7]

Legend has it that the initial connection that linked the twins to Wilkes County formed during an exhibition in New York, when visiting small-town doctor James Calloway saw the twins and, learning of their interest in hunting and fishing, invited them to visit his home of Wilkesboro. This account comes from Shepherd M. Dugger's fanciful *Romance of the Siamese Twins*, published in 1936. There is so much that is clearly untrue in the publication, which Dugger claimed to be a corrective informed by family members and neighbors of the twins, that we have much reason to dismiss its contents. And yet there is enough plausible information to make some of his claims worth a second glance.[8] One segment of society with which the twins regularly formed relationships was the medical community. Doctors had played an important role in the twins' early career, and they occupied prominent positions for the rest of the twins' lives. What is more, the twins did socialize with Calloway and his wife in Wilkes and through them created a series of connections with important county residents, including other doctors.

There was a sizable medical community in Wilkesboro—four doctors—all of whom had received their medical training in Philadelphia. One of these, with whom the twins were also acquainted, made his name through his attempts to manipulate the human body. Wilkes native Robert C. Martin earned renown in the region fixing clubfeet and cross-eyes. "He is becoming to be quite a celebrated physician here," one Wilkesboro woman wrote to her younger sister in Salem. "He has straightened club feet, and performed an operation upon a lady who had cross-eyes with so much success that her eyes are as straight as anyone's." About his surgical skills, the Salisbury newspaper gushed, "The patient has since expressed her willingness to undergo twenty such operations rather than to remain afflicted as she had been." Referring to Salisbury's doctors, the paper asked, "Will not our Physicians let it be known to the afflicted . . . that they may be healed? or are they not qualified to undertake such a job?" Clearly there was demand for medical services that could fix physical anomalies, to take deformities and make them fit the ideal human form, though there is no evidence that the twins consulted any of the Wilkesboro physicians about their own condition. But these doctors were also able to use the twins to build their own reputations in other ways. For instance, when Martin later sought a letter of credit for a trip to Europe, he asked Chang and Eng for a letter of introduction to their banker in New York.[9]

The twins' relationship with the medical community smoothed their entry into the elite society of Wilkes. Martin, for one, a member of a prominent family, was also the subject of (tame) gossip engaged in by daughters of Wilkes's finest. Calloway, meanwhile, was a great-nephew of Daniel Boone, a flourishing medical practitioner who was beginning to dabble in land speculation, and a future politician. Calloway had also married a daughter of the county sheriff, Abner Carmichael, and thus into one of the most powerful political families in the northwestern part of the state. The twins took advantage of these connections to participate in public social events and to ground themselves in Wilkes society. In their first month, for instance, Calloway's wife, Mary, took the twins to a camp meeting, offering Chang and Eng the chance to attend alongside a prominent woman as observers—perhaps participants—but not as the object of display.[10]

The Carmichael family, in turn, ran a boardinghouse in Wilkesboro, at which Chang and Eng stayed for a couple of months in 1839. Later, after they had moved to another part of the county, the twins continued to entertain at the Carmichaels' and lodged there when on extended business in the county seat. Also resident at the inn was James W. Gwyn Jr., the county's superior court clerk, whose signature marked every order the court issued. He stayed at the Carmichaels' only when court was in session; otherwise, he lived, in 1839, with his newlywed wife, Mary Ann Lenoir, at the Fort Defiance plantation of her father, Thomas Lenoir, the county's largest slaveholder (with thirty-eight) and the son of a county founding father.[11] Gwyn came to know the twins not only through his work on the superior court but also through commercial transactions. From Calloway and Martin to Carmichael and Gwyn, Chang and Eng used these networks to enter Wilkes society.

In all this, Charles Harris remained their companion. It is impossible to overemphasize this point. For many years, the twins' welfare had been linked closely to Harris. Since 1831, he had managed the details of the twins' performances, arranging transportation, deciding which cities to visit and for how long, purchasing day-to-day necessities for the twins, and getting them out of scrapes with the law. He had written down their angry complaints against the Coffins and stood by their side as they declared their independence from the sea captain and his wife. Of course, he received handsome compensation from the twins, as their expense accounts reveal, and he had accumulated substantial savings. But after so many years on the road, he, too, was tired of travel, and the decision to settle down in Wilkes likely was as much his as that of the twins.[12] Once in Wilkes County, the twins continued to tie their fortunes to Harris, and the accomplished Harris was able to open doors for them. He also carved out a significant place for himself. For instance, he appears often in county criminal action papers, not for wrongdoing but as guarantor of people who needed bonds to pledge their appearance in court. He used his contacts in northern cities, especially New York, to procure special orders of fine china and cutlery for the county's high society. And he used his vast experience sending and receiving letters across the country to assume the position of postmaster at Traphill, a community about twenty miles northwest of Wilkesboro, where he and the twins had settled by October 1839.[13]

That month, the twins and Harris pursued courses of action that fundamentally strengthened their ties to the area. First, each of them petitioned the superior court in Wilkesboro for U.S. citizenship. The twins volunteered that they were "natives of the kingdom of Siam, in Asia," Harris that he was a "native of Ireland, within the Kingdom of Great Britain and Ireland." All three asserted that "they have behaved as men of good moral character" and that they were "attached to the principles of the Constitution of the United States and . . . well disposed to the good order and happiness of the same." They renounced their allegiance to their respective monarchs, the twins to the "king of Siam," Harris to "Victoria, Queen of Great Britain & Ireland." In open court, James Gwyn administered to his boardinghouse neighbors the oath of allegiance to the United States and the state of North Carolina. Chang, Eng, and Harris were citizens of the United States and of North Carolina.[14]

The twins' successful application to obtain citizenship carried more significance than did Harris's. A 1790 congressional act limited naturalization to "free white persons." But the twins were not alone in their success. At least one Chinese-born male had been naturalized by the time the twins took the oath, and a handful of others became citizens before anti-Asian attitudes hardened in the late nineteenth century.[15] That later Chinese immigrants were excluded from citizenship on the grounds of the 1790 act reveals much about the growing pervasiveness of a common racial imaginary across the nation. That the twins and a handful of other early Chinese settlers were able to gain citizenship despite the congressional prohibition speaks not to a more accepting early republic ideology but to the limited presence of a "national" racial discourse, at least as it applied to Asians in America, and to the localized nature of citizenship during these years. Until the 1870s, county officials determined a person's fitness for citizenship. Local standards, not national laws, influenced the process. The twins were applying in a county that had very few immigrants and no other Asians, in a region whose color line was drawn decisively between white and black, in a court where they had been neighbors with the man administering the oaths. The twins were able to take advantage of the community's standards and its social networks to gain citizenship.

The second major development of October 1839 was the twins' purchase in midmonth of 150 acres along Little Sandy Creek, near the Roaring River and Traphill, for $300. This transaction was the function of a new set of social networks among a different sector of the Wilkes County population. The twins' initial contacts with the medical and legal communities had given them access to some of the county's most prominent families. Those ties centered on Wilkesboro, the county's commercial seat and a remarkably diverse town. In a county in which whites accounted for 87 percent of the population in 1840, in Wilkesboro they were just 64 percent. Enslaved blacks accounted for 19 percent of Wilkesboro's population (compared with 11 percent countywide), and free persons of color made up 17 percent of the town's population. (This figure compared with just 1 percent countywide. Out of 117 free persons of color in the county, 61 lived in the county seat.) Not surprisingly, most county residents employed in commerce lived in town, and many town residents were also engaged in manufacturing jobs, likely in sawmills, or as makers of carriages and wagons. The county seat, with its courthouse and jail, its stores, and its doctors' offices, served as a central meeting place for the county's residents, in both official and personal matters. The town's diversity, density, and commerce likely gave Wilkesboro a familiar feel for the twins, but these were not the qualities Chang and Eng were after. They wanted space and isolation.

As did most town residents, the prominent citizens with whom the twins engaged had close ties to other parts of the county. Through marriage, for instance, Gwyn had ties to the county's southwestern tip, at the headwaters of the Yadkin River, which held the county's greatest concentration of slaveholding wealth and, not coincidentally, families of influence.[16] Altogether, the county's southwestern tip had a proportion of slaves—30 percent—approaching that of the state overall. Of the county's thirteen people who owned twenty or more slaves, four lived in this census district; only two other districts had two, and the rest had one or none.[17] Their doctor acquaintance James Calloway had land along Hunting Creek, east of Wilkesboro, and the Martins of Wilkes County congregated along North Hunting Creek, as did the family of William Masten, the county court clerk with whom the twins also became acquainted. This district also enjoyed rich agriculture and larger farms; it was home to two planters and had the highest number of slave-holding households in the county.[18] But the twins did not use these connections to settle in those districts. Land in these richer parts of the county was scarce and expensive. Plus, with the number of large plantations, any home the twins built for themselves might seem inconsequential in comparison. Instead, the twins, and Harris, turned to a mountainous region in the northeastern extreme of the county.

Small, white farming families formed the bulk of Wilkes County. Out of 1,953 total households, only 241 had slaves; in other words, 88 percent of the county's households did not own slaves. Of the 241 slaveholding households, 78 had just one slave and 32 had two. More than half had three or fewer. Some districts had percentages of whites as high as 95 percent. Spicer's District, of which Traphill formed the base, was 92 percent white. Yet the district had 22 slaveholding households, more than any other district save one. Ten households had just one slave (tied for the most in the county), and seventeen had five or fewer. These numbers are deceptive, however. Of the twenty-two households, five were Johnsons (with a total of twenty-three slaves), three were Spicers (for a total of twelve), and three were Holbrooks (with nine between them). This is to say, half of the households, accounting for 59 percent of the district's enslaved population, belonged to three families, and two of these, the Spicers and the Holbrooks, were connected by marriage.[19]

After settling in Traphill, the twins would forge relationships with each of these families. But their initial connection to this neck of the woods was with farmer Robert J. Baugus, one of the other slaveholders in the district (with five), who also ran a boardinghouse.[20] Traphill was near the natural landmark Stone Mountain, also known then as Rock Mountain, which attracted a fair number of visitors, who often stayed overnight in the village. We do not know for certain how Chang, Eng, and Harris first came upon Traphill and the lodgings afforded by Baugus, though the possibility of traveling to see the mountain is as good as any.[21]

In mid-October, the twins purchased 150 acres from a Caleb Martin. This transaction showed early connections already being made; the witnesses for the deal were Charles Harris, of course, but also Samuel J. Baugus (son of Robert) and Captain John Johnson, the district's most wealthy man in land

and slaves.[22] In other words, the twins continued to align themselves with very important people, socially and economically. Chang and Eng immediately had a house built and stocked. They also briefly tried their hand as merchants in the village. The burst of economic activity thrust the twins into a variety of relationships with their neighbors, as customers, suppliers, and employers.

They bought goods—primarily produce, meat, and livestock—from the prominent slaveholding families. They sold textiles and dry goods to a wide assortment of neighbors, prominent and obscure. (One name mentioned frequently in the store account book was Alston Yates, their future brother-in-law.) They hired several local women for extended periods to keep house and a number of slaves to perform other types of labor. The twins were, judging from various lists of expenses and income, the picture of industry. And even though they were building bridges with the county's elite, they presented themselves as common people. "We have wood and water in great abundance and our neighbours are all on an equality, and none are very rich," they wrote in 1842. "People live comfortably but each man tills his own soil." They were men who proved good on payment for services in kind, to whom neighbors could turn if they needed something, and for whom wives and daughters could work without scandal. Quickly, Chang and Eng worked their way into the economic life of Traphill.[23]

At the same time, the twins set themselves apart from—or above—many of their neighbors through a flamboyant display of wealth. The house they built, "with its singular dormer windows, and long piazza, and its parlors and spacious chamber, and neat bedrooms . . . was considered uncommonly elegant," Jesse Franklin Graves wrote some forty years later. And while his description may have been embellished, the twins did not spare much expense. Harris made a special run to New York to purchase items for the house, including six silver table forks ($29), six silver tablespoons ($26.25), twelve teaspoons ($22), two dozen ivory knives and forks ($9), two dozen buck knives and forks ($2.63), and three tea trays ($3.31). For their persons, Harris bought a dozen silk handkerchiefs ($15), four ribbed lamb's-wool shirts ($10), four pair of lamb's-wool drawers ($8), and a suit of double harness ($25). The twins intended to entertain and to look good doing so. In all, the "articles purchased for the private use of CE" on this trip cost $467.25. Their determination to improve their land and make a home for themselves paid dividends too, at least in how they compared with their neighbors. By the early 1840s, only two other properties in the district received a higher valuation for tax purposes—the twins' property was valued at $1,000—and both of those had substantially more land.[24]

As Chang and Eng carved out a new place for themselves in the mountains of northwestern North Carolina, newspapers continued to follow them closely. The *Carolina Watchman* of nearby Salisbury offered the first report of the twins' presence in the area: "Our old acquaintances, the Messrs. Chang & Eng, have purchased a tract of land . . . where they intend establishing for themselves a home." The twins did not plan to exhibit much more, if at all; they might visit Siam, their native country, but they would return to Wilkes County; and they made application for U.S. citizenship, showing "considerable interest in the affairs of the County and their neighborhood, and what speaks for their taste as well as intelligence, they are GENUINE WHIGS." (Wilkes County and Salisbury's Rowan County, and indeed much of western North Carolina, were Whig strongholds, and the *Watchman* was a Whig paper.) Other papers quickly picked up the story and added details of their own. They had bought a farm and gone to farming. They had purchased subscriptions to the *New York Gazette* and the *New World*. They were "as happy as lords."[25]

The paper closest to home, the *Watchman*, reported the twins were "much delighted with their mountain settlement," and "they appeared in their unconstrained condition much more amiable and interesting than when encountering the gaze of the wondering crowd." Papers elsewhere—in the North, especially—produced the requisite jokes mocking the idea of the twins as political citizens or as tillers of the soil. "They drive a *double* team, and ought to raise a *double* crop," the *New-Yorker* teased. "We should like to see them mowing together," a Massachusetts paper commented. "How many votes would they be entitled to?" asked a New Hampshire paper, while the *Philadelphia Gazette* surmised that the twins' ultimate goal was to run for Congress.[26] These jokes ridiculed the twins for engaging in the most mundane (and, hence, the most profound) acts that ordinary people (and, thus, *not* the twins) performed. But none of these first articles reporting the twins' new residence speculated or teased at the possibility of intimacy with their female neighbors. This was, perhaps, an oversight on the part of the papers. After all, written into the very contract of landownership—into every such contract—was the stipulation that the land now belonged, in perpetuity, to the new owners, their assigns, and their heirs.

Sexual Networks: Marriage and the Bonds of Respectability

In addition to becoming citizens and buying land, the third major development of October 1839 was Charles Harris's marriage to Frances "Fannie"

Baugus, the daughter of the man who played host to the twins and Harris during their first months in Traphill. This relationship had a tremendous impact on the course of the three men's lives, though this assertion rests on a preponderance of speculation. Perhaps it was a flicker of attraction between Charles Harris and Fannie Baugus on a trip to Traphill that motivated the men to move to Traphill in the first place.[27] Perhaps the spark emerged after the men were already lodging at Robert Baugus's house.[28] Perhaps the courtship and looming marriage drove Harris to apply for citizenship and the twins to purchase land (perhaps to give the twins, Harris, and his new bride space to build a future, or perhaps to give the twins a place of their own away from Harris and his new family). Perhaps the wedding of Harris and Baugus provided that first opportunity for Chang and Eng to spot and start romancing Adelaide and Sarah Ann Yates.[29] Or perhaps these inroads were made a year later when Fannie Baugus's older brother married the Yates girls' older sister, making Harris related by marriage to the Yates family. All of these "perhapses" cannot be true, but some of them certainly are, and it was these that shaped the events that occurred next. The specter of illicit sexual relations between men and women and the prospect of sanctioned sex that marriage offered came to dominate the lives of the twins for the rest of their time in Wilkes County.

In truth, issues of courtship, marriage, and sex outside of marriage—adultery, fornication, and bastardy—dominated much of the public's attention as well. Newspapers regularly printed prescriptive literature that laid out clear frameworks for how relationships between men and women should proceed. Many Americans believed they were living in degenerate days, a belief derived from perceived instability that shook accepted norms. Nationally, utopian communities experimented with alternative forms of family, and North Carolina newspapers ran cautionary tales on atypical marriages. In 1839, the state legislature took a step to strengthen normative marriage by prohibiting marriage between free persons of color and white persons and by declaring any such marriage already entered into to be null and void.[30] And local newspapers followed the Massachusetts General Assembly's debate over repealing that state's ban on interracial marriage. Just as the popular press and political discourse aimed at imposing a standard of behavior on individuals, individuals used rumor and gossip to keep friend and family in line. One daughter of the county elite proclaimed she would not attend a ball, despite the presence of several respectable chaperones, because "I do not think the company will be exactly *comme il faut*," or, in other words, proper. And strange men who came to town were met with suspicion. "There is a Mr. Crider & a Mr. Allison here again," James Gwyn wrote to his wife. "I would not be surprised if they have a notion of courting some of our Wilkes Ladies. I thought Mr. C. liked to look at & talk to our Cousin MLG today very well. . . . I don't know anything at all about him; he does not look like he was of much account."[31] So when our three newcomers, Chang, Eng, and Harris, showed up, we might imagine how the community responded to the prospects of these men's relations with its "Wilkes Ladies."

The marriage bond of £500 offered by Charles Harris and John Holbrook Jr. on October 31, 1839, made clearer a couple of points surrounding the move by Harris and the twins to Traphill. First, the support provided by Holbrook—a slaveholder and now a neighbor of the twins—further illustrated the connections being made with influential residents. Harris and the twins were newcomers, but they were able to make allies with important people. Second, it showed familiarity with, and a predilection to follow, the law. Statute required a marriage license and, to get that, a marriage bond, which guaranteed that the two parties were in fact eligible to wed each other. In practice, however, this law was often ignored. In countless adultery proceedings, for example, a common response was that the accused couple had indeed been married, by a man of the gospel if not by authority of the state.[32] Despite his impressive social connections, Harris would not have accumulated in the span of a few months the social capital necessary to attempt a union sanctioned by family, church, or community but not by law.

What the available documentation cannot reveal, however, are the motives behind the marriage. There was, after all, an unusually brief courtship; Harris had been in the county just four months and in Traphill for no more than two. In this instance, Harris's status as an outsider most likely accelerated the process. A man such as Harris, with means but without roots, would have presented an unacceptable flight risk to a father such as Robert Baugus. And if romance was in the air, as Jesse Franklin Graves has suggested, it follows that Baugus would have required a commitment from Harris—citizenship, property, especially marriage. Only in this way could Baugus guarantee that his youngest daughter would not be taken advantage of and left behind with any burdens, such as a soiled reputation or a child out of wedlock. Unless, of course, Fanny Baugus was already with child; this possibility offers another clear motive for marrying so quickly. Bastardy was one of the most common criminal offenses of antebellum North Carolina, behind only assault and battery and affray, and in 1839, the state legislature deliberated a pair of bastardy bills. But the first child of Charles and Fanny Harris did not arrive until 1842, and so a pregnancy outside of marriage—perhaps one of the first possibilities that flashed through the minds of many community members when they learned of the marriage—does not offer any light on the first family that the Siamese twins grew close to in Wilkes County.[33]

The second family with which Chang and Eng grew intimate, the Yateses, became related to Harris and the Bauguses by marriage in November 1840. If the twins were not already familiar with the women who became their wives, the union between Letha Yates, older sister to Sarah and Adelaide, and Samuel J. Baugus, Fanny Harris's older brother, certainly provided that opportunity. The first Yates, John, came to the Yadkin River valley from Virginia during the Revolutionary War and by 1780 had taken a wife and settled down. David Yates, Chang's and Eng's future father-in-law, was born on Lewis Fork in 1792, the third of John's eight children. In 1814, David Yates married Nancy Hayes, of the Warrior Creek area, and soon after the couple moved just east of Lewis Fork to the Mulberry Creek area, northwest of Wilkesboro. By 1828, they had six children: two sons and four daughters. Sarah Yates, born December 18, 1822, was David and Nancy's fourth child and their second daughter. Adelaide Yates came along ten months later, on October 11, 1823.[34] By 1829, David Yates had accumulated 500 acres of land (valued at $1,000), and by 1830, four slaves, all females, the youngest being under 10 and the two oldest somewhere between 24 and 36. By 1840, he owned seven slaves. Three were women, one of them 10 to 24 years old, the other two between 36 and 55; the four boys were all under 10. The Yates household also had one free person of color, a woman aged 10 to 24 (perhaps one of the enslaved women from 1830?). With these seven slaves, David Yates was the largest slaveholder in his 1840 census district.[35] David Yates and his family had a respectable amount of land and enslaved resources. But they were not part of the county's elite. In a variety of ways, the Yateses found their lives shaped by cultural, social, and legal forces that the county's elite did not.

The documents that tell their story are not letters, diaries, or journals but criminal action papers. In February 1840, for instance, a Wilkes County grand jury issued a bill of indictment against a "single woman" named Sarah Yates, charging that she and a man named Aron Church, both being "evil disposed persons," did "unlawfully live, bed, and cohabit together as man and wife, they not being intermarried, & not being man and wife."[36] This Sarah Yates was not the future Mrs. Eng but rather her first cousin, just two years older. Nevertheless, the incident reveals both family and social networks that connected the David Yates household to its neighbors. (The charged Sarah Yates was the daughter of David's older brother Hugh; Aron Church lived in close proximity to David and had long been a neighbor of the Yates family.) What is more, these same sources shed light directly into the David Yates household.

These sources reveal that illicit sex was unlawful but not uncommon and that these were public, not private, affairs, involving entire communities. On June 27, 1840, David Yates signed a bond for the sum of $200 to guarantee the support of a bastard child that his oldest son, Alston, was alleged to have fathered. Unlike charges of fornication or adultery, which the state viewed as a threat to the community's moral underpinnings but most often carried a relatively light fine, bastardy was treated by the state simply as a question of support. The child born to an unwed mother became a potential ward of the state, and so the court aimed at identifying a father and wresting from him a guarantee of support, often about $200, for the child's first few years of life. The mother's testimony in this case, in which she stated for the permanent court record her name and status as a single woman, as well as the age, sex, and father of the child in question, is no longer extant. What does exist is the bond, which states the mother's name, but because it is torn in an unfortunate place it offers only "Rachel H." This is most likely a Shumate's District neighbor of David Yates named Rachel Hall, in 1840 a twenty-something single woman living with four children under age ten. In the court hearings that followed and lasted into 1841, neighbors and relatives were called to testify: Yates's younger brother, Jesse; first cousins Nancy, Jesse, and Sally Hays, who also lived nearby; longtime neighbors John and Nancy Havenor, in addition to Barbary Stamper, Nancy Ballard, and Eli Brown; and more distant acquaintances Wellborn and Nancy Adams.[37] The community came out to discuss the propriety or impropriety of Alston Yates's sex life, and David Yates saw a child's supposed sexual deviance come under public scrutiny, not for the last time.

This story did not end with the Alston Yates hearings. In Wilkes County, many cases involving illicit acts of sex—bastardy, adultery, or fornication—grew in scope, ensnaring other community members in further allegations.[38] In 1841, a finding of fornication and adultery was made against Rachel Hall and Reubin Hays, and a warrant for their arrest for trial was issued. Like Hall, the forty-something Hays was a neighbor; he had grown up on his father's land on Mulberry Creek, near the Yates residence. Hays was also related by marriage to David's wife, Nancy. And the witness list was almost identical to that of the Alston Yates bastardy hearings. This all makes the timing of the indictment peculiar. Rachel Hall had been having children out of wedlock since before the 1830 federal census, and an 1841 school census for the county lists Hays next to Hall, with six children between them, some of the children in Hays's listing bearing the last name Hall. By 1841, these two had been in a relationship for more than ten years. (Their oldest child, Riley Reubin Hall, was born in 1829.)[39] Yet it was not until Alston Yates was charged with fathering a bastard child with Rachel Hall that the relationship between Hall and Hays attracted the attention of the court. Did David Yates level the accusation against the two as retribution for the allegation against his son? Regardless, the significance was twofold. Unlawful sex was neither uncommon nor out of public view. As such, once allegations were made, large numbers of neighbors and relations became involved, receiving subpoenas and putting bonds to ensure their presence at court to testify. Sex was a very public act. Entered into on the sly, it became the state's—and the community's—business. Entered into publicly within the institution of marriage, a veil of privacy descended, and the sex became sanctioned.

There had long been speculation about the twins' capacity for sexual relations. Despite the label of "monster" that Chang and Eng carried and despite early public portrayals as young boys, observers in 1829 immediately noted the potential for romance that existed for the newly arrived eighteen-year-olds, and the twins themselves talked about their desire for attractive women. Reporting observations he had made during the twins' first trip to England in 1830, a doctor commented that women were a very common topic of discussion between the brothers. An American researcher noted that Eng, when asked what he considered "the handsomest object, or as possessing the greatest beauty," immediately offered women as his answer. And the twins themselves held attraction for some women. An affectionate letter to the twins in 1831 poetically urged Chang and Eng to "think on her thou leav'st behind": "Thy love, thy fate dear youths to share / May never be my happy lot / But thou may'st grant this humble [plea] / Forget me not! Forget me not!"[40]

Most often, however, newspapers treated tales of attraction between the twins and women as jokes. Throughout the 1830s, newspapers passed along stories about love affairs that the twins had reportedly entered into. One story held that Chang had interfered in a "love intrigue" of Eng; the brothers would have engaged in a duel, "but the parties could not agree on a distance." This story was dismissed as "malicious" by a report that carried the joke a step further: One brother would never wish to conceal his love interests from the other, went the punch line. A couple of years later, a woman from Wilmington, Delaware, reportedly caught the eye of the twins.

She took a fancy to Chang but objected to marrying them both. "The fate of poor Chang is hard, as a divorce from Eng, his brother, is not to be obtained on any terms," the *Virginia Free Press* concluded. Another paper said it was Eng who wanted to marry, but his brother was "inclined to a life of single blessedness." This particular affair prompted a London poet, "Rueben Ramble," to write a few lines:

The lady's is a sorry case,
    And really must dishearten her;
Why did you creep into her grace?
    For you could not want a partner.

Already you'd your other half;
    Why long, then, for three quarters?
Oh, Chang, you are too bad by half,
    For any Yankee's daughters.

Yet should the lady take Eng too,
    How sweet were your community;
And how astonished eyes would view
    Your Trinity in Unity.[41]

The punch lines in these stories inevitably came down to the nature of the twins' physical anomaly. The London poem was unusual in that it not only took Chang to task for even desiring a mate but also in the sense that it emphasized explicitly that this would be a union across racial and national lines—"You are too bad by half / For any Yankee's daughters." (There is also the possibility that the poet was ribbing the "Yankee daughter" as well; no Brit would deign marry them.) Implicit in every report about Chang's and Eng's love interests was the question of interracial relations; after all, the phrase "Siamese twins" referred to both their physical anomaly and their national origins. But other reports also looked for laughs by matching the twins up with Asian women. In the summer of 1838, newspapers were abuzz with reports that "one of the Siamese twins" would soon be married to Afong Moy, "the little Chinese lady" who performed at such places as Peale's Museum. This reported union between Asian entertainers nevertheless closed with a punch line at the twins' expense. The "happy bridegroom" invited his brother to be his groomsman; "we wonder," the *New York Mirror* asked, "if his brother will stand up with him."[42] The foundation of condemnation had roots in the twins' deformity and the fact that any union with a woman would be, in effect, a marriage between two men and one woman, a "Trinity in Unity." In publishing stories about the attraction that the twins felt for some women and that some women felt for the twins, newspapers could only present the possibility as farce. The thought of these two men, attached forever, joining with a woman was either too funny or too perverse to take seriously.

Indeed, themes of fear, repulsion, or disgust permeated popular representations of the twins as sexual objects. While some writers criticized the sexualized Siamese twins through their ridicule of attraction, others voiced their criticisms through frightening images. The prospect of the twins engaging in sexual relations with women disturbed sensibilities. Objections were made on account of the twins' race and their physical anomaly. On the one hand, the twins understood these objections as aimed not at their conjoined state or their position in society but at their race and nationality. By 1840, there were relatively few Chinese in the United States; most were concentrated around port cities on the East Coast, especially New York City. But a discourse of Orientalism—in which an expansive America consumed "Oriental" goods and bodies but also dreamed of civilizing the Orient and of which the twins were a central element—had emerged since the earliest days of the nation. On the other hand, various concerns existed about the impact that the twins' conjoinedness might have on women of childbearing age. An illustration of the twins in one newspaper caused a correspondent to call to mind "the number of monstrous births, miscarriages, &c. . . . caused by such exhibitions, even by the mere representations of them." French authorities reportedly refused entry to the twins in 1831 for fear that mere proximity to the twins would prove disturbing—and dangerous—to French women. In 1833, speculation soared after a Kentucky woman who gave birth to still-born conjoined twins claimed she had seen numerous representations of the twins in newspaper advertisements around the time she conceived the children, which "affected" her imagination.[43]

This stillbirth resulted in repugnant speculation by newspapers. Had the Kentucky twins lived, one paper wrote, "they might have been given in marriage to the boys of Siam, and thus have become the mothers of a new race of bipeds or rather *quadrupeds*."[44] In this example, the newspaper walked an increasingly well-worn path of using "humor" to interrogate the possibility that the twins might marry, but it grounded its discussion in a number of grotesque propositions. One was the suggestion that these infant girls, who were in fact stillborn, would be given in marriage to two adult men, who were being blamed for the deaths of these very girls. Another was the prospect of this union creating "quadrupeds," or animals. The potent juxtaposition of Kentucky, Siam, race, and quadrupeds offers us today a rich illustration of the intimacy and interconnectedness that race and deformity shared. To many readers in the 1830s, however, it likely offered an unsettling glimpse into the specter of hybridity, intermarriage, or amalgamation, terms used at the time by early practitioners of racial science to describe practices and products of sexual relations across lines of race or species. It also probably reaffirmed for those readers notions of what was natural and what was not.

A profile first published in 1840 in the *Tennessee Mirror* reported, "It is said they have serious thoughts of marrying, and thus more fully dividing the sorrows and doubling the joys of this life."[45] Unlike other stories that used the idea of the twins getting married to put forth a punch line, this article did not try to make a joke of the twins' desire, nor did it use scary images to turn people against the idea. Perhaps this shift occurred because the twins had settled down and become naturalized citizens. Throughout the 1830s, newspapers speculated constantly on when Chang and Eng would return to Siam. Even if the twins were not going home, they were always transitory, in town for a day, a week, or, in the case of New York City or Philadelphia, perhaps a month or two but always leaving. With their purchase of land, their naturalization, and their stated desire to become farmers—all widely reported around the United States—the prospect of their getting married and settling down was no longer a joke.[46]

This is not to say that a stark change occurred in the views Americans held of the twins and marriage. Newspapers continued to print stories that discouraged the idea. In early 1841, just three months after the first reports that the twins were considering taking wives, newspapers spread word that the twins had fallen in love with a woman who, though she favored one over the other, was willing to marry both. Her lawyer warned her off, however, saying she would face indictment for bigamy. The veracity of such a report may be in doubt, but the moral of the story is not all that dissimilar from earlier reports suggesting that the possibility of marriage for the twins was undesirable.[47] This story eschewed usual attempts at humor or scare tactics by placing the threat in a foundational discourse that everyone understood—the law. The twins' marriage could be considered a crime against the state.

How much, if at all, the twins feared public criticism of the prospect of their getting married, or whether they held concern over the legality of their marrying, we do not know. By 1842, however, Chang and Eng still harbored dreams of marriage. In a letter to Robert Hunter, the adventurer who "discovered" them in Siam, the twins said: "We enjoy ourselves pretty well, but have not as yet got married. But we are making love pretty fast, and if we get a couple of nice wives we will be sure to let you know about it."[48]

And so it was that on April 13, 1843, Eng married Sarah Yates and Chang married Adelaide Yates. These weddings received national attention, yet in a community very concerned with policing illicit acts of sex, with a state government concerned with enforcing prohibitions on marriage across racial lines and a local medical community concerned with "fixing" physical anomalies, the marriages of the Siamese twins appear to have been tolerated without much fuss.[49] The preceding sentence goes against what many students of Chang and Eng have written, and so before I can write more about these weddings—a story built on documentary evidence—I must deal with the ways that authors have treated them over the past forty years.[50] Scholars have focused on an act of violence that mars the love story, violence that, as far as I can tell, was introduced in a 1964 popular biography by Kay Hunter. Earlier chroniclers consistently wrote that the women who attracted the interest of Chang and Eng were daughters of a well-to-do farmer in Wilkes County. Both women, Adelaide and Sarah Yates, had their fair share of suitors as they came of age in the early 1840s. The Bunker brothers built their case by befriending the family, both parents and daughters, and often dropping in for dinner on their way home from doing business in the county seat. Over the course of several years, Chang and Adelaide developed a mutual affection, while Sarah's interest in Eng was slower in coming. On these points, the various narratives varied little.[51]

Kay Hunter, though, introduced conflict. The two couples made their intentions to marry known to the community (and the Yates family) by riding together in an open wagon through the town of Mount Airy, Hunter wrote, and all hell broke loose. A few men "smashed some windows at his [David Yates's] farm house, and generally made life very uncomfortable for the family." Some of Yates's neighbors "threatened to burn his crops if he did not promise to control his daughters." Their hopes dashed, the twins retreated, no doubt, Hunter speculated, developing hatred for each other and their condition. Luckily for them, "they had secured the affections of such strong-willed girls as the Yates sisters, who were not to be easily put off." The sisters arranged for a secret meeting, which led to others, and soon the sweethearts had agreed to marry, despite continuing disapproval from the community.[52]

Later narratives and analyses made much of the key detail that seems to have debuted in Hunter's book, namely, the violence aimed at the Yates household. Hunter did not disclose her sources for this specific detail. One possible source is Joffre Bunker, a grandson of the twins who acted as family historian, collecting family papers and, Hunter said, sharing stories with her about his ancestors, but here I am engaging in pure speculation.[53] What is clear, however, is that Hunter's account itself became a rich source for later narratives about the twins' weddings.

The 1978 biography by the father and daughter team Irving Wallace and Amy Wallace borrowed liberally from Hunter's book—indeed, it escalated the rhetoric. Now, "several groups" advanced on the Yates house rather than a "few men," the sisters were "fair maidens," not simply "local girls," and the marriage was an "unholy alliance."[54] The Wallaces built on Hunter's account with details from an unpublished biography written after the twins' death in 1874 by Jesse Franklin Graves, a later acquaintance of the Bunkers who was fourteen years old in 1843 and lived a county away, and a folksy story written in 1936 by Shepherd M. Dugger, who also claimed to have met the twins.[55] Neither Graves nor Dugger mentioned a community outburst and so did not advance the Wallace narrative in that respect, but Graves asserted that "the father and mother were both indignant at the prospect of such a union and forbade their daughters any further communication with their lovers." Graves wrote, and the Wallaces reported, that Chang and Eng believed the Yateses' objection arose not "from any want of character or social position for in point of morality, probity [and] strict integrity they sustained a spotless reputation, but it had its origins in an ineradicable prejudice against their race and nationality."[56] The Wallaces rightfully noted (as did Hunter) that the twins' physical anomaly no doubt also played a central role in marking this marriage as violating community norms.

Hunter's *Duet for a Lifetime* and the Wallaces' *The Two* were popular biographies. While each made use of primary sources—the amount of research that comes through in the Wallace book, especially, is impressive—there are also times when these works clearly strayed from easily verifiable facts. For instance, in describing the Yates family, Hunter made mistake after mistake. David Yates did not have nine daughters but four daughters and two sons. The Yateses were not Quakers of Dutch and Irish descent but Baptists of English descent. And the two couples would not have ridden into Mount Airy to announce their engagement. Although they did eventually move to Mount Airy, a community two days distant, the town in which they would have made their intentions known would likely have been the county seat of Wilkesboro or perhaps Traphill, the small village that the twins called home.

Nevertheless, the story of the wedding propagated by these two books has informed the consideration of the twins by academic scholars over the past several years. Citing only the Wallaces, Gary Y. Okihiro used the story of the neighbors pelting the Yates house with rocks as an illustration of the ways in which nonwhite men and white women who dared to fall in love were subject to the inspection and violence of white society. In an otherwise careful reading of the antebellum literature about Chang and Eng and the specter of sex, Allison Pingree took elements from Hunter and the Wallaces to illustrate the community uproar surrounding the twins' marriage. Meanwhile, David L. Clark and Catherine Myser used other suspicious portions of Hunter's narrative of the engagement and wedding in their discussion of the voyeurism surrounding conjoined twins. And yet, while all these studies spoke of the violation of or subjection to community norms and the impact these norms have on the individual, none of these works focused attention on the broader community itself.[57]

Even more problematic, not one of these scholars paid attention to the historical record in writing about the marriage. None of the twins' associates spoke of mob violence or unrest in their letters that mentioned the wedding, and in a community in which letters often dealt with gossip about courtships and marriages and at times included discussion about the twins, no extant letters even mention the weddings. Newspapers welcomed the opportunity to take digs at the twins and the women who married them, but none mentioned any unrest. And county court minutes and criminal action papers make no reference to trespassing, assault and battery, or destruction of property allegations that remotely relate to the Yates family or the weddings of the Siamese twins. This void does not mean anything in and of itself; perhaps it should not even be surprising. Historians have discussed at length the challenges in uncovering evidence of interracial sex and its ancillaries; legal records, for instance, often fail to reveal acts of violence committed in response to sex across racial lines, often because no one wanted to acknowledge the sex act or because the violence did not seem to deserve notice.[58] Yet there is no ambiguity about the fact of this relationship, and it seems significant that, of these two marriages, about which much would be written—and much of that negative and scandalous—the prospect of violence was never raised for more than a century.

The weddings were supported by bonds in the usual sum of $1,000 each, taken out by Chang and Eng for the one party and Jesse Yates for the other, and a marriage license signed by county court clerk William Masten. Baptist preacher Colby Sparks officiated the ceremony. At a time when it was not unusual to ignore the letter of the law and not obtain a bond, for instance, or simply to live together in unwedded bliss, Chang, Eng, and the Yateses followed each step as laid out by law.[59]

To prove the fact of their wedding and of their legal right to be married, the twins had the marriage documents published, "for the satisfaction of those who are disposed to doubt the truth of their marriage."[60] This response, several years after the fact, probably stemmed from the incredulity expressed by so many newspapers and other commentators after news of the wedding spread. Apparently, no documentation of the community's reaction exists, but newspaper reports from around the state and the country offered a wide range of reaction. The *Carolina Watchman* published a brief announcement, titled "Marriage Extraordinary," closing with the hope that "the connection will be as happy as it will be close." Many other North Carolina newspapers published announcements without comment. The strongest response from a southern paper was framed as a joke on the twins' physical anomaly. "Ought not the wives of the Siamese twins to be indicted for marrying a quadruped?" the *Louisville Journal* asked. The most outspoken criticism came from northern papers. One paper called the marriage an "enormity." Another commented: "Extraordinary indeed. So much so that were it not for the evidence daily afforded of what unnatural things men and women will do, we should pronounce the account incredible. What sort of women can they be who have entered into such a marriage? What sort of father to consent? What sort of clergyman to perform the unnatural ceremony?"[61]

Abolitionist papers ramped up the condemnation, placing the responsibility for the union squarely on a South contaminated by the sin of slavery. The *Emancipator and Free American* printed its wedding notice in a column titled "Southern Scenes," filled with murder, matricide, duels, drunken assaults, robberies, judicial corruption, and insanity. The *Liberator* spewed vitriol: "None but a priest whose mind had become besotted by the impurities of slavery could 'solemnize' so bestial a union as this; and none but a community sunk below the very Sodomites in lasciviousness, from the same cause, would tolerate it."[62] We have no more direct commentary on the weddings from these sources, but the graphic nature of the abolitionist condemnations offers several approaches to considering why the reaction of northern papers seemed so much stronger than that of southern papers.

Certainly, the denunciation is an example of the abolitionist—but also, to a lesser extent, northern—tendency to view the South as an utterly depraved land, whose sexual peccadilloes were reported in such detail as to be almost

Engraving of Adelaide, Chang, Eng, and Sarah, which served as the frontispiece
in J. N. Moreheid, *Lives, Adventures, Anecdotes, Amusements, and Domestic Habits
of the Siamese Twins*, 1850. North Carolina Collection, Wilson Special Collections
Library, University of North Carolina at Chapel Hill.

pornographic. Enslaved men and women were forced to walk almost naked
in the fields and in the plantation houses, among masters and mistresses
who did not bat an eyelash, whereas their northern counterparts would be
mortified. Slaves seduced their masters' daughters, and of course, in the most
common scenario, masters took their female slaves, sometimes against their
will. Everyone was debased.[63] Most northern publications, while not using
the sensationalistic language of the abolitionist press, nevertheless raised
the identical question—What kind of people would allow such a thing to
happen?—and the answer, left unspoken in their pages, may very well have
flashed across their readers' minds: southerners. Such representations of the
South provided for northern readers a mirror image of how they supposed
themselves to be. This is to say, the South was as much an "other" to the North
as the "Orient" was to the "West" or as the Siamese twins were to Americans.

Of course, this explanation goes only a short way toward explaining the strong tones taken by the abolitionist papers. What was it about this marriage that made it so "extraordinary" and worthy of such contempt? At one level, such condemnation seemed out of character. Garrison and the *Liberator* sought immediate emancipation, as did the *Emancipator*; as such, they advocated racial equality. From the *Liberator*'s earliest days, Garrison spoke out against the Massachusetts ban on interracial marriage, and by the 1840s the campaign had reached the state legislature. (It was this very debate that North Carolina papers were following when the twins first settled in Wilkes County.) These views earned immediatists the label of "amalgamationist"—someone who favored the mixing of black and white blood through sexual unions—and put them at odds with the majority of northerners, not just antiabolitionists but also advocates of gradual emancipation and colonization, who despised the institution of slavery but also feared the possibility of living alongside free blacks—fears that fed off the prospect of economic competition but also the possibility of amalgamation.[64]

But Garrison and his abolitionist allies were not always consistent in their rhetoric. Garrison repeatedly turned around against southerners the question of whether he would allow a daughter of his to marry a black man, saying they were in no position to cast aspersions on amalgamation, this after prefacing his response that, of course, he had no daughters. One scholar takes Garrison's response to mean that "no, he would not let her intermarry," and then documents other immediate abolitionists stating that, no, they did not support amalgamation. When the question left the realm of the hypothetical, tempers flared and violence occurred. The 1853 example of William G. Allen showed how an abolitionist community could react to the possibility of marriage across racial lines. Allen, a "quadroon" college professor in New York State, had to flee a lynch mob after his intentions to marry the white daughter of an abolitionist minister became clear. The strong language employed by the *Liberator* at the twins' weddings and at other examples of southern "depravity" also provided abolitionists the opportunity to take the heat off themselves and place it on the slave South, perhaps mollifying tensions within the North.[65]

Lastly, the strong language employed by the *Liberator* might also be attributed to the other characteristic that made the marriage extraordinary: the twins' conjoined state. Indeed, the paper's charge of "bestiality" parallels the Louisville paper's use of "quadruped," each suggesting that the twins were not human. The criticism could thus be seen as a reproach against the uncomfortable images that the twins' physical anomaly suggested for the marriage bed. By the time of their marriage, the public had understood Chang's and Eng's condition for fourteen years. To say that the Siamese twins had married carried with it the understanding that these two "abnormal" men, connected forever to each other, would be sharing the same bed with "normal" women.

To some, however, the suggestion that the twins had married two white women—two *sisters*—seemed too incredible to believe. For fourteen years, newspapers had amused their readers with exaggerated—or fictional—stories of the twins' exploits. Reports of their marriage might similarly have originated in an editor's imagination, and the joking tone taken by several of the southern papers suggests that this might indeed have been the case. In May 1844, however, newspapers began to report that the wives of Chang and Eng had each given birth to daughters. The evidence of children forced people to take seriously these "extraordinary" marriages. Earlier reports of the weddings had been "treated as a hoax," one correspondent wrote. "I incline to think that public opinion settled that the twins were still living in *single* blessedness. To my surprise I find that the supposed hoax is a literal fact; and that these distinguished characters are married men!"[66] In the practice of illicit sex, the arrival of a child often served to mark the relationship—and the baby—as illegitimate. In the case of the twins, the arrival of children proved to be the content that gave legitimate form to the marriages.

At a national level, the multiple layers of criticism and incredulity that met the marriages of the Siamese twins revealed a disjuncture between legal and popular understandings of deformity and race. In the eyes of the public, the twins were clearly different. From the first published reports of the twins' arrival—the *Boston Daily Advertiser* reported that they "have the Chinese complexion and physiognomy"—people commented on the brothers' swarthy skin, their thick hair, and the folds over their eyes.[67] From 1829 to their retirement in 1839, the acts of exhibiting themselves, of being onstage, of traveling from town to town in a private carriage, of subjecting themselves to the constant gaze of the audience and of physicians, had served to magnify their difference and had kept them apart from the public. In their retirement, however, leaving the exhibition hall, settling in a single town, away from the public eye, had served to highlight their almost-normalness and to make them a part of a community. In the eyes of the law, in 1843, the twins were white because "Asiatic," "Mongolian," "Oriental," or even "Chinese" had not received sanction as an official category, and they clearly were not black. Chang and Eng became naturalized citizens, something limited to free white persons; the census listed them as white (and continued to do so even in 1870, when "Chinese" became one of the possible categories); and they had married two white women, despite state laws that prohibited interracial marriage, between whites, on the one hand, and blacks and mulattoes, on the other. Legally, the mechanisms necessary to isolate the twins were lacking; socially, the twins had slipped under the radar and emerged as landholding citizens and family men. The public's sense of surprise at the breakdown of social enforcement mechanisms— What kind of preacher would perform such a ceremony? What kind of father would consent to such a marriage? What kind of women would enter such a union?—highlights the central role that local communities played in policing social behavior.

The Wedded Siamese Twins and the World of Wilkes County

And yet, what if a mob—or even just a handful of neighbors—did throw rocks at the Yates house? In a community preoccupied with rumors about sex, in which stories about flirting, courtship, inappropriate actions, and weddings took up a lot of letter-writing energy—and into which *the Siamese twins* had landed—it seems significant that no mention was made of any such controversy.

In addition, Wilkes County was a violent and litigious society. The thirty-four adultery cases that I examined over the ten-year period from 1835 to 1844 were dwarfed by the number of cases of assault and battery and destruction to property. People were eager to assign blame and to reclaim damages. And David Yates was a man who in the years before the wedding had become increasingly schooled in legal action, who sat on grand juries, who knew how the court system worked. He knew how to pursue criminal charges if his property had been destroyed. Of course, his knowledge of the system, of the public parade of summonses and court hearings, may have discouraged him from pressing charges. But, as historian Bertram Wyatt-Brown has shown, there were other, extralegal ways that southern communities enforced their moral codes. Mob actions that could include "wedding-day jest to public whipping and tar-and-feathering" were common forms of policing that provided community members the chance to exhibit their censure while still allowing the controversial act, in this case the engagement or wedding, to proceed. The most serious violators of accepted behavior, including "both women and men who made marriages deemed incongruous," faced a grimmer fate, including public banishment.[68] There is no evidence that any such public act of shaming or disciplining took place in Wilkes. If it had, given the twins' celebrity, it almost certainly would have been widely reported. But what if I am missing the one piece of evidence that could prove the attack happened? Or, what if there simply is no evidence, but it really did happen? To what extent would it change the story unfolded here?

Most serious, it might strike a blow against the sectional differences that lurk in this chapter. We would have, in essence, a counterpart to the example of William G. Allen, except that Allen was kept from marrying his white sweetheart, whereas the twins were successful. Further, Wilkes County residents committed acts of violence against neighbors over sex (and for other reasons) regularly. None of those cases of documented violence involved the county's women having sex with or getting married to conjoined twins or Chinese men. This observation is not to dismiss the significance of the unions that took place on April 13, 1843. It is safe to assume that the news of the wedding—and the news of the engagement, to whatever extent there was any—stunned many people in the community, just as it did newspaper editors across the country. It is safe to assume that this news staggered family members. This wedding, between two white sisters and two Asian conjoined twins, was, and is, a big deal. But if there was violence committed against the Yates home, it took a form recognized by the community as a way to articulate dissatisfaction with a public act of sex. The fact of the violence, if any, would not necessarily have carried any larger significance, in and of itself.

Stepping away from speculation and back toward the evidence, I want to close this chapter with the consideration of two pieces of correspondence, both involving local characters. These are the only letters I have found that were produced in the months following the wedding that refer to the twins and their domestic situation. The first shows the highly personal characteristics that relations could take when long histories and uncomfortable conflicts shaped the dynamic. The second illustrates the structured nature of social relations, in which social forms allowed for smooth interactions, among community members who did not necessarily know each other well and between individuals who were not on the best of terms.

In May 1843, James W. Hale, who from 1829 to 1831 preceded Charles Harris as manager of the twins, wrote to his former colleague. The letter, written from New York, was clearly a response to a communication from Harris about Chang and Eng. "Give me all the particulars of the marriage— of your difficulty with them," Hale requests of Harris. "I am *very* anxious to know how they got into such a stupid scrape. If they only wanted *skin*, I think they might have managed to get it for *less* than for life." Two months later, Hale responded to another letter. "I am so desirous of knowing . . . the difficulty between yourself and Chang Eng. You may imagine that I am in a wonder how they could do or say any thing which should have offended one who has been to them so true a friend as you have been," Hale wrote. "I . . . hope that they will yet find that your friendship and kindness is too valuable to be thrown away."[69] The close proximity between the particulars of the marriage and Harris's difficulty with the twins suggests that there was a falling out and that the wedding was at the crux of the issue. The tension between Harris and the twins was the result of family politics.

An interview with the twins in 1849 indicated that the disagreement was "in consequence of his [Harris] not marrying to the taste of Mrs. Chang and Mrs. Eng."[70] Of course, Harris married Frances Baugus years before Adelaide and Sarah became "Mrs. Chang and Mrs. Eng." Nevertheless, in the four years since Harris had wedded Baugus, circumstances had changed. The 1840 marriage between Samuel Baugus, Frances's older brother, and Letha Yates, Adelaide and Sarah's older sister, was not going well. He began to drink heavily and repeatedly threatened her with violence.[71] At the same time, Harris, who had spent years looking after the twins' interests (and, judging from Hale's words, perhaps arranging sexual trysts when necessary), likely was suspicious of the Yates sisters' motives in marrying Chang and Eng. The sisters never spoke of this, but people at the time wondered if they were perverted, if they wanted fame, or, most commonly, if they wanted fortune.[72] Harris likely voiced his concerns to the twins—we have no idea how aggressively, of course—but it is clear from the Hale letter that the result was a fracture between the men who had traveled the world together. Violence did occur as a result of the wedding—not *physical* violence, but violence takes many forms. As in most cases in which conflict breaks out over sexual relations, however, the people most affected were those who were closest to the situation.

A second letter, written in 1844 from one Wilkesboro elite to another, sheds a different light on the marriage of the Siamese twins. Writing to his brother, a young town resident related how a group of friends and family went with "Mr. & Mrs. Harris" to visit "the Twins" and, from there, a local natural wonder called Rock Mountain. After spending Thursday night at the twins' house, "Fryday-morning we set out with one of the young Mr. Baugus's as a guide to visit Rock-mountain & the Water-falls springhouse, etc," he wrote. "We got back to the Twins about 3 Oclock in the evening just when it commenced raining and it rained until Saturday-night, which detained us there until Sunday-morning, though we enjoyed our-selves verry well indeed."[73] Eighteen months after the wedding, the twins and their wives merited no special commentary—no commentary what-soever, really—on their unusual circumstances. Indeed, the letter portrays the twins and family as fine hosts who welcomed visitors and showed them a good time, even for unexpectedly long stays. This is to say, it por-trayed the twins and family in a generic fashion; this was how countless correspondents portrayed visits to other fine hosts. Charles Harris's role was just as revealing about the function that social roles—social forms—played. Despite his conflict with the twins—and correspondence from Hale to Harris at roughly the same period reveals that there was still a rift between Harris and the twins[74]—Harris was able to play the role of agent, bringing others into the world of the twins to facilitate a smooth social transaction, to maximize the enjoyment of the party. And the display of the twins' family went off seamlessly. The adherence to accepted forms of sexuality allowed Wilkes County residents to navigate more effectively a social world fraught with conflict. But even as the path was smoothed for some, others suffered from the constraint and burdens that these forms imposed on them.

CHAPTER FOUR

Asiatic Americans

Many in the United States were not entirely sure what to make of Chang and Eng. The itinerant Oriental curiosities had become nested southern farmers, the formerly bonded laborers had transformed into the owners of men, the conjoined brothers were now conjoined brothers-in-law. The young "boys" who had arrived as eighteen-year-olds in 1829 were now aging men and fathers, and in 1849, they hit the road again, with their sons and daughters, branding themselves the "Siamese Twins and children." Their ability to adapt to new circumstances, to mold themselves again and again into new roles, meant that people who had last seen them years before might be surprised at what they saw at the next opportunity.

In 1853, on their way north for a summer exhibition with two of their children in tow, the twins passed through North Carolina's capital city, allowing the local newspaper to comment on the celebrities. "It is a phenomenon, not, perhaps, to be witnessed again in the Country, to see Asiatics transformed to good American citizens, not only in language but in feeling," the *Raleigh Register* reported. "They have lost every vestige of their native tongue. . . . In fact, they speak English fluently, and almost without foreign accent. A few words seem to be impracticable, but they are chatty and communicative, and hence their perfection in our language. They are altogether American in feeling."[1]

But even as the twins changed, the country around them was transforming too. Debates over abolitionism, sectionalism, and nativism dominated the public discourse, and the growing Chinese population in the West raised questions about Chang and Eng's position. "I think I noticed, by a decision of the Supreme Court of California, that Chinese are not considered to be citizens of that State, and can neither vote nor give testimony against a white person in certain cases," a reader of the Washington-based *National Era* newspaper wrote from York Springs, Pennsylvania, in December 1854. "I would like to know how it is with the Siamese Twins in North Carolina. I understand they are both landholders and slaveholders. Are they permitted to either vote or give evidence, in consequence of their being slaveholders, or are they debarred from it, like the Chinese of California?"[2]

Chang and Eng Bunker were landholders and slaveholders, they had filed criminal charges against white persons, and they could vote, not because they owned slaves but because they were citizens of North Carolina and the United States. They were, as they stated in interviews, American. Yet, the letter writer was taking a meaningful leap, drawing a connection as he did between the Siamese-born brothers and Chinese laborers who had been emigrating to work in California since the late 1840s. While much of the publicity surrounding the twins in the 1840s and early 1850s highlighted the ways these "Asiatics [had] transformed to good American citizens"— and, in essence, engaged in a discussion of what "good American citizens" were—developments in the 1850s served to reemphasize Chang's and Eng's foreignness.

The Bunker family negotiated its way through shifting identities of "Asian" and "American" in the late 1840s and the 1850s. In the late 1840s, Chang's and Eng's "Asianness" was measured in comparison to Asians (Chinese and Siamese) in Asia (Siam and China). Their "Americanness," though certainly rooted in the South, was the product of an emerging southern middle class that engaged actively with the bourgeois culture of the North. By the late 1850s, the twins' "Asianness" was gauged by the growing presence of Chinese in the United States—California, specifically—while their "Americanness" was shaped by fierce sectionalism and ultimately undone by disunion.[3]

This chapter explores these themes in four parts. First, it looks at representations of home life both in Siam and in North Carolina to get a sense for where the twins had been and where they were now in the late 1840s. Second, it interrogates the story of the twins as part of a royal Siamese embassy to Vietnam as well as the Taiping Rebellion in China to understand the international forces that shaped the way Americans understood Chang and Eng in the early 1850s. Third, it fits the twins' experience as slaveholders within a larger debate over slavery, abolitionism, and nativism to explore the ways in which race and class were used to negotiate or police social hierarchies. Fourth, it follows the twins' children as they go on tour as proof of their father's masculinity and class standing but also as proof of their father's foreign origins. Reminders of the Orient acted as a check on the twins' self-representation as Americans; the twins were almost American, but not quite.

Domestic Scenes

Within their corner of North Carolina, the twins continued to make connections with the local elite. Despite moving from Wilkes County to Surry County in the latter half of the 1840s, the twins' relations with an emerging southern middle class—merchants, lawyers, and doctors, most of whom kept one foot in the agricultural game too—built on shared desires for educational opportunities, close economic relations with northern capital, and a fixed racial hierarchy underpinned by chattel slavery. Further abroad, however, the rest of the country made its own connections when it came to the twins, linking them to developments in immigration, abolitionism, and racial science in the United States, as well as efforts to "civilize" the "heathens" of Asia.

In the late 1840s, missionaries in Siam continued to write about the twins and the family they had left behind. By the mid-nineteenth century, American Protestant missionaries had become the most influential Westerners in Siam. They introduced smallpox inoculations, surgery, and Western ideas of obstetrics. They also created schools for boys and girls, as well as importing the country's first printing press that could accommodate the Siamese alphabet. Through such efforts, missionaries sought to bring Christianity and "civilization" to Siam. They were also prolific chroniclers of their work, travel, and observations, and their descriptions of the country often were of a dual nature, both ethnological and evangelical. These characterizations held as well for accounts of the twins' family in Siam.[4]

The twins' mother, stepfather, and siblings lived in the same village in which the twins had been born, Maklong, a town of about 8,000 to 12,000 that was some sixty miles southwest of Bangkok. Floating houses lined the banks of a river, and most villagers, the twins' family included, supported themselves by fishing and raising ducks. According to the Americans who visited the village in 1844, however, industry did not accurately characterize the population. Early in the morning, villagers had already drunk themselves into a stupor, and rather than pay attention to Christian sermonizing, the villagers groped the missionaries' clothing. The old and the sick who were poor and had no one to look after them were left abandoned under trees or "thrown away" at temples to die. Intemperance and selfishness were certain signs of adherence to false religion, and missionaries attributed these qualities to both ethnic Chinese and Siamese.[5]

The population of Maklong was heavily ethnic Chinese (Taechieu), and the old questions about the twins' racial origins returned. The twins' mother and siblings spoke the Siamese language more fluently than they did Chinese, although apparently their older brother was able to write the latter and not the former.[6] The mother's complexion was lighter than that of most women, and her father was said to be from China. Coupled with the fact that both her husbands were Chinese, a missionary concluded that "the twins are in no sense Siamese, except that they were born in Siam."[7] But they *were* born in Siam, as was their mother, they *did* speak Siamese, as did their mother, and they *did* believe in Siamese Buddhism (or had; this point was still up for debate), as did their mother. Yet, in formulations such as those offered by the American missionary above, it was the paternity of the twins and not the cultural characteristics drawn from their environment and their everyday lives that determined their race or nationality.

Nevertheless, these missionaries believed they could convert the Siamese to Christianity, and when they found the twins' mother, they thought they had a useful strategy. She was much gratified to learn of the sons she had not seen in fifteen years. She had concluded they were dead, but the missionaries assured her that they were alive and had recently married two sisters in the southern states. Grateful to learn this, their mother expressed her affection for them and her "strong desire to see them again." The missionaries encouraged the mother to embrace the religion of Christ so that she could see her sons in heaven. Seek Jesus as her savior, the Reverend W. P. Buell told her, "and should you leave this world soon, you may go where you and your children may meet and be forever happy together; provided they also love this same Saviour; and as they now live in a Christian land, I hope they certainly will become the friends of Christ, if they have not already." When the twins had first arrived in the United States, Christians hoped they would convert to Christianity, return to Siam, and act as an example. That had not happened, but missionaries were able to assimilate them into a frequently used proselytizing device, the promise of seeing loved ones in the afterlife. The missionaries vowed to call again, though we have no evidence that any did until 1849, after she had died. Instead, they continued on with their proselytizing efforts, stopping next at a temple where they proceeded to get in an argument over the gospel. For his refusal to take the Bible they offered and consider the truth of its teachings, they labeled one of the priests "stubborn," "obstinate," and "the most bigoted [man] we had yet met with."[8]

Despite the hopes they had for converting Asians to Christianity, missionaries experienced very little success. The American missionaries in Siam, as well as the growing number of missionaries in China, increasingly explained their failures through descriptions that came to be identified with

Asians as a race—their loose morals, duplicity, obstinacy, and, ironically, their hostility to foreign ways. The hope for cultural transfer transformed into a rigid embrace of racial intransigence. Of course, the idea of cultural transfer had always been seen as one-way—from the Christian American to the heathen Asian—and these descriptions of the sinful, narrow-minded Siamese came through the lenses of frustrated and, often, prejudiced missionaries. There were, nonetheless, some successes, and by the late 1840s, American missionaries were bringing Chinese converts to the East Coast and the South, not only to educate them further so they could return to their homeland and spread Christianity but also to show off to American audiences the fruits of missionary labors abroad. Churchgoers saw these converts in person, while others read about them in newspapers and journals.[9]

Similarly, the twins' adoption of American ways was a focal point for curiosity seekers. As visitors to their homes in North Carolina showed, Chang and Eng were busy crafting the lives of southern farmers for themselves. No sooner had they completed construction on their Traphill home in 1840 then reporters began calling to see the brothers in their new domestic setting. When Chang and Eng married and then fathered children, newspapers kept the country informed. As the families expanded and in increments moved from Wilkes County to neighboring Surry County, curiosity seekers tracked the Bunkers down and wrote about the twins' dress, physical appearance, pastimes, religious beliefs, and dining habits and about their wives, children, and slaves. These conjoined twins from Siam, their young brides from North Carolina, and their ever-growing brood of mixed-race children became a southern household on display.

In 1845, the twins took the first steps toward establishing a residence in Surry County. On March 1, they bought two tracts of land, totaling more than 650 acres, and a small dwelling along Stewart's Creek, about five miles south of Mount Airy, for $3,750 in hand. In the fall, Chang and Eng bought three black children from another Mount Airy resident for $625, and over the next year the twins continued their acquisition of various types of property in the area. By 1847, Surry County was a part-time home for the brothers, who were referred to in a manner that no doubt reflected the drawl of their southern neighbors as the "Sime twins."[10]

Chang and Eng split time between the two properties, with one wife at each, for a simple reason: Their families were growing rapidly. By June 1847, Adelaide had given birth to four children, Sarah had delivered three, and the combined population of enslaved blacks approached twenty. To make the commute more practical, the twins were building another house about one mile from their Mount Airy property. Until that new house was completed, the dual residences—the twins retained their property near Traphill, forty miles to the southwest, at least through 1853—thwarted the intentions of some curiosity seekers. A correspondent from the *Biblical Recorder* in Raleigh was disappointed when he arrived at Mount Airy only to find that the brothers were at "their plantation" in Wilkes. Meanwhile, the twins' absence from their Traphill residence surprised another visitor, a Richmond journalist who had no idea the twins had acquired property in Surry County. Each of these groups—wives, children, and slaves—in time received its share of attention in the public eye. The bulk of the printed word, however, continued to focus on Chang and Eng.[11]

According to some accounts, the twins appeared very much to be members of southern gentry. Visitors always referred to their Wilkes County residence as a plantation, and their new farm just outside Mount Airy was said to have a blacksmith shop and a shoemaker's shop. A Wilkes County neighbor wrote to a Raleigh newspaper to attest that the twins lived in "quite splendid style," kept "several hands to work," and, as did a select class of southerners who also invested in new forms of agricultural technology, had "a splendid assortment of farming utensils, and seem to have superior knowledge of how to use them." Inside their homes, the twins surrounded themselves with fine furniture, ate off dishes purchased from the North, and, significantly, used knives and forks rather than simply consume their food with a spoon. Socially, they were accommodating hosts who kept their company engaged in interesting conversation and often gave parties and dinners. "Messrs. Chang-Eng . . . are well-to-do planters," a Boston paper concluded.[12]

Portraits of the twins as southern gentlemen of great wealth appeared often in reports published during the late 1840s and the 1850s. An 1850 booklet, published by Erasmus Elmer Barclay, made the portrait most explicit. Its frontispiece featured an engraving of Chang and Eng, finely dressed in tuxedos, flanked by their wives in evening gowns. The title page presented a detailed engraving of the Surry County residence, in which "they . . . are at present residing," a two-story structure with numerous large windows, a covered porch that wrapped around the house, two chimneys, with a smaller house—servants' quarters?—in the background. Another engraving of their Wilkes "mansion house" had four stories, with several wings or quarters attached to it, imposingly set amid a wide clearing of farmland, with mountains in the background. The twins, the pamphlet stated, had invested some $10,000 in their North Carolina residences—including land, slaves, and

Engraving of the marriage of Chang and Eng Bunker to sisters Adelaide Yates
and Sarah Ann Yates, from *An Account of Chang and Eng, the World Renowned Siamese
Twins*, 1853. North Carolina Collection, Wilson Special Collections Library, University
of North Carolina at Chapel Hill.

other personal property—and had an additional $60,000 under the management of an import merchant in New York. They were free to engage in agriculture and merchandizing "on a small scale" while living off the interest accruing from their New York investments. They were citizens who exercised the franchise, they legally adopted an American last name—Bunker, "in honor of a lady in New York who treated them with great kindness"—and they married two fine North Carolina sisters.[13]

In 1843, when Sarah and Adelaide married Eng and Chang, respectively, no one outside Wilkes County knew anything about these sisters. By 1850, this was no longer the case. Their experience was unremarkable in almost every respect save one: their choice of husbands. That they were the wives of the Siamese twins meant that their lives, their homes, and their families became the subject of public discourse. In a time when society considered wives to be a purifying force on their husbands, popular representations of Sarah and Adelaide served more to highlight racial, cultural, and religious differences between the sisters and the twins and to raise the question of just how possible assimilation was.[14]

Visitors to the Bunker estates almost always commented on the wives, often because the women were the only ones present to greet them. Sarah Bunker, also called "Mrs. Eng" by many publications, initially remained in Traphill, while Adelaide Bunker, or "Mrs. Chang," moved to the Mount Airy property once the brothers acquired it. Sarah lived simply. Described as "close and saving"—references to her thriftiness—she kept a neat house but provided an excellent supper. She exhibited "good sense and shrewdness" in her conversation though she was clearly "uneducated." She had "rich, auburn hair, fine teeth, and hazel eyes," but she tended toward corpulence; Sarah was "a bouncing woman of some two hundred pounds." Adelaide, meanwhile, was taller, more slender, and apparently more intelligent than her older sister. She had "a free and open countenance," her home was more tastefully arranged, and her "dress and general appearance all indicated a degree of tidiness that Mrs. Eng lacks." Unlike Sarah, Adelaide "excelled in personal beauty" and "indulge[d] in dress and various other expenses." Indeed, the people of Mount Airy "all say" that Adelaide "is mighty townified."[15]

The noted dissimilarities between the two women offered observers the chance to comment on the twins' tastes in women and how they differed from the white American male. The first accounts of the courtship reported that Chang and Eng had had to decide between themselves which brother would court which sister. Both brothers, it seemed, were interested in "the more portly fair one," Sarah, and not the "good-looking, intelligent woman,"

Adelaide. In the end, Chang "had to content himself" with his second choice. The reports offered the twins' racial origins as explanation for their baffling preference: "To any but an oriental taste, [Adelaide] was much the prettiest, being, in fact, a handsome and showy brunette."[16]

But much more than racialize the twins or their wives, the descriptions of each suggested a clash between differing ideals of class and gender in the antebellum South. A southern bourgeoisie was appearing that pursued cultural and economic ties with a northern middle class and promoted internal improvements, investments in cities, and virtue in hard work, and Surry County and Mount Airy, unlike Wilkes County and Traphill, had a vibrant manufacturing and commercial sector, at least in comparison with their neighbors in northwestern North Carolina.

Demographically, Surry was similar to Wilkes and some other mountain counties. In 1850, 88 percent of Surry was white, and enslaved blacks accounted for 11 percent of the population. (In Wilkes, the breakdown was 89 percent white, 9 percent enslaved. Statewide, the breakdown was 64 percent white, 33 percent enslaved.) In a state where in 1850 the average farm was 369 acres—96 improved acres and 273 unimproved—Surry's farms averaged 270 (69 improved, 201 unimproved). The cash value of Surry farms was almost half that of the state average—$641 to $1,192. Unlike mountain counties, however, Surry had a substantial manufacturing sector. In 1850, the county had 168 people employed in manufacturing, had $123,455 invested in manufacturing, and produced $99,979 annually in manufacturing. None of the surrounding counties approached Surry in terms of manufacturing. As farmers, the twins became identified more with the agricultural sector. But the relatively mixed economy, in a community that had very few large plantations, provided the opportunity to find a place within an entrepreneurial slave society.[17]

Several aspects of the twins' representations made it clear that Chang and Eng were separate from southern aristocracy. First, there was the issue of their labor, namely, their apparent proclivity to engage in a wide range of hard labor on their farm. One visitor came upon the twins "busily engaged in shingling a house." With four hands, they proved extraordinarily effective chopping wood, either placing all four hands on a single ax at the same time or each taking alternate blows with separate axes. The Richmond correspondent observed that the twins had made "a good sized frame house . . . without any assistance; from foundation to roof," while a Greensboro reporter wrote that they were "excellent hands to carry up a corner of a log house—exceeding all their neighbors in cutting saddles and notches in corner logs." From 1849 into the 1850s, the image of the industrious twins followed them after they returned to the exhibition circuit. "During the last ten years, as they assured me, they . . . work constantly and laboriously on their farms," a Washington correspondent wrote in 1849. "They are enterprising farmers, and though very well off they work hard in their fields, early and late," another paper reported.[18]

The twins "attended very industriously to the business of their plantation [and] were always ready and willing to turn their own hands to something useful, and would plough, and reap, and grind, chop wood, and do all sorts of farm work," the *New York Herald* wrote after Chang and Eng visited its establishment in 1853. "Then, when business was not urgent, they would devote their time to field sports, and were among the keenest hunters, fowlers and fishermen of their district. In fact, they lived as real country gentlemen, ready to drink a glass, or fight a round, as occasion required."[19] The key word in the last sentence is not "gentlemen" but "country." Representations of Chang and Eng, shaped it would seem by the brothers themselves, drew on assertions of industry and physical strength to portray a particular type of masculinity. The twins' interest in making such a move is clear. Exhibitions of strength and self-sufficiency—mastery of skills beyond their able-bodied neighbors, even—all stood to invest the twins with a vitality that outshone their deformity. (A similar strategy had, in the 1830s, marked earlier representations of the twins as neither Chinese mandarin nor Siamese slave but as independent merchants, free labor of the Far East.)

Even their decision to resume touring marked them as men of the southern middle class. Certainly, their return to exhibitions served to place their difference on display again, and this time, as we will see, they capitalized also on the display of their children. And, as historian John Kuo Wei Tchen has argued, their going on the road to find work to support the family back home could be viewed in the tradition of the Chinese "sojourner." But it fit just as easily into the increasingly common practice of southern professionals traveling to the North for business trips that lasted as long as several months. Letters between the twins and their families and neighbors reveal the strains such travel placed on household business—there were crops to sell, supplies to buy, and sicknesses to deal with—but they also show the ways in which the family had quickly made connections with leading members of Mount Airy society who checked in with the family, assisted the twins in legal matters, and paved the way for business contacts in northern cities.[20]

"'Chang' and 'Eng,' the World Renowned United Siamese Twins," lithograph, 1860. Chang and Eng Bunker Papers #3761, Southern Historical Collection, Wilson Special Collections Library, University of North Carolina at Chapel Hill.

The engagement of the twins and other southern businessmen with the North made economic and cultural sense. Northern markets offered much better credit, choice, and status, while northern books and magazines espoused middle-class ideas about work, religion, and gender roles. But such connections also revealed points of contention in a mid-nineteenth-century South that was expanding and experiencing unprecedented social and spatial mobility. Some, for instance, saw commercial relations with the North as undermining southern mercantile trade, while others believed they were essential for southern economic health. Some worried that the changing South was undermining traditional gender roles, while others celebrated what they saw emerging as a more virtuous model of womanhood.

The representations of Sarah and Adelaide embodied the clash over gender roles. Adelaide, who was beautiful, slender, intelligent, and indulgent of expensive purchases, might have brought to mind the opulence or excessiveness of a plantation mistress; Sarah, who was plain, portly, unadorned, but generous, might have been read as a simple farmer's wife or as a sensible middle-class woman with means who eschewed the profligacy of southern aristocrats. Reports affirmed that Sarah and Adelaide were daughters of respectable parents and placed the sisters as members of the Baptist Church who attended worship regularly. These reports, coinciding with the sectional schism of the mid-1840s that resulted in a Southern Baptist denomination, may have led readers to conclude that the sisters embraced a conservative or reactionary religion that embraced slavery and withdrew from a national body to preserve antimodern southern ways. Or, perhaps their church membership signified support for missionary activities, education, and the consumption of newspapers and books, as well as the embrace of "a Christian slavery," not a "proslavery Christianity," as one historian phrased it.[21]

But if religion was to be a modernizing or civilizing force, people had to believe, and in this some press accounts painted the twins as lacking. American missionaries in Siam assumed the twins had converted to Christianity. American newspapers were reporting something different. In September 1847, Raleigh's *Biblical Recorder* commented briefly that the twins "occasionally" accompanied their wives to church. In August, we know, the twins did attend a service given by itinerant Methodist pastor Sidney Bumpass, joining the preacher the next day for breakfast. "In conversation they are quite agreeable," Bumpass noted in a letter to his wife. "They pay good attention to preaching." In providing their husbands the opportunities to attend worship, even if only "occasionally," Adelaide and Sarah set the moral example expected of wives.[22]

But the wives' work in this regard was cut out for them because of the twins' utterly foreign nature, according to reports. Richmond's *Southerner* included a lengthy discourse that purported to reflect the twins' *beliefs*, not simply their occasional attendance at church: "'What are your notions about the Christian religion? Do you believe in our religion?' 'We not like your religion, you quarrel 'bout him too much—too much different church, all say him right and t'other wrong, we never quarrel about our religion.'— 'What do you think will become of you when you die?' 'We go in hog first, and stay till we repent for do bad in this world, then we go in horse or deer, or some good animal, and stay always.' 'Do you believe that if you are in a horse that you will be used in drawing a buggy, ploughing corn, hauling wagons, etc.?'—'Yes, we know this is true, our religion tells us so, and all our people, when we in our country, tell we same thing.' 'Do you ever go to church?' 'We go sometime wid we wife,' (wives.) 'Do you believe what the preacher says?' 'Preacher no speak true all time.'"[23]

The twins' commentary on the divisive, contentious, and doctrinaire characteristics of American religion most likely was meant to reflect both the nature of the camp revivals they had lived through during their almost twenty years in the country and the recent sectional divisions in the Baptist and Methodist churches. As always, national and local developments in politics and culture influenced the ways people thought about the twins.

The report also reinforced the public's mental picture of the twins' foreign origins and their racial difference even as the twins made claims to whiteness through their citizenship, political participation, landownership, marriage, and, as we will discuss shortly, slaveholdings. Some of the phrases attributed to the twins did this work. The use of "our religion" and "our country" created distance between the twins and their American audience, as did the imagery suggested by the notion of "going into" hogs, horses, and deer. Offering its own commentary on the *Southerner* report, the *Trumpet and Universalist Magazine* spelled out this notion for its readers: "Their religious views embrace the Eastern doctrine of transmigration of souls." The phrasing offered in the *Southerner* report, which suggested foreignness through broken syntax, became further racialized in later reprints. The twins said—"in their own simple words"—that they would stay in the hog "until we repent for de bad in dis world; den we go in horse, or deer." As for their opinion of men of the cloth, "all de preachers say *him* right, t'other church wrong, and they no speak true all de time."[24] The broken English of the nonnative speaker was accentuated by the addition of an exaggerated black dialect—"de" for "the," "dis" for "this," "den" for "then." The northern publication's introduction of this dialect suggests an attempt perhaps to color Chang's and Eng's home as southern—northern fears of racial amalgamation and disgust at what they saw as the decadence of the South certainly did not fade in the late 1840s and 1850s. The diversity of this North Carolina plantation—"heathen" and Christian, black and Asian and white—at once belied a fabled white America and foreshadowed a multicultural America.

On the World Stage

In 1849, Chang and Eng left retirement and their North Carolina home for New York City. Their motivation, they said, was to earn money to support their growing families—they had a combined seven children by this point—and they took with them their two oldest daughters, aged five. That year's tour was a bust, however, thanks primarily to incompetent management, and they faded from the public eye for another few years. Their next effort, in 1853, was more successful. Again, they took two children along, and again they framed their tour as a necessity to support their children—by then a total of eleven. With their children's polished manners and evident book learning, the Bunkers might have appeared as a distinguished southern family on display except for the fact that no family of distinction would exhibit itself to the public. Instead, developments abroad and in the United States framed the twins even more explicitly in the context of the Orient.

The 1850s saw a renewed American interest in Asia. In Siam, change in leadership, commercial treaties, and the continued missionary presence captured the interest of Americans, and publications invoked the Siamese twins to ground their readers in some sense of the familiar as they wrote about this distant land. A newspaper reporting on Siam's royal succession allowed that most people knew nothing of the country save that it produced the famous brothers. To give readers some sense of Siam's history, the country's three events of world-historical importance were identified as the introduction of Buddhism from Ceylon in the seventh century; a Siamese embassy to France in the seventeenth century (which had raised hopes of a religious conversion); and "the appearance of the Siamese twins." And the *New York Herald*, concerned with Britain's rising fortunes in the East, urged the Senate to ratify the Harris Treaty so that the United States could begin to take advantage of Siam's immense commercial potential, which, the paper opined, had so much more to offer than simply the Siamese twins.[25]

In 1853, New York publisher and engraver Thomas W. Strong published *An Account of Chang and Eng, the World Renowned Siamese Twins*. At ninety-one pages, the book-length biography was longer and offered more details than any other work yet published about the twins. Just who wrote the book is unclear, although the "elegantly illustrated" volume featured Strong's engravings and was commissioned by promoters Seth B. Howes and Avery Smith. These two men wrote to Chang and Eng in December 1852, explaining that the book would be sold in the exhibition room and requesting more recent and detailed information of their lives since they had married.[26] The resulting *Account of Chang and Eng* was widely read, portions of it being reprinted in newspapers and magazines, and it had a large impact on the story of the twins that eventually became part of the legend, especially with respect to their early years in Siam.

Almost two-thirds of the book's ninety-one pages focused on their years in Siam. (By 1853, the twins had lived twenty-four of their forty-two years away from the country of their birth.) It purported to follow the brothers from their births, through the intense curiosity that their conjoined state drew from neighbors when they were newborns, to the challenges of learning to walk, swim, and fish. It went with them after the king of Siam summoned them to visit the palace in Bangkok, and it chronicled their service to the king on an embassy to Cochin China in the early 1820s, in which they were included as examples of the fantastic wonders that came out of Siam. Many writers have assumed this account provided an accurate description of their lives.[27] A close reading of this section of *An Account of Chang and Eng*, however, shows it for what it really is: a retelling—sometimes word for word—of John Crawfurd's journal of his embassy to Siam and Cochin China in 1822 as envoy for the British East India Company, in which Crawfurd and his mission have been excised and the twins have been inserted in his place as leading characters.

In many ways, the 1853 account stayed faithful to the Crawfurd text. The fact of the twins' Chinese father allowed *An Account of Chang and Eng* to copy extensively Crawfurd's observations on the Chinese in Siam; in so doing, it privileged the position of the twins, as Chinese, vis-à-vis the Siamese they lived among, as had earlier exhibition pamphlets. The substantial number of Chinese migrants made up the "most energetic and business like portion" of Siam's population, they intermarried with Siamese women, they adopted the Siamese religion, they paid a head tax that exempted them from corvée labor and military service, and they had a near monopoly on the country's free labor, which served to place the twins and their parents in a special category in their homeland.[28] Virtually all learning and science was to be found among the Chinese; the Siamese were beholden to superstition and pagan religion, and this proved almost catastrophic when Siam's finest medicine men pondered what to do with the newborn conjoined twins.[29] The Siamese arts were "destitute of ingenuity," but they provided memorable entertainment to the young brothers.[30] And the Siamese, the two publications agreed, despite being extraordinarily unsophisticated, looked down on "outside barbarians"; for instance, they called Africans "pepperheads," Americans were the "Markan," and the English became "Angrit," and all these peoples came from small, insignificant lands.[31]

At times, the 1853 publication pulled events in the twins' lives published in the earlier exhibition pamphlets (almost always taken word for word) and used these as a framework in which to fit material from Crawfurd. Early bouts with smallpox and measles and their father's death led into lengthy discussions of Siamese funeral rites, cremation, and mourning rituals. The economic hardship that followed the death of their father led to a discussion, again taken almost word for word from Crawfurd, about the ways that Siamese religion and superstition were obstacles to individual success. Whereas the borrowed material in the first pages of *An Account of Chang and Eng* placed the Chinese brothers, heirs to a rich civilization, against the ignorant Siamese, the discussion of disease, death, and economic hardship served at once to mark the twins as survivors but also as victims of a backward social and religious order. Religious precepts hindered free enterprise, and criminal cases were decided not by law or reason but by superstitious tests.[32]

A dramatic shift occurred in the final part of the *Account* that dealt with the twins' lives in Siam. Rather than events in their lives serving as portals to tangentially related content in the Crawfurd text, Chang and Eng assumed the place of the British officer as he paid a visit to the Siamese king and then led an embassy to Cochin China.[33] Just as Crawfurd approached Bangkok by river, taking note of the Buddhist temples "glittering with gold" and the "mean huts and hovels of the natives," as well as the row of "floating habitations" that gave way to the enormous Chinese junks, so did the twins arrive by boat from their village and marvel at the same sights.[34] They passed through an outer gate, progressed down a long avenue lined by fantastically adorned guards, took off their shoes before entering the innermost sanctum that was decorated with golden plates and images, performed obeisance to the throne and had an interview with the king, before being led out through a hall of curiosities and the temple of the emerald Buddha, given a load of presents, and returned to their vessels.[35]

The king included the twins as part of an embassy to Cochin China because, the 1853 publication claimed, "the appearance of such a wonderful *lusus naturae* as the twins . . . could not fail of giving the Cochin Chinese a high opinion of the resources of Siam."[36] The *Account* then followed Crawfurd's journal closely, chronicling stops in Cape St. James, Saigon, and Hue; encounters with giant elephants and curious onlookers; confinement in close quarters; and a fight between a tiger and an elephant. In addition to the spectacle of the twins on display in an exotic land—indeed, a land presented in the book as even more exotic than the twins—the opportunity was taken to provide details on Siam's trade with other Asian countries (China, especially), as well as the types of resources available in Cochin China, details that were not irrelevant to a United States that was, at that very moment, about to engage in commercial treaty discussions with these countries.[37]

An Account of Chang and Eng drew heavily from Crawfurd's *Journal.* Yet, at times, it made notable departures, which often took the form of asides that made the Siamese seem even more superstitious, ignorant, or incompetent than Crawfurd's text alone suggested. The most significant differences, however, had to do with placing the twins into the text not simply as actors who substitute for Crawfurd but as Chinese who possess characteristics that make them more recognizable to an American public. For instance, in his discussion of the Chinese in Siam, Crawfurd wrote that the Chinese adopted Siamese ways in all aspects except that they retained their native style of dress.[38] The *Account* repeated that the Chinese adopted Siamese ways in all aspects except that they retained their "long 'tail' of braided hair." Before resuming its recitation of Crawfurd's journal, the *Account* then stated that the public would remember that the twins, too, had a queue when they first arrived, "which they retained until becoming naturalized citizens of the United States, when they cut it off, together with their allegiance to all foreign potentates."[39] This departure fit into the popular image of the twins, as it explicitly stated, but it also reflected public stereotypes of the current crop of Chinese immigrants, both their attachment to their "tails" and concerns about their national allegiance. This could be read as a source of anxiety—the Chinese in America clearly had thus far retained their allegiance to China, if the meaning suggested in the account was to be believed—but also of hope. The twins, after all, had cut their queues and pledged their allegiance to the United States.

A second significant departure similarly painted a hopeful picture of Chinese immigration. After taking Crawfurd's description of the Chinese as Siam's "free labour," who came from a land "overstocked with labor" to a country (Siam) with an "abundance of good, unoccupied land [and] great commercial capabilities," the *Account* went further.[40] "It is not strange that thousands yearly avail themselves of the opportunity thus presented of improving their situations," the *Account* stated. "The character of the Chinese is generally wholly misunderstood. Very few have any idea of the shrewdness and industry they possess as a nation. They may be justly termed the Yankees of Asia, for their migratory propensities, as well as their aptness in striking a bargain."[41] The twins, the reader was reminded, were born of a Chinese father. Clearly, this type of description fed into earlier descriptions of the twins as foreigners who came to the United States and through hard work and business acumen molded themselves into successful Americans. But it also spoke in broad, general terms of the *Chinese* as Yankees of Asia. Could they not also come and make a life for themselves here? Again, there were multiple responses to this question. Some Americans were eager—for a variety of reasons, as we will see—for Chinese to come to the United States. Others had already come to resent their "shrewdness and industry" and worried that they would be so successful as to challenge white Americans.

Various strains of Orientalist thought came together in the pages of the 1853 publication. On the one hand, there was an Orientalism informed by overseas encounters, especially that articulated by the very specific figure of John Crawfurd in the late 1820s. Also drawing on what historian John Kuo Wei Tchen has called "patrician" ideas of the Orient, ideas that similarly carried more weight among Americans when Crawfurd was writing, this strain of thought praised the Chinese for their ancient civilization and aligned China with American ideals of republican virtue.[42] They were, after all, hardworking and industrious, these "Yankees of Asia." On the other hand, a discourse that was informed by a domestic vision was also present. The Chinese as well as other Asians (the Siamese in this instance) practiced a pagan religion, followed backward superstitions, and bowed to despots. They were an ill-bred mass of people who, when numbering just a few, were a curiosity but, when numbering thousands and tens of thousands, became a threat to the American way of life.[43] This vision was more negative. These ideas, in the pages of the *Account* at once very specific to Chang and Eng and yet also carrying a broader resonance, became caught up in a larger discourse that was being shaped by relations with China overseas and with Chinese at home.

In the 1850s, a rebellion in China burst into the American consciousness in a way that no other single event in the country would over the course of the nineteenth century. American publications devoted unprecedented coverage to the Taiping Rebellion and the Chinese, which also provided an opportunity to place the twins squarely in a Chinese context. This internal struggle for control of the country, which began in 1850, grabbed the public's interest largely because initial reports suggested that the rebels were an indigenous Protestant sect whose leader had studied the religion with an American missionary. By 1854, it became clear that a successful rebellion would not introduce Christianity to China, and early exuberance gave way to bitter disappointment. So, while editors suggested in 1853 that Americans would have to revise their stereotypes about the funny eyes, tails, and unsavory eating habits (such as dogs and rats) of the Chinese, by 1854 newspapers were reporting that the Chinese were blasphemous, duplicitous, and insufferably xenophobic, much as they had been seen before the rebellion.[44]

A biography of the rebellion's leader published in 1857 is significant because it inspired a meditation on Chinese the world over that featured the twins prominently. An unsigned review of the book, printed in *Putnam's Monthly Magazine* in April 1857, first ridiculed the Chinese as a people impossible to take seriously because of their tails but then poked fun at the tendency of Americans to view all Chinese as alike; this was similar to the English and French saying that all Americans were the same, the author noted.[45] The review's author had traveled widely, and he offered examples of variations in Chinese from San Francisco, Honolulu, Hong Kong, Singapore, Penang, Calcutta, and London. The very first example the reviewer gave, from New York City, was Chang and Eng.

"My own earliest idea of the Chinaman was derived from the Siamese Twins," he wrote. "While yet an urchin, I had the rare honor to be admitted to personal intimacy with that famous lusus naturae. . . . From all they said, or did, or were, I derived notions, droll or shocking, as the occasion was, of three hundred millions of pig-eyed people, . . . notions that have not altogether left me to this day." He noted their long hair and their funny way of speaking English and, of course, their conjoined state. "And therefore, deduced I, all Chinamen are born double."[46] Even though this conclusion made clear the absurdity of drawing broad conclusions about an entire people from a single example, it also suggested that conjoinedness had become imagined by some as a racial feature. (One characteristic of the twins that did apply to the larger Chinese population, he said, was their "duplicity.") Despite the author's recognition of diversity within the Chinese population, he nevertheless assigned them firm physical features—"pig eyes" or slanted eyes, long hair drawn back into tails. The portrait he painted was not favorable; rather, it was made up of many different shades of undesirable. He also placed the Chinese in San Francisco and New York—including the twins—squarely in a community that spanned the States, the Pacific, East and South Asia, as well as Europe, at a time when the United States was experiencing an influx of migrants from China and playing a more active role in Asia.

Nevertheless, it is important to keep his initial criticism in mind: It was absurd to let one example—Chang and Eng, for example—shape how Americans saw all Chinese; rather, the important lesson here is to consider how increasing encounters with Chinese, abroad and at home, shaped Americans' views of the twins. Indeed, the letter to the editor of the *National Era* that began this chapter makes it clear that the Chinese presence in California provoked new questions about Chang and Eng. We must also keep in mind, however, that the growing discourse about the Chinese, and the changing discourse about the twins, was not playing out simply in a binary that pitted Chinese and white Americans on opposite ends of the spectrum, and it did not simply complicate a black-white binary either. Rather, divisive debates over sectionalism, abolitionism, and nativism influenced the direction that discussion of the twins and their families took in the late 1850s.

Slavery, Nativism, and the Siamese Twins

Indeed, the letter writer implicitly touched on all these issues: sectionalism, abolitionism, and nativism. The Pennsylvania resident compared the "nominally free" state of California to the slave state of North Carolina, remarked on the California court's restrictive decision against Chinese, and ended his letter wondering "how Slavery works with the Siamese twins." Given the fact that he was writing to the *National Era*, one of the nation's most radical abolitionist newspapers, several questions present themselves. To what extent was the letter offering commentary on the rising anti-Chinese sentiment in California, and to what extent was it making an observation about the larger nativist sentiment in the country? Was it suggesting the twins ought not to have political rights, or was it expressing sympathy for the California Chinese who had been stripped of rights? And what moral statement was it implying with respect to the slave-owning twins?

Since the mid-1830s, the twins had been crafting a public image that rested on ideals of masculinity, race, and class. The decision to retire from touring in 1839 and settle down in rural western North Carolina as gentleman farmers and slaveholders can be seen as strategies to assert white manhood for themselves. As a result, the fact of their slaveholdings had been no secret. The earliest reports from their Mount Airy residence made reference to their "negroes" or their "servants," common euphemisms for enslaved blacks, and some articles discussed outright their "slaves."[47] And these slaves became a central part of the public presentation of the Bunkers as southern family men.

No evidence suggests the twins' mindset as they became the owners of men, women, and, predominantly, children. They grew up in a country where most of the population was subject to corvée labor under a feudalistic system, though, notably, the Chinese were exempt. In Siam, there were also enslaved debtors who earned their freedom on payment of their debt, as well as prisoners of war who were offered as rewards to army officials or kept as slaves of the king but who, it seems, were treated similarly to free men.[48] Pamphlet literature explained that as the sons of a Chinese father, the twins were exempt from forced labor; in their native land, they occupied a higher level in the social order than those who might be enslaved. In the United States, Chang and Eng responded strongly when Americans talked about them as being bought and sold. During their traveling days in the 1830s and in their initial months in Wilkes County, they regularly hired the services of slaves.[49] Perhaps they stumbled into slaveholding; anecdotes suggest that they received their first slave as a wedding present from their father-in-law. It is likely, though, that they quickly understood the advantages to be derived from owning slaves; their ability to do so quickly established their mastery over one group of people (blacks), their superiority over another (poor whites), and their ability to rub shoulders with the elite of northwestern North Carolina.[50]

Attempting to reconstruct Chang's and Eng's experience as slaveholders is no exact science. In addition to the woman they received as a gift from David Yates, extant records reveal purchases from Surry County neighbors of a three-year-old boy for $175 and two girls, aged seven and five, for $450, in September 1845, and a girl, age unknown, for $325 in February 1846. In 1848, the brothers told a newspaper correspondent that they had thirteen slaves. Two years later, the census slave schedule listed nine males and nine females, including men aged fifty-five and twenty-four, a woman aged thirty, five between the ages of eleven and nineteen, and ten younger than eight. That same year, the twins added three more slaves. Arriving in New York City in 1853 to embark on a yearlong tour, the twins said in an interview that they had thirty slaves. In the mid-1850s, the twins ended their "copartnership" and divided their property between them. In truth, the transaction merely formalized separate living arrangements that had been in place since the late 1840s. Nevertheless, the formal partition of the households had a significant impact on the property of each twin, including their slaveholdings; as part of the division, Eng sold ten slaves to Chang for one dollar in November 1855, which, if the 1853 information was correct and had remained stable, left Eng with twenty. In return for taking the fewer number of slaves, Chang received more land, about 625 acres in Stewart's Creek and White Plains. The full impact of this transaction would be felt at the end of the Civil War. The 1860 census, the last before emancipation, recorded Eng with sixteen slaves and Chang with twelve. Of Eng's slaves, one was thirty-five years old, three were in their twenties, six were teenagers, and six were ten or younger (four of these were younger than four); ten were female. Of Chang's slaves, the oldest was forty years old, one was twenty-two, five were in their teens, three were ten, and two were two years old or younger.[51]

What the twins did with their slaves is even more difficult to discern. Their predominant youth, for example, posed some issues. "Some few of their slaves were valuable to them, for their present ability to labor," a contemporary biographer wrote, "but much the greater number of them were an absolute burden but very valuable on account of the marketable price and prospective usefulness." In 1850, ten of the twins' eighteen slaves were aged seven or under. While the immediate utility of these slaves in servicing the family in the field or in the house was minimal, the long-term possibilities were more promising. Indeed, judging solely from a comparison of the age and sex of the slaves, there is the distinct possibility that most of these young slaves provided the bulk of teenage laborers that were present in 1860. On their farms, the twins raised cattle, sheep, and swine and grew wheat, rye, corn, oats, and potatoes in large quantities but, unlike many of their neighbors, no tobacco, suggesting perhaps that much of the output was intended to provision the two families—numbering nineteen in 1860, with five more children to come in the next eight years—and their many slaves.[52]

Unquestionably, however, the slaves also provided a useful resource on which Chang and Eng could build their reputations as among the "better class of farmer." It was not merely a question of owning slaves, however, that bestowed honor on the master but also of how well one treated his slaves. Owning slaves also gave critics ammunition to attack the twins. In 1852, a North Carolina newspaper published a profile of the twins that included praise—they had raised "remarkably" well-behaved and intelligent children, they were "thorough-going" businessmen, and they had embraced "a strong Christian faith or belief and [were] regular attendants at Church . . . where they deport themselves as becomes good citizens of the land of their adoption"—but also undermined other positive representations of the brothers. Neighbors questioned the twins' shooting skills, and the brothers were belligerent and had several run-ins with the law. Additionally, the Greensboro paper reported that the twins were merciless toward their slaves. "In driving a horse or chastising their negroes, both of them use the lash without mercy. A gentleman who purchased a black man, a short time ago, from them, informed the writer he was 'the worst whipped negro' he ever saw." The story was picked up by New York and Philadelphia papers, and the New England press, including the *Liberator*, ran briefs that characterized the twins as "severe taskmasters." The truth of charges such as this cannot be verified, but their importance to the twins' reputation cannot be denied. Within the South—and the story originated just sixty miles to the east in Greensboro—the ideological tenets of paternalism caused many neighbors to look down on brutal masters as men who could not control their tempers, were unpredictable, and, worst of all, disturbed the delicate balance between kindness and cruelty, callousness and care, on which the southern ideology of paternalism rested. Slave owners feared that a cruel master made those less cruel seem weak, perhaps provoking the latter's slaves to try to take advantage of his softness.[53]

Chang and Eng responded immediately to the 1852 report, writing a letter to the editor of that same newspaper. "That portion of said piece relating to the inhuman manner in which we had chastized a negro man which we afterwards sold is a sheer fabrication and infamous falsehood." A statement from thirteen of their neighbors attesting to the "good character, peaceable demeanor, and strict integrity" of the twins accompanied the letter. In the 1853 booklet that coincided with that year's tour of the North, the twins appear as the real laborers on the farm: "Chang and Eng not only superintend all their work personally, but accomplish themselves more actual labor, than any four of their servants." And in an interview with a New York newspaper that year, the twins portrayed themselves as kind, humane father figures. "The respected heads of families . . . left their plantation, their wives, children, and slaves" to come to New York. In their absence, "Madame Chang devotes her time to the general supervision of the slaves . . . while Madame Eng charges herself with the care of the young masters and misses, and keeps a school for their tuition and that of the negroes." The message was clear: The Bunkers did not drive their slaves but supervised them; what is more, they gave them an education.[54]

Despite the twins' assertions, their property in slaves was essential to the running of their farms. Letters from the twins to their wives during the 1853 tour have many references to their slaves and the work they did. Adelaide was instructed to have slaves sow the rye and oats, look after the stock, get pigs ready for market, and kill hogs. Adelaide was also hiring out slaves, primarily young girls, to work for neighboring families. At some points in the correspondence, it becomes clear how the twins might have earned a reputation among some neighbors as being ruthless, though not necessarily toward their slaves. When Adelaide wrote that dogs had gotten into the property and killed some sheep, the twins' response was straightforward: "Why Berry have not shot them[?] . . . You may tell Berry that we want him to kill all dogs that come in side of our fents & throw them in the creek & say nothing about it." In some places, the twins speak of their slaves with paternalistic fondness. When an acquaintance wrote to them that "our folk have made good deal of corn," they instructed Adelaide to "tell all of them that when we come back we will bring them all some things," language that the twins also used when talking about their own children. On occasion, the language was less family-friendly: after a discussion of Berry's work, they told Adelaide "to gave our old pant & coat to the niger."[55]

The twins understood social hierarchies, and they also seemed proficient in recognizing connections between one's skin color and one's place in the hierarchy. So, to answer one of the questions posed in the *National Era*, slavery provided the twins a racialized, subjugated group of people—black slaves—whom they could position themselves against, alongside a racialized but privileged group of people—white slaveholders. In so doing, however, it might have been argued that they were in some way undermining the slaveholding class. In a system based on white supremacy, what did it mean for there to be slaveholders of color who often received prominent public attention? In other places in this chapter and in the book I argue that the twins were making claims to whiteness through their adoption of certain roles, slave owner being one of them. In terms of legal whiteness, it is a valid point; they became U.S. citizens, married white women, were listed in census reports as white. Yet, time after time, press reports and letters identified the twins clearly as something other than white. What implications did the twins, and other immigrants from Asia, hold for slavery in the United States?

The role of slaveholder that the twins had adopted was infinitely more complicated than their simply embracing symbols of whiteness. In the early 1850s, the country was caught up in debates over free and slave labor, the promise and perils of assimilation by immigrants generally, and the place that free people of color—including Chinese—should occupy in America. And developments in the western states and territories were fraught with implications for the Atlantic states, northern and southern.

In 1854, a fateful year that saw not only the Kansas-Nebraska Act, which repealed the Missouri Compromise of 1820, but also the rise of both the antislavery Republican Party and the nativist American Party, also known as the "Know-Nothings," the weekly *National Era* introduced a "Voice of the People" section, usually taking up much of the last page, that featured long and thoughtful letters from readers of many stripes. (This is the column in which the inquiry about Chang and Eng in light of anti-Chinese sentiment in California appeared.) Readers concerned that the allegiance of Catholics rested with Rome and not the United States butted heads with readers who worried that nativism undermined the political and moral power of the antislavery cause. Some expressed opposition to slavery but fear of the free Negro, while others insisted on the equality of all men and the need to bring people of color into the political and economic body of the country. Politics dominated discussion, and countervailing emphases on ethnicity and religion versus slavery and abolition clearly marked the debate. Underlying these threads of thought, however, was pressing anxiety about shifting racial and cultural categories that controlled access to economic, social, and political power.[56] The way these issues played out shaped the remaining years of the twins' lives.

In addition to a changing racial landscape, the 1850s saw shifting political, ideological, and sectional allegiances as well. As the second party system collapsed, the issues of slavery and nativism threatened to split a northern coalition that aimed at wresting political power from Democrats. The division was apparent even to readers of the *National Era*, who almost entirely saw themselves as antislavery. The paper's editor, Gamaliel Bailey, routinely condemned Know-Nothings as going against the nation's traditions of civil liberty, religious freedom, and opportunity for immigrants, and many readers agreed. These charges rattled his Know-Nothing readers, and many canceled their subscriptions. Others engaged in debate. Aside from cultural and religious concerns, nativists argued that the recent influx of immigrants supported the Democratic Party and had few qualms about slavery. Radical abolitionists argued that not only were nativists ripping apart a coalition that could compete against the real threat—the Slave Power, the name used by antislavery activists to describe what they understood to be the control of the federal government by slave owners—but also that, in their prejudice, nativists had much in common with proslavery sympathizers.[57]

The conflict was not simply black and white, however, as the immigration of tens of thousands of Chinese in the ten years after 1848 made clear. The introduction of cheap labor from Asia fueled debates over slavery and immigration as much as the latter two influenced the public's reception of the growing Chinese presence. The 47,203 Chinese who arrived in San Francisco from 1848 to 1855—and who made up the vast majority of Chinese arrivals during these years—were of course dwarfed by 853,484 Irish and 684,654 Germans who arrived in the United States from 1847 to 1854. Nevertheless, the Chinese quickly became the largest minority in California and as such received the brunt of prejudice and discrimination. Just as Know-Nothings nationwide pursued immigration and naturalization reforms, California Know-Nothings explored ways to restrict Chinese immigration and constrain the activities of Chinese already in the state.[58]

The Chinese in California complicated discussions of American slavery in two ways. Most profound, they posed the specter, or the promise, of a new category of bonded labor. In the 1840s, the British pioneered a "coolie" trade that shipped contract laborers from China to British possessions in the West Indies and in Peru. The brutal nature of the coolie trade was soon apparent; workers were often recruited fraudulently, the conditions of their overseas passage evoked memories of the slave trade, and their labor was exploited ruthlessly. The Chinese who went to California were free emigrants and not contract labor; nevertheless, the stigma of the coolie trade, coupled with their non-European origins, made the Chinese a type of bonded labor in the minds of many Americans. In the early 1850s, there was discussion of undermining the slave economy in the South by introducing Chinese coolies for a daily pittance. Reports of the brutality of the coolie trade, including the deaths of more than 200 migrants on a Boston-based trading ship in 1855, led to discussion through the rest of the decade that centered on either regulating or outlawing the trade. The 1862 congressional act to prohibit the coolie trade was just the latest legislation at the local, state, and national levels designed to limit the immigration of Chinese. Such constraints attracted attention nationwide, causing consternation among antislavery advocates and knowing smiles from supporters of slavery. The first step toward slavery in California was the legislature's authorization of "Chinese peonage," the *Richmond Dispatch* reported. "The next step will be African slavery."[59]

Conceptions of American slavery were also complicated by the consideration of slavery in China, of the Chinese as slaveholders. On the part of the abolitionist press, slavery in China provided an opportunity for comparative study, most often to show just how backward the fact and practice of slavery was in the American South. Whereas the South was made up of so-called Christians who, sinfully, owned slaves, the pagan Chinese practiced slavery through ignorance. The possibility that the Taiping Rebellion might introduce Christianity to China tickled observers. "It would be a singular spectacle to see China renounce domestic slavery, under the influence of a semi-Christianity, whilst America, boasting of her freedom and her religious and political institutions, clings to the abomination," the *Anti-Slavery Reporter* opined. The poverty of parents who had nothing and wanted only to be freed from the obligations of raising a child fueled slavery in China, not the greed of a master class. The slave child was taken into a family and often raised as a member. There was no auction block, families were not forcibly separated, and slaves were citizens nonetheless (albeit citizens of a despotic empire). "Since master and slave are both of the same race, there is no line of separation, as in the case of African Slavery, and the slave is received into the family, faring as other members," the *National Era* reported.[60]

The discussion of Chinese slaves bought and sold departed substantially from the tale told by Chang and Eng of the Chinese in Siam who were exempted from corvée labor and worked as independent merchants. Similarly, the image of Chinese masters buying and selling reflected on the twins and their claim to whiteness as slaveholders. And, as we have seen, the twins were increasingly identified as Chinese and associated with China. (Indeed, reports began stating that the twins were actually from China.) At this same time, Chinese in America began to be "Negroized," as one historian has phrased it. They were marginalized in courts of law. They were excluded from certain types of labor and relegated, instead, to the least desirable and least profitable positions. They were employed in challenges to free labor. In visual images and verbal depictions, Chinese were described in ways that had previously been limited to African Americans. In 1854, when the California Supreme Court announced its *People v. Hall* decision that prohibited Chinese from offering testimony against whites, the *Liberator* likened the decision to the South's slave codes, describing the state as taking "rapid strides toward slavery." In 1857, *Lippincott's Geographical Dictionary of the World* said the Chinese "bear a considerable resemblance to the Negro."[61]

Proslavery Americans used the image of Chinese slaves and masters to argue for the legalization of a slave trade with China. Contending that the Chinese in California were enslaved by mandarins in China (the laborers' contracts were often held by Chinese firms until the laborer paid off the cost of his passage), proslavery Americans reasoned that the state could engage in a similar business. For a fraction of the cost of an African slave, "the Californian may have a laborer who will answer all the purpose of a negro." In response, the *National Era* claimed that the prospect of enslaving Chinese presented a slippery slope. "The Chinese have no African blood in them, and their enslavement would at once destroy the peculiarity of Slavery in this country, of being confined to the African race. Slaves would cease to be distinguishable by the color of the skin and by the hair." If this step succeeded, it would be "more than a half-way step to the introduction of white Slavery." Similarly, in the editor's response to his reader's query about the Siamese twins, Gamaliel Bailey responded that he did not know the specifics of the twins as slaveholders but that in one Virginia county, the largest landholder was a black man who also owned slaves but, because of his race, could not vote or testify in a court of law against a white man.[62]

The introduction of a critical mass of Chinese laborers raised all sorts of questions that made the position Chang and Eng occupied increasingly unstable. The shifting boundaries of race did not necessarily obliterate the position the twins had carved out for themselves. But it did open room for ambivalence and uncertainty. As men who were clearly not black, they had been able to make legal and social claims to whiteness. As we have seen, however, the popular imagination continued to envision the twins as Chinese, and Chinese were increasingly lumped in a generic "nonwhite" category. Discussions of the direction slavery might take now focused on forms of nonwhite—and not necessarily black—labor. And slaveholding itself, long a marker of whiteness in the South, also was coming to be discussed as something that did not guarantee a white racial consciousness or community. Where did the twins fit in?

An essay published in the *National Era* argued for a united human race, claiming that race in the United States had nothing to do with skin color and everything to do with descent. The reason some abolitionists saw such a slippery slope to white slavery (aside from the shock value it added to their campaign to raise public opposition to the institution of slavery) was this conception of a common humanity. Framing "The United States of the United Races" around the fact of Chinese immigration and the prospect of Hungarians, Italians, and Turks soon "swelling the tide," the author argued that the country's political and religious traditions could provide the foundations on which these newcomers could adapt and prosper, learning the language, "marrying your cousin," and running for Congress. It dismissed claims by ethnologists and phrenologists that a person's race or national origins suggested an essential nature, and it denied that such considerations ought to play a role in America's social order. "A negro is a slave, though an albino, with alabaster skin, pink eyes, and silver white hair. Trace the whitest and handsomest woman in Charleston to the stock for two centuries devoted to the American yoke, and she goes to the auction block, and the darkest colored white man in the nation may buy her and be her owner. It is not color but kindred that settles the question." And the Chinese, though not "white," descended from a great civilization rich in fine arts, literature, and trade.[63]

This counterpoint to the emerging racial sciences and legal definitions of the day was not alone. But, as might be expected, this questioning of the racial hierarchy was not widely embraced and in fact became contentious. Within the abolitionist community—even among readers of the radical press—there was opposition to allowing the emancipated Negro to mingle with whites. One reader of the *National Era* proclaimed his support of all the paper's abolitionist and antinativist policies, "save the idea of a full extent of American negro suffrage and a place in legislative halls. This I cannot consent to." This Virginia native who had recently emigrated to Iowa wanted instead "an entire separation of the two races—negroes to live where God designed them." His comments reflected rifts in the abolitionist movement—between gradual and immediate emancipation or colonization and racial integration. Chinese in California protested the trend they identified of placing them alongside blacks and Irish, and an advocate of the Chinese decried the practice of some newspapers of describing them as even lower. The Irish "have never fairly amalgamated with republican Institutions," and the Germans "have published a series of resolutions against our present Institutions." As for those who compared the Chinese with blacks, they should be considered mentally ill, the advocate suggested. "We protest against making targets of the poor Chinese, and say, it is only fair, that Republicans should warmly encourage, cherish, and protect every effort to diffuse the spirit of Christianity and Republicanism amongst this interesting race."[64]

The Siamese brothers in North Carolina had received the opportunity to attach themselves to a number of American institutions. They were citizens, they attended church with their white wives, and they owned slaves, even though, as observers commented, they were not white. In their actions, they were described as "good citizens of the land" but also as ruthless men who took punishment of slaves to an extreme. They were ambivalence embodied, themselves a cultural hybrid that puzzled observers, their families an example of the promises and perils of amalgamation. The themes of racial and cultural fluidity that surrounded the twins and influenced the way Americans discussed Chinese in America proved too much. The twins' example might have served as an inspiration for Californians to give Chinese immigrants the room necessary to engage with American institutions; instead, the prejudice against Chinese that many white Americans felt began to be directed also at the twins and their children.

The Bunker Children on Display

It was not native Californians who drove the anti-Chinese movement. It was, rather, newcomers to the state. Many native-born white Americans moved to California from the Atlantic states and expressed disgust at the sheer number of Chinese they found there.[65] One such example was Hinton Rowan Helper, an abolitionist-racist whose claim to fame rests most largely with his 1857 book, *The Impending Crisis of the South*, which advocated the overthrow of the South's planter class and the removal of all blacks from the United States, lest amalgamation occur between black and white. What made this argument for abolition particularly explosive was that he was a son of the South, although his family did not own slaves. What makes him especially intriguing for this study is that he was from Rowan County, North Carolina, which neighbored Wilkes County, where Chang and Eng had first settled. No direct evidence exists that connects the twins to Helper, although scholar Robert G. Lee speculates convincingly that he likely knew of the famous brothers and the mixed-race families they were raising nearby. Helper was ten years old when the twins married, and he apprenticed as a clerk in Salisbury, the home of the same *Carolina Watchman* newspaper that featured stories on the twins. After his apprenticeship, he moved to New York City and then to California in 1850. His attempts to get rich quick failed, and his writings documented the unfortunate circumstances of many whites from the Atlantic states who similarly had traveled to the Pacific to make money and instead found themselves penniless and living in squalor.[66]

In 1855, Helper published *The Land of Gold*, a polemic that promised to uncover the ugly truths of life in California that promoters tried to hide. He condemned the filth, debauchery, lawlessness, and loose morals of men and women that greeted him upon arrival. He lamented the "human menagerie" he found, "probably one of the most motley and heterogeneous that ever occupied space . . . Americans, French, English, Irish, Scotch, Germans, Dutch, Danes, Swedes, Spaniards, Portuguese, Italians, Russians, Poles,

Greeks, Chinese, Japanese, Hindoos, Sandwich Islanders, New Zealanders, Indians, Africans, and hybrids." And, in the only chapter devoted specifically to a certain group of people, he chronicles the Chinese in California, his authorial voice dripping with distaste. Their facial features, hair, dress, and manners, as well as their "xanthous," or yellow, complexion, made them appear exactly like each other but unlike anyone else. Though most were slaves to their wealthier countrymen, Helper wrote, the Chinese thought so highly of themselves that none would deign serve a white man. What few Chinese women were present knew nothing about good morals, and the men habitually wasted their time in gambling dens. They were so disdainful of American ways that they continued to work and lay bets on the Sabbath. In the end, Helper argued that they were not suitable for immigration. "Our population was already too heterogeneous before the Chinese came; but now another adventitious ingredient has been added."[67] Further, their presence would hinder the introduction of virtuous white American women necessary to cultivate the moral values that the frontier society required.

Robert G. Lee links Helper's "anxiety about Chinese immigration and interracial amalgamation" to an obsession with "barrier[s] to 'normal' family development."[68] The Bunkers of Surry County, meanwhile, though still considered extraordinary by most Americans, nevertheless did their best to embody the values of a "normal" white family. Many of the sons' names were celebrations of American and English history—Christopher Wren, an acclaimed English architect; Stephen Decatur, a noted U.S. naval officer; James Montgomery, a British poet; Patrick Henry, a founding father of the United States. Lest the names be overlooked, the twins purportedly made the point themselves in a letter published in the New York *Courier*.[69] As we will see, other publications consistently commented on the children's education, their manners, and their respect for their parents. And yet, putting aside for a moment the conjoined state of their fathers and their own mixed-racedness, these children led lives that differed vastly from that of the "normal" American. After all, they spent much of their childhood on display, in newspapers, magazines, and exhibition halls, certainly, but also at home. The very attempts to document their normality simply reinforced their difference.

Ultimately, of course, the children could not be separated from the identity of their parents. The birth of the first two children—Sarah Bunker gave birth to Katherine Marcellus on February 10, 1844, and on February 16, Adelaide Bunker welcomed Josephine Virginia to the world—at once legitimated the unions between the sisters and their husbands; they were *actually* married, it was not just a joke. It also set tongues wagging. Children, after all, were public proof of a very private, often unspeakable, act. Friends of the twins were astounded by the proximity of the births. "That was pretty close work—within 6 days of each other!" James W. Hale wrote. Newspapers up and down the Atlantic coast reprinted a *South Carolina Spartan* report celebrating the arrival of a "fine, fat, bouncing daughter" for each. The closest any publication came to discussing the sexual unions occurred in one of the early profiles, in 1848: "I wish the ladies distinctly to understand that in their courtship there were no secrets among them," the *Richmond Southerner* reported. "The ladies will also understand that they were married on the same evening, by the same Preacher, and retired to rest about the same hour." To drive the point home, the reporter noted the proximity in birth dates between the cousins thus born. In addition to the six-day difference between Katherine and Josephine, Chang's son Christopher was eight days younger than cousin Julia. In all, Eng and Sarah Bunker had eleven children, Chang and Adelaide had ten. Together, the twins had twelve daughters and nine sons. Two died before age three (both apparently from burns), and two were deaf. Neither Chang nor Eng had twins.[70]

As the Bunker offspring grew up, however, observers showed interest in how these mixed-race children would turn out, and they expected the process to be in the public eye. Almost within months, newspapers speculated on when the twins would hit the road again, this time with their wives and children. "It is said that Chang and Eng, with their wives and children, contemplate making a tour through this country in the course of a year or two," newspapers reported. The twins would "doubtless prove more interesting and attractive in their second tour than they did in their first over the civilized world. Having families to provide for as prudent husbands and fathers, they may think their bachelor fortune insufficient for all the little Changs and Engs of which they now have the promise."[71] Perhaps signifying its spectacle, a Boston paper ran the news of the birth directly below a notice, titled "Curiosities," that a ship from Africa had arrived carrying an ourang outang, two chameleons, and two monkeys of the rarest species, all ready for display.[72] Americans did not have to wait long until the details of the children's appearance also became available for public consumption. In the years before the twins returned to exhibition, people began converging on the Bunker households to see the children and shared their impressions. The same reports that chronicled the twins working on the farm and the wives looking after the home commented on the children. They looked healthy but had "their father's features clearly stamped upon them. You could readily single them out of ten thousand children."[73]

The short-lived tour of 1849 featured five-year-olds Katherine and Josephine. People had assumed that their mothers would go along as well, either reflecting the central role that women played in child-rearing, especially of their daughters, or the strong desire by many Americans to gaze upon the wives of the Siamese twins. Indeed, the earliest articles from New York, the ultimate destination, reported incorrectly that the twins and their wives and children had left home and were exhibiting in Richmond. The absence of Sarah and Adelaide, however, effected a representation of the girls—and, ultimately, of all the children who toured with the twins—that while inevitable was nevertheless notable. The girls were their fathers' children; the advertisements said so: "The Living Siamese Twins Chang-Eng and Their Children." The constant proximity between father and child on the public stage made statements about their resemblance to their fathers predictable. Although none of the children shared the unique characteristic that marked their father and uncle (and, in truth, the absence of physical deformity proved noteworthy in almost all references to the children), the physical characteristics of Chang and Eng marked their children in other ways, articulated and given meaning by the observing public. Newspapers and private correspondents remarked frequently on the children's "Siamese cast of countenance," their "coarse black hair" and "swarthy" complexion.[74] The Bunker children carried the markers—visible and invisible—of their fathers as they became public exhibits, both away and at home.

But, Chang and Eng believed, the children marked the twins just as significantly. Children were the most tangible evidence of their manhood, and these children, raised to be well-spoken and elegant in their manners, supported the twins' claim to a certain type of masculinity that spoke to both race and class, the southern gentleman farmer. Publicity that accompanied the 1853 tour made this explicit. The twins wanted to provide their children with a good home and a liberal education, as did all parents, the literature stated. The twins' emphasis on the importance of educating their children was a central component of their strategy to create a normative, privileged family. Indeed, the justification offered for resuming touring and exhibiting was the need to raise funds to educate their children. "To educate a large family, thoroughly, requires a considerable expenditure of money," the 1853 booklet that coincided with their northern tour reported, "and as their children manifest remarkable aptness and superior capacity, they have determined to spare no expense where the cultivation of their minds is

Chang and Eng with their wives and children, from *Gleason's Pictorial Drawing-Room Companion*, 1853. Ronald G. Becker Collection of Charles Eisenmann Photographs, Special Collections Research Center, Syracuse University Libraries.

concerned." Southern elite, including the middle class, generally sought to educate their children, sons and daughters, in knowledge and virtue. Boys tended to receive a classical education, whereas girls obtained a more practical education that stressed their future roles as household managers and mothers. The Bunkers thought enough of education that, at least for a time in the 1850s, they moved to the nearby town of Mount Airy for schooling under the tutelage of two clergymen. Later, the Bunkers and their next-door neighbors built and shared a schoolhouse on the farm, hiring a young man to teach. The effort apparently paid off. Almost all reports about the children reflect the favorable tone taken by the Raleigh newspaper. A profile in another North Carolina paper called the children "a credit to their parents and the community in which they live."[75]

So, the children's success reflected well on the twins as parents, in some respects. But whether the children succeeded in marking the twins as anything other than racial and national outliers is doubtful. In one interview, the twins used their families to suggest they would never return to Siam:

"We have wives and children here, all Americans, and we are Americans now too," they said. Another version of the same interview appeared thus: "We never going back, have wife and children here, all 'Merican, and we 'Mericans now too."[76] Not only did the twins fall short of being full Americans, their wives and children did, too, through association.

The twins' children provided a case study in the effects of sex between the races and between monstrosity and normality. The fears—or perverse curiosities—fell along two lines of thought, which, in truth, were two sides of the same coin. On the one side, would the Siamese twins have Siamese twins for children? On the other, would the mixing of races produce children with other defects? The years during which the twins were having children, 1844 to 1868, coincided with early scientific theories on hybridity, or the mixing of the races.[77] Concerns surrounded the health and viability of mixed-race offspring. For instance, American physician and surgeon Josiah Clark Nott argued in 1844 that mixed-race children tended to be short lived, less smart than their white parents, prone to chronic disease, and unable to endure hardship or fatigue. Although Nott specifically referred to the children that resulted from black-white relationships, the taxonomy that he developed included Mongolians—referring to Chinese—and later theorists developed similar critiques about the mixing of Asian and white races based on Nott's work.[78]

When Chang and Eng passed through Raleigh in April 1853 on their way to a summer exhibition tour of the North, a local newspaper commented on the son and daughter—Chang's Christopher and Eng's Katherine—who accompanied the twins. Aside from the children's dark complexion, "the blending of the Caucasian and Mongolian blood would seem in this case to defy the investigations of those who deny the unity of races; for nothing in them betrays a foreign origin." Others were not as kind. "Their flat, swarthy features, black coarse hair, and low, retreating forehead, indicated clearly their Siamese paternity," one publication reported, while another believed the boy "looks more like an Indian than a Siamese" and "the girl has more of the Chinese features." What is more, the article commented on Katherine's mannerisms in a way that did not necessarily reflect poorly on her, though it did not reflect favorably on her father. "She looks sad and unhappy, as if she had much rather have her liberty . . . than be surrounded with people all day, staring at her, and asking her questions, as it seemed a great effort for her to behave as she evidently had been instructed to do."[79]

Although it might have seemed to some observers that the twins were mistreating their children by placing them on exhibit, personal letters between the twins and their wives suggest instead that the twins doted on their children. Each letter from the brothers is full of reports on the well-being of Katherine and Christopher (the two children traveling with them on this tour) as well as inquiries about the children who had stayed home. The twins bought gifts of rings and earrings for their daughters and asked about what their sons might like. But their concern for the children came through in an extraordinary and heartfelt exchange between Eng and Sarah in late 1853:

> Dear Sarah, we just received bad news of your acciden & we sorry to hear that our child has been so badly scalded—can you tell us who is to blame we should like to know pleased inform us by the next— hope this acciden would make you all more care full here after—we have wrote to you often befor to take good care of the children— However hope to hear no more of it—Dear Sarah i am not mad with you but i want you to be care full about all the children—i do not want you to work at all—want you to look after the children first— then if you can do some thing well & good but must take care of the children *first*.[80]

Family was not just a performance for the twins, despite the claims of some critics. And while most letters were not about such dire circumstances as the above, they all focused on the long distance that separated the family and the desire to be reunited. The twins wrote that "we think the little children at home will forget us by the time we get back," while Adelaide said to "tell Christopher I am mighty sorry he has forgotten me." Responded the twins, "We will always be glad to hear from all—we wish you will write offener," and then, "Be sure to write to us. Love to children."[81]

Still, just as privately the twins understood what they were doing as a sacrifice for the good of their families, many in the public understood what the twins were doing as sacrificing their families for their own benefit, and the viewing public was rendering judgment upon the brothers. Certainly, the twins were earning money. But they were also making claims for middle-class normality. Inhabiting parlor settings and invoking themes of a domestic gentility, their viewings came to be called "levees" and involved sitting, talking, mingling, and some degree of acceptance. The setting allowed the twins to show off their political insights, their wit, and their good English. But as the years passed, the twins' age began to show and became a point of dismay for their audiences. One disappointed reporter wrote that "seen from behind, Chang and Eng looked like lads who had just thrown their arms about one another in sport," but from the front, they betrayed "their age and the great Asiatic division of the human family to which they belong."[82] These levees also were intended to allow the twins to show off their bright and intelligent children. But while the children proved remarkable for their intelligence and appropriate behavior, there were many more comments on their "swarthiness." Their features—coarse hair, dark skin— marked them as different, as foreign. And, as the comment about Katherine showed, their Chinese ancestry was not far from the minds of their audience, and the influx of Chinese immigrants in the early 1850s only made this more so.

Even those who considered the Chinese the most civilized people in Asia and lauded their prowess in manufacturing and trade drew distinctions between elite Chinese and those who made their way to America. "The class of Chinese in California are generally of the lowest order," U.S. representative Milton S. Latham of California said in a speech that actually promoted trade between the two countries. "This class are from the scum of the Chinese population, and cannot be considered a valuable acquisition to any community."[83] Increasingly, the large presence of Chinese on the West Coast created a range of positions into which Chinese could be situated. For Chang and Eng, this meant that earlier efforts to present them as analogous to American merchants of the privileged race became more difficult. And, by December 1860, when the twins arrived in San Francisco with two of Eng's sons, anti-Chinese sentiment had festered for the good part of a decade.

In the first week of October 1860, the Siamese twins and two sons appeared in New York City, where they had, for the first time, contracted with P. T. Barnum to exhibit themselves for little more than a month at his American Museum. In New York, they performed alongside "Zip the Man Monkey"—the son of former slaves, whose small head resulted from microcephaly—and the "Albino family," in front of such illustrious guests as the Prince of Wales. But the twins were just passing through. On November 12, they set sail for California aboard the steamer *Northern Light*. Eight days later they arrived in Aspinwall, crossing the Panamanian isthmus by train, then boarding the steamer *Uncle Sam*. The final leg of the voyage from Panama to San Francisco took sixteen days, the twins and sons arriving on the morning of December 6. Northern Californians had been following Chang's and Eng's first journey to the West Coast, and large posters with a full-length cut of the twins advertised their visit.[84]

The San Francisco that the twins visited was a rapidly growing city of more than 55,000 people. The city was relatively young—in 1850 its population was just 21,000—and most of its residents came from elsewhere. Most of the Americans living in the city were born in other states, and 50 percent of its population was foreign born. More than 2,700 of the city's population were Chinese, and these immigrants had begun congregating in an area that came to be called "Little China."[85] Local politics in this city of immigrants—from the Atlantic states as well as from across the Pacific—was definitely colored by developments a continent and an ocean away.

On the one hand, there was the "Chinese Question," as local newspapers termed it. The question was whether California should prohibit Chinese from immigrating to the state; whether California should make conditions for Chinese so unbearable, through higher taxes and laws that restricted court testimony and other forms of civic participation, that they would choose to leave and not return; or whether the state should place no limits on immigration or the Chinese living in California. On the other hand, there was the question of union: Lincoln's election and the talk of secession by some southern states had a major impact on the twins' California trip.

A coalition of middle-class merchants and reformers argued for the importance not only of protecting the rights of Chinese immigrants but also of providing more opportunities to study, labor, and cultivate the land. Such cooperation, they hoped, would benefit both the Chinese and white Americans. By giving Chinese an education, they could take to China American ideals of religion, business, and diplomacy and share these ideas with native Chinese in a way that American missionaries never could. The success of one evening school for Chinese was evidence that "American ideas will creep with the alphabet, into the brains of pupils of every color, climate, and nation," the *Daily Evening Bulletin* reported on December 13, a week after the twins arrived.[86] Similarly, giving the Chinese the opportunity to work freely without prohibitive taxes or restrictive laws meant that they would continue to be consumers of American food and manufactured goods; they could labor prodigiously on projects (such as the railroads) that white laborers would struggle with, which projects would then provide an infrastructure through which white Americans would profit greatly; and they would return home with positive things to say about the United States and make the millions of Chinese back home more eager to do business with Americans.[87] Additionally, pro-Chinese merchants and reformers believed that encouraging these migrants to begin cultivating California's swampland with rice or its barren desert with other crops would add wealth to the state's economy and make the Chinese more attached to the land, encouraging them to invest further in the country as consumers and also to adopt republican values.[88]

The white laboring class, as well as some small merchants, resented the Chinese presence and agitated for exclusion or more restrictive laws and higher taxes. For many of these people, the Chinese represented not only an economic threat but also a symbolic threat that challenged their position in society. "The Chinese coolies are vampires on the existence of the poorer portion of the laboring classes," one miner wrote.[89] The "poorer portion" of which this miner was specifically speaking was Irish; he stated this explicitly, and he also compared the work ethic and abilities of the Irish favorably to those of the Chinese. Indeed, his juxtaposition of the wealthy Chinese with the poor coolie—comparable to an African slave—served at once to cheapen Chinese labor and raise up the Irish. As we saw earlier, the slavery paradigm continued to inform the ways in which Chinese were viewed, especially poor Chinese workers.

In much the same way, letters that praised Chinese labor implicitly criticized other groups. Lauding the Chinese hard work ethic—and their willingness to do any job—as well as their thrift and rich civilization was often designed to place them favorably against the so-called ignorant and lazy Negro and Irish. In San Francisco, racial lines occasionally became obscured. At times, this was intended, as in the *Hall* decision, which blurred categories of nonwhite peoples to strengthen the division between white and nonwhite. In so doing, however, the California court also provoked questions that had the potential to destabilize the category of white. "Who is white?" one publication asked, offering the possibility that Chinese, Hindus, and American Indians were, but not revealing the court's answer. Newspapers, meanwhile, published reports of "white Chinese babies that were, apparently, the offspring of European men and Chinese women.[90] Even though distinctions between white and Chinese seemed to be taking root, there was nevertheless the danger of more fluidity in the future.

The Chinese in California similarly attempted to position themselves vis-à-vis other racial and ethnic groups. Most commonly, Chinese expressed their dismay at being compared to African Americans. Occasionally, they turned their anxiety elsewhere. Responding to the conclusion reached by many Americans that the "Chinese are the same as Indians and Negros," a San Francisco newspaper that was bilingual in Chinese and English titled the *Oriental*, or *Tung-Nai Sau-Luk*, responded that "Indians know nothing about the relations of society—they know no mutual respect—they wear neither clothes nor shoes—they live in wild places and in caves." An English-language editorial published in the Chinese-language newspaper *Golden Hills' News* of San Francisco belittled the Irish and Germans in contrast to the Chinese. "Why, the Celtic-race have never fairly amalgamated with republican Institutions," while "the Germans of Louisville have published a series of resolutions against our present Institutions!"[91]

Just as Chang and Eng had portrayed themselves against other racial and ethnic groups in an attempt to position themselves favorably in mainstream society, so did the Chinese in California. But while the twins were a very particular example that did not pose a larger risk to many people, if any, the arrival of tens of thousands of Chinese threatened the interests of several other groups, and so their attempts to position themselves favorably were unsuccessful. San Francisco's *Daily Evening Bulletin*, which earlier in 1860 had published a very open debate on the "Chinese Question," in June came out in favor of immigration restrictions of some sort. All but a few people would "admit that the Chinese are an undesirable population" who would undoubtedly "overrun" the state's population "unless their coming is checked." The Chinese person, while not as "low down in the scale of humanity as the pure African," was "lower than the white man[,] whose political equal he can never be allowed to become." If the nation's forefathers could have seen the "evils that have grown out of the importation of African laborers," the paper opined, they never would have unloaded the first cargo of blacks in Virginia. Similarly, Chinese should not be allowed to come into the country any longer. The Chinese, in other words, were analogous to enslaved blacks; they were "slaves, peons, and colored apprentices" and could never be citizens.[92]

Into this climate Chang, Eng, Patrick, and Montgomery Bunker arrived in California. And while their visit to San Francisco, Sacramento, and surrounding towns apparently went without incident, the twins and their children nevertheless found themselves linked with Chinese in America in a way they never had been before. Earlier in their lives, the twins had been able to negotiate between races, positioning themselves against blacks and alongside whites; now, they were placed alongside a people whose growing numbers, unfamiliar ways, and apparent success proved threatening to American society. The arrival of the twins and children was celebrated, to be sure. Newspapers, as they always had, urged an "admiring public" to visit this "greatest of living curiosities," who had "made much noise in the world, and are certainly worth seeing." The twins and their sons at turns sat in the center of the hall and mingled with their visitors. They shook hands with those who "craved the privilege," and they conversed with their guests "freely and pleasantly in good English." The twins were "venerable with age," their sons "bright and intelligent."[93]

And yet, the trip to California also made explicit language about their race and their nationality. Reports surfaced that the twins were circulating Chinese-language flyers among San Francisco's "Celestials," "describing the twins, and urging (we suppose) the children of the Flowery Kingdom to visit them."[94] Such reports evoked a number of images: of the twins as Chinese speakers, perhaps, and of their ability to engage in stealth communications with a certain notorious portion of the population, as well as the possibility of Chinese visitors alongside whites in the exhibition hall. To reformers, it might also have suggested the chance that the Americanized twins—dressed in Western suits, speaking English, and, reportedly, practicing Christianity—would provide a good role model for Chinese immigrants to follow and, perhaps, work toward assimilation.[95] As peril or promise, however, the report suggested a connection between the twins and the Chinese community.

Also on this trip, newspapers used the color "yellow" to describe the twins and their children for the first time in America. This usage suggests a shift of at least two dimensions. On the one hand, the twins and their children, whose skin color had previously been described as dark or swarthy and who most often had been compared in color to American Indians, now were being characterized by a color that was, increasingly in America, becoming associated with Chinese. On the other hand, "yellow" was becoming racialized in the American context to signify Chinese heritage. In the Atlantic states, "yellow" had commonly been used to describe mulattoes, especially in the South, where runaway slave notices provided frequent opportunities to articulate the skin color of enslaved laborers as descriptively as possible. Beginning in the 1850s, however, "yellow" was increasingly attached to the Chinese, popularized in Gold Rush–era ditties such as "Get Out Yellowskins!"[96] Their trip to California was not the last time the twins were described as yellow; later reports from the Northeast would similarly paint the twins as Chinese.

But while the presence of Chinese in California influenced the ways in which the twins were represented during their trip to the Pacific, it was the onset of war in the Atlantic states that ultimately determined the scope of their visit. The twins left New York in mid-November with the knowledge of Lincoln's election. By the time they arrived in California, South Carolina was on the verge of seceding, which it did on December 20, and by the time they left, on February 11, 1861, six more states—Mississippi, Florida, Alabama, Georgia, Louisiana, and Texas—had also seceded. War seemed increasingly likely, which probably influenced the decision to return when they did. (There are no records or newspaper reports about the return journey. Assuming it took a similar three and a half weeks to get back to New York City, then another week or two to return home to North Carolina, the twins and the children would have arrived home before mid-April, when fighting broke out at Fort Sumter and President Lincoln declared the lower South to be in a state of insurrection. North Carolina did not secede until May 20.)[97]

The coming of civil war refocused the gaze of most Americans back on domestic affairs; the trauma of the war and of Reconstruction has been associated in part with the decision by the United States to step back from imperial relations in East and Southeast Asia for most of the late nineteenth century, for instance. The months leading up to disunion similarly returned the twins, briefly, to a very American paradigm. Even as the twins traveled to California and came to be Orientalized once again, they—or, more precisely, their conjoined state—became a metaphor for the Union.

CHAPTER FIVE

Southern Curiosities

The Siamese twins had long been used ironically as symbols of American nationalism. The earliest pamphlet about the twins published in the United States in the early 1830s featured a title page image of a flying eagle carrying a banner that read "E Pluribus Unum," and beneath that was the phrase "United We Stand." This appeared opposite a frontispiece that pictured the twins as dark-skinned boys wearing queues and loose Oriental garments. The 1836 pamphlet published under the twins' direction similarly featured a bald eagle clutching the national shield, beneath which were the words "Union and Liberty, one and inseparable, now and forever." Analyzing the Siamese twins and American identity, scholar Allison Pingree argued that these exhibition booklets, which juxtaposed the parlance of the day describing conjoinedness—"united brothers" or "united twins"—with the symbolism of the American eagle holding an "E Pluribus Unum" banner in its beak, were playing to political concerns of the period. Even as nationalists appropriated the bond to symbolize union, proponents of states' rights could claim that "connecting the states too closely was 'monstrous' and excessive."[1]

This symbolism of the 1830s carried even more resonance in 1860. By this time, with the twins famously slaveholders and family men, representations of the twins and union were framed around the theme of a house divided, brother against brother, and the absurdity and tragedy of the moment. The political imagery began in July when the *Louisville Journal* took aim at discord in the Democratic Party. "It is said that Chang and Eng, the Siamese twins, differ in politics," the widely reprinted "news" item reported. "Both are veteran democrats, but Chang is now for Breckinridge, and Eng for Douglas."[2] The idea that the twins, longtime Whigs, supported either Democratic candidate—Illinois senator Stephen A. Douglas, who many southerners believed would not protect slavery, or Vice President John C. Breckinridge of Kentucky, who was staunchly proslavery—apparently proved too much for a Surry County neighbor. The twins "are not now and never have been Democrats [and] they say they never expect to be Democrats," the neighbor wrote to the *Fayetteville Observer*, which had published the report from Louisville. Instead, the anonymous neighbor wrote, they both supported John Bell of Tennessee, a pro-Union slaveholder who was running under the Constitutional Union Party, a coalition of former Southern Whigs and Know-Nothings that performed well in northwestern North Carolina but did not carry Surry County.[3] True or not, the significance of these assertions is the symbolism each carries: In the first report, the brothers were at odds, spelling doom for party and country, whereas in the second, Chang and Eng saw eye to eye and backed a candidate who similarly promised union.

Stories that used the twins to illustrate the sectional divide continued to pit brother against brother. A *New York Tribune* report claimed to describe a confrontation that occurred between the twins while on exhibit at Barnum's American Museum in early November. Chang, "a North Carolinian and a secessionist"—and apparently quarrelsome—first insisted that the ligament connecting the two brothers be painted black, suggesting to readers the centrality of slavery to the Union. When Eng voiced his preference for its natural color, Chang demanded that the union between the two brothers be dissolved. Eng, "of a calmer temperament," persuaded Chang to wait at least until March 4, 1861, when the new president would be inaugurated. Meanwhile, a "Dr. Lincoln" was called in and offered the prognosis that the surgery would be "dangerous for both parties" and that "the union must and shall be preserved."[4] The *Baltimore American* similarly predicted that separating this union would cause mortal injury. "If one of the Siamese brothers . . . rudely tears himself away, snapping asunder a bond that God and nature intended to be perpetual, he inflicts upon himself the same precise injury that he inflicts upon his fellow. . . . He commits fratricide and suicide at once." A North Carolina newspaper reprinted the item, observing that the report "likens secession to a supposed separating of the Siamese twins." The paper, however, titled the report "A Forcible Comparison," suggesting that it did not see such dire consequences in the prospect of disunion.[5]

The most elaborate analogy came out of another state that straddled the growing divide between North and South. For border states such as Missouri, Maryland, and Kentucky, which allowed slavery but, because of their strategic locations and profoundly divided populations, felt themselves tugged mightily in both directions, the imagery of the united twins perhaps had the greatest resonance: united they stand, divided they die.

Missouri's governor, Claiborne Fox Jackson, had led proslavery forces into "Bleeding Kansas" in the 1850s and now was determined for his state to "bind together in one brotherhood [with] the States of the South." The military commander of the U.S. arsenal in St. Louis, Captain Nathaniel Lyon, had faced off against Jackson in Kansas and had pledged to keep Missouri aligned with the Union. That state was about to undergo as bloody an internal struggle as any other over the question of secession.[6]

It should come as little surprise, then, that a Missouri paper published one of the most violent and grotesque analogies pitting the twins against each other. In February 1861, St. Louis's *Daily Missouri Republican* related an incident while stating that it "does not vouch for its truth." At some unspecified point in the past, the paper reported, Chang had emancipated his slaves and wanted Eng to do the same. Eng refused and, what was more, wanted to use his slaves to work "an *outlying lot*, which had been considered more than the rest of their plantation a piece of *common property*." Chang forbade this, and the two quarreled. Eng threatened to cut their tie; Chang defied him to do so. Eng insisted that Chang had wronged him and demanded redress; Chang argued that Eng had no cause to complain and refused to consider his brother's demands. Finally, slaveholder Eng, "tired of remonstrating and offering compromises, suddenly cut the tie and the two stood apart, no longer one!" Chang fell upon his brother, and the two engaged in a bloody fight. "It is doubtful whether both, or indeed, whether either of them will survive the cruel and unnatural encounter," the author commented.

On both sides, the families were the victims of the brothers' falling out. Some troublesome neighbors robbed them of valuables, a "scoundrelly land-shark" had set up fictitious claims to their lands, and each brother was killing and crippling children of the other. Chang even set Eng's slaves "to pillage him and take his life." Throughout, Chang insisted that Eng was still tied to him, which Eng derided "as ridiculous and nonsensical." "The warm pulsations, flesh and blood tie, which once joined them has been separated and can never be reunited, any more than the dead man can be brought to life," Eng told his brother. Of course they could be joined once again, Chang responded, suggesting that a rope could be tied around Eng's neck and Chang's waist, and if Eng failed to follow the path set by his brother, Chang could drag him along. This proposal suggested to doctors that Chang's mind was "disordered."[7]

Although the analogy to the greater sectional conflict was obvious, there were also in this report some notable parallels with the lives of the twins and families. They had, for instance, divided their estates, both in slaves and in property. This was a legal divorce of sorts, which some observers pinned on conflicts between the families and others on overcrowding. In fact, the division of estates codified living arrangements that had been in place since the years immediately following their weddings.[8] The report's drift into fiction was equally obvious. Of course the twins had not killed any of their children or, as far as we know, come to physical blows of any sort. And, for those paying attention to the several analogies appearing in newspapers around the country, there were clear inconsistencies. The Missouri example posed Eng as the intransigent slaveholder, while the Maryland paper had placed Chang in that role. The significance of these analogies was not their relation to the actual lives of the Bunker brothers but the metaphor the united twins offered for a nation in crisis.

For readers of the *St. Louis Republican*, the coming war between the states—as well as the ongoing battle within Missouri and the recent memories of Bleeding Kansas, in which many Missourians participated—provided the real framework for this mournful account of the twins and their families. The fears about deadly violence were clear, pitting brother against brother, of course, but also involving uncles killing nephews and family members unleashing slaves against other family members. And for what? For outsiders to come and lay claim to the land, to plunder and pillage while the women and children were weakened and the brothers were mortally wounded. The article came down harshly on Unionists, that is, Chang. They placed onerous demands on slaveholders, they clung stubbornly to their own beliefs, and their proposals for reunion amounted to little more than placing a leash on a disobedient mutt. But secessionists, that is, Eng, received criticism as well. They were hotheads who acted rashly and, in rushing to sever the tie that bound the two together, mortally wounded each and unleashed misery on their families.

The *Republican* concluded:

> All the real friends of these unfortunate parties are much concerned at this unhappy quarrel and its results. How it will finally terminate cannot be wholly foreseen. But this case seems to be hopeless. The *constitution* of neither of them can probably withstand the injuries and sufferings they have incurred; and that which should, and with an ordinary exercise of moderation and good sense would have remained a goodly heritage for their children, will be divided among strangers.[9]

The article spoke fondly of the twins, of the promise of a secure and bountiful future they had offered to their families. The united brothers had become symbols of the American union and the promise it offered to its citizens. Ultimately, however, the twins were scorned; they had become symbols of the nation's disunion.

In truth, the twins themselves did not separate; their union held. But as the nation approached its greatest crisis, the twins made their stand clear, hurrying from California to North Carolina, to their plantations, their slaves, and their families. The Bunkers were southerners, and they would remain southerners after the war, at home and abroad.

Snapshots from Surry County

Chang and Eng returned from California in early 1861 to a North Carolina that was the last state to secede. Statewide, as well as in Surry, the Southern Democratic candidate Breckinridge won the popular vote, but most state Democratic leaders denied that Breckinridge—who insisted that slavery must be protected in the western territories—was a disunion candidate. But as Confederate forces attacked Fort Sumter on April 12, as Lincoln called for 75,000 troops—including from North Carolina—to put down the rebellion, and as Virginia, their neighbor to the north, seceded, North Carolinians, united by anticoercion sentiment, rallied behind the southern cause, joining the Confederacy on May 20. "When the war come," one western Carolinian said, "I felt awful southern."[10]

The twins returned to farms that were portrayed as modest but were, in truth, among Surry's richest. In 1860, Eng owned 300 acres of land, and his real estate was valued at $1,100, placing him in the Mount Airy district's top quarter. He owned sixteen slaves in a county where 90 percent of slaveholders had fewer than fifteen, and only fifteen owned more than twenty. His personal estate was valued at $6,000—placing him in the district's top 7 percent—of which slaves made up perhaps two-thirds. His estate was dwarfed by his brother's, however. Chang's farm, just a mile away, was on 550 acres of land worth $6,000, and his personal estate was valued at $12,000—each measure in the district's top 5 percent. Chang owned eleven slaves in 1860.[11] Together, the brothers' farms raised swine, sheep, and cattle and cultivated corn, oats, wheat, and sweet potatoes, for consumption at home and for market.[12]

Over the course of the war, the twins' estates grew. While the size and value of their real estate remained steady, Eng's slaveholdings increased markedly. The 1860 slave schedules show Eng with sixteen, then county tax lists show him with nineteen in 1862 and twenty-one in 1863 and 1864. Perhaps the rise was from natural increase—although Mount Airy neighbors with more slaves did not experience similar growth—or perhaps Eng was taking slaves off the hands of smaller holders; there are no records of sales available.[13] Whatever the reason for the increase in numbers, the value of Eng's slaveholdings soared. In 1862, his slaveholdings were valued at $6,000; the next year, the value was $17,850, and in 1864, $17,050. This almost threefold increase can be explained in part by a rapid inflation in the value of slaves between 1862 and 1863. For example, Chang's holdings, which decreased in number from eleven to ten between those two years, rose in value from $4,000 to $10,150. The value of the district's (and county's) largest slaveholder, Hugh Gwyn, jumped from $12,000 (for forty-four slaves) to $30,050 (for forty-six). One neighbor, Robert Gilmer, saw the value of his fourteen slaves jump from $5,000 to $8,950, while another neighbor, William Rawley, saw the value rise from $6,000 to $9,300 despite the fact that his holdings decreased from eighteen to sixteen. The numbers suggest that even as the value of Surry County's slaves inflated unnaturally during the war, that of the twins did so disproportionately. And, in 1864, while Chang's investments in land and slaves were proportioned more evenly—$6,000 in land, $9,500 in slaves—Eng's investments—$1,000 in land, $17,050 in slaves—were strikingly unbalanced.

Their households changed in other ways during the war years. Just days before fighting broke out, on April 2, Adelaide gave birth to Jesse Lafayette, Chang's eighth child. She added another, Margaret Elizabeth, in October 1863. Sarah, meanwhile, gave Eng a daughter, Georgianna Columbia, in May 1863 and a son, Robert Edward—their eleventh and final child, named after Confederate general Robert E. Lee—days after the fighting ended, on April 17, 1865. (Adelaide and Chang's last child, Hattie Irene, was born in 1868, when Chang was fifty-seven and Adelaide was forty-five.) Eng and Sarah lost two daughters in 1865; Julia Ann died in February at age twenty, and two-year-old Georgianna died in September.[14] Two sons fought in the war. In April 1863, Chang's son Christopher enlisted with the 37th Battalion of the Virginia Cavalry in Wythe County, which neighbored Surry County to the north and in which other young men from Mount Airy enrolled. His cousin Decatur enlisted with the same company in January 1864. Decatur ended the war wounded and in hospital. Christopher, meanwhile, was captured at Moorefield, Virginia, in August 1864. Described in a list of prisoners held in Wheeling, West Virginia, as brown-eyed, black-haired, and dark-complexioned, he was sent as a prisoner of war to Camp Chase, Ohio, where he contracted and was treated for smallpox. He was exchanged in early March 1865 and returned home later that month.[15]

By the early months of 1865, Mount Airy was ready for an end to the fighting. "Every body is talking about peace and I hope that we will not be disappointed," a schoolgirl wrote to her sister in February. But on what terms, no one was clear. "Some think we are going back in to the union and some think that the confederacy will be established." But before peace arrived, Union troops under General George H. Stoneman pushed through the area as part of a larger foray through southwestern Virginia and western North Carolina. Stoneman's raid struck the homes of familiar names such as Gilmer, Hollingsworth, Prather, and Graves, taking food, primarily. "I expected they would destroy every thang and burn the houses," the schoolgirl wrote, but they did not, and the real distress for many of Mount Airy's landowning population came afterward.[16]

The enslaved men, women, and children who had been bought and sold like animals were now free. In Surry County, this was 12 percent of the population. For many former slaves, freedom meant the opportunity to break their ties with their former owners; they traveled throughout the South looking for husbands, wives, parents, and children from whom they had been separated, and they tried to establish farms for themselves and set the stage for economic self-determination as well. Others stayed put, in communities in which they had lived perhaps their entire lives, where their loved ones already resided.[17] They legitimated marriages in the eyes of the white law, often under the authority of their former owners. Joseph Banner and Pocahontas Galloway, the "former property" of two of the twins' Mount Airy neighbors, attested that they had been married since December 1849 "and that they had always since that time recognized each other as man & wife and that they were now living together and wish to remain together." The certificate was signed and sealed by the man's former owner. Their last names often reflected who their owner had been. Caroline Bunker married Henry Banner, and Betty Bunker married Thomas Davis; all formerly belonged to Mount Airy slaveholders. Some continued to live with their onetime masters. In the Eng Bunker household in 1870, for instance, Grace Gates, who had been a gift from David Yates more than twenty-five years before, lived as a maidservant. (Another man identified as black—Peter Karzy—lived in the Eng household, and three—identified as Jacob, Jack, and James—lived in the Chang household.) Others, meanwhile, established residences for themselves.[18]

The experience of the former Bunker slaves was representative of the larger black experience postemancipation, and their freedom was a blow to the finances of their former masters. In 1864, the county's largest slave-holder, Hugh Gwyn, had combined holdings in land and slaves worth $50,050; in 1866, his taxable holdings in land were $17,750. William Raw-ley, from whom the twins had bought their first tract of Surry County land in the 1840s, had sixteen slaves in 1864 and a combined value of $14,800; in 1866, his landholdings were worth $6,475. T. F. Prather, who sold three young slaves to Chang and Eng in 1845 and owned just five slaves in 1864, saw the value of his taxable property shrink from $12,900 to $5,500. Rela-tively speaking, these men were still wealthy, but their wealth now resided almost entirely in the land they owned. In 1864, Chang's combined holdings were worth $15,500; in 1866 his landholdings were valued at $6,000. For Eng, the contrast was even more remarkable, from $18,050 to $1,000.[19] With combined households now exceeding twenty members, the Bunkers had to rebuild their financial foundation. They would do so in a social and racial order that differed markedly from antebellum America.

Reconstructing the Twins

By 1864, the twins no longer were a metaphor for union, at least not a union that was palatable to many northerners. Instead, they came to symbolize other facets of American society that threatened the health of the nation: the prospect of bending political principles to accommodate traitorous views, the specter of newly freed blacks, and the image of the unrepentant southerner looking to pick up as if nothing had happened. Their fortunes destroyed, their slaves freed, and desperate for northern capital, the twins seemed to northern eyes the symbol of southern sins and the peril that the South posed to the nation.

During that year's presidential race, for instance, Republicans labeled Democratic candidate George B. McClellan, the one-time Union commander, and his running mate, Ohio antiwar congressman George H. Pendleton, as "Siamese twins," a pair with opposing interests who, to advance their own circumstances, tied their fortunes together. The Democrats' platform com-ing out of their August convention in Chicago called for a cease-fire and peace conference, which McClellan did not support, although he had been a vocal critic of Lincoln's plans for emancipation. Under a column titled "The Siamese Twins," the *New York Times* noted that "the Copperheads are still struggling like madmen to save Slavery from destruction. . . . Slavery, we know, was [the Democrats'] tower and buttress once, but it is too far gone to help them now."[20] McClellan attempted to distance himself from the apparent nod to proslavery interests in his party's platform, but Republicans chided him. "The Presidential candidate of the Democracy . . . forgets that as a candidate he is born with the platform, and united to it, as the Siamese twins are united together, so that the two cannot be separated," Massachusetts abolitionist Senator Charles Sumner said in a speech. "As well cut apart Chang and Eng as cut apart McClellan and Chicago. The two must go together."[21] As the election neared, a Boston paper opined that "the Siamese twins, McClellan and Pendleton, are sure to be drowned next week in the strong current of public opinion."[22]

The most graphic articulation of the objectionable union was an editorial cartoon called "The Political 'Siamese' Twins."[23] Subtitled "The Offspring of Chicago Miscegenation," the illustration portrayed McClellan and Pendleton standing together, bound at the chest by a band of flesh, just as Chang and Eng were; the connecting ligature was labeled "The Party Tie." The pair was flanked on McClellan's side by two Union soldiers, one wounded, expressing their sense of betrayal at their former commander's political bedmates. "I would vote for you General, if you were not tied to a PEACE COPPERHEAD who says that Treason and Rebellion ought to triumph!!" one said, while the other bid "little Mac" goodbye. McClellan, true to Sumner's criticism, protested the characterizations: "It was not I that did it fellow Soldiers! but with this unfortunate attachment I was politically born at Chicago!"

On Pendleton's side, the "twins" were flanked by former Ohio congressman Clement Vallandigham—author of the Democratic platform—and New York's Democratic governor, Horatio Seymour. Each was driven entirely by political calculations designed to promote their own self-interest. Making fun of McClellan's letter-writing prowess, Pendleton said, "I don't care how many letters Mac writes, if it brings him votes; for every vote for him counts one for me!!" Vallandigham, a "Peace Democrat" who supported the Confederacy and had been arrested for disloyalty and banished to the South by Lincoln, concurred: "Yes Pen, that's the only reason that I support the ticket; if you are elected both Jeff and I will be triumphant." Seymour, meanwhile, said the Democrats would accept any kind of peace that "our friends" in the South asked for. The words put in the mouths of these three politicians expressed contempt for Union soldiers, disloyalty to the cause of the North, and support for Jefferson Davis and the Confederacy, all for the opportunity to occupy political office.

"The Political 'Siamese' Twins, the Offspring of Chicago Miscegenation,"
published by Currier & Ives, 1864. Library of Congress.

These political Siamese twins were the antithesis of principles that
characterized the Union cause by 1864, especially as the war came to be
identified with ending slavery outright. The use of the newly coined "miscegenation" in the cartoon's subtitle was just one indication of the racially
charged times. The use was, of course, an ironic poke at the Democrats,
whose supporters had coined the word in late 1863. In a pamphlet titled
*Miscegenation: The Theory of the Blending of the Races, Applied to the
American White Man and Negro*, two anonymous Democrats posed as Republicans who were excited about the prospect of emancipation because
it would allow for the mixing of the two races. The authors designed the
pamphlet to be a political attack against Lincoln and the Republicans in
the 1864 elections.[24] While the "Political 'Siamese' Twins" did not mix the
races, the political pairing appeared to be a mixing of ideals, and the result
was monstrous, a *lusus naturae* that made a mockery of principled politics. In other words, the illustration suggested that the Democratic Party
had become degenerate. Granted, the targets were not racially mixed—the
Democratic platform called for slavery to continue, and the party preyed
on the fears of northerners that emancipation would result in sexual
unions between blacks and whites—but the word "miscegenation" and the
imagery of the Siamese twins suggested a racial dimension that could not
be ignored: this political union was not natural, and it was not acceptable. It followed that miscegenation itself was undesirable, something to
ridicule or fear.

About this same time, a theater performance about the Siamese twins evoked completely different images of the twins that showcased the anxieties of some in northern cities nonetheless. In May 1863, a troupe performed a Charles White burlesque sketch called *Siamese Twins* at the American Theatre on Broadway. The story featured a slick businessman named Mr. Skinner who was being kept from his darling by her father, the wealthy Dr. Grabem. Skinner planned to distract Grabem—who was "very fond of curiosities"—by taking two men off the street to impersonate the Siamese twins; Grabem would not notice when Skinner eloped with his daughter and snagged "the snug sum of money" that came with her. The first person Skinner met was a "loose careless style of darkey" named Dan Crow, who was on his way to whitewash Mrs. Martin's pigpen. Skinner told Crow he would pay double the four dollars he was due for the whitewashing job, and the job would take much less time. "How much will dat be?" Crow asked. Persuaded by the prospect of easy money, Crow lied to Martin about why he would be delayed. Dan Crow embodied the anxieties many felt about the presence of a free black labor force in the North. He was uneducated and, it was assumed, easily led from honest labor to nefarious plots. The next man Skinner set his eyes on was Ned Malone, a "fresh Mick" with a bundle and stick who similarly agreed to participate in the trickery.

And so, at the end of the first part of the sketch, we have a Negro—a white man in blackface—and an Irishman who were called upon to impersonate the Siamese twins. The joke here was threefold. First, there was the act of placing together these two men and passing them off as twins. Second, the duo was not simply pretending to be twins, but *Siamese* twins—*the* Siamese twins—which is to say, conjoined twins of Asian origins. Third, as became apparent by the end, they were successful. Crow and Malone donned short Chinese breeches, Chinese-style coats, and turbans to mask their physical appearance, and they used a rubber tube as the conjoining ligament. When Malone took a sip of brandy offered to him, Crow smacked his lips; when Crow took a sip, Malone did the same. Offered a cigar, Malone let Crow take a puff while Grabem's back was turned; then, when Malone drew from the cigar, Crow blew out the smoke he had held in his mouth. Grabem was sold. The clever cooperation between Irishman and Negro had succeeded in swindling the good doctor. The jig was up when Crow responded to the amazed doctor's pondering of how to account for this wonder: "Oh, it all goes frough dis ginger rubber tube," Crow said. In the end, however, the doctor was separated from his finest spirits, smokes, and his daughter, who did indeed run off with Skinner while the "twins" preoccupied her father.

Despite the ludicrous scenario, the juxtaposition of ideas of black, Irish, and Chinese served to illustrate their generically "nonwhite" nature. It was one thing to look at each group individually and declare them different from and inferior to "white" Americans. In the years after the 1854 California court decision in *People v. Hall* provided a legal framework for clumping together "nonwhite" peoples, it became increasingly commonplace for cultural representations to clump black, Irish, and Chinese together, portraying their collective difference and inferiority. The threat was not simply difference and inferiority, however. There was also the prospect that cooperation between these groups might serve to undermine the authority of whites and strip whites of things they held dear. *Siamese Twins: A Negro Burlesque Sketch* was one early example of this practice in popular art. Over the next ten years, other forms of popular culture similarly placed these groups together.[25] The successful impersonation of the Siamese twins by a "darkey" and a "Mick" was farce, but in postbellum New York, and the North more broadly, it was a scenario that became increasingly commonplace in the popular mind as newly freed blacks imagined life outside the South, Irish continued to immigrate, and Chinese laborers migrated East and as, together, these groups occupied common urban areas.

These two examples of popular representations of "Siamese twins" in the final years of the Civil War foreshadowed northern sentiment that Chang and Eng had to confront after the war. The Confederate cause came to be seen as immoral, and cooperation with former slaveholders, especially on terms that they set, still threatened the nation. Such feelings were exacerbated by the lenient path to reconstruction pursued by Lincoln's successor in office, Tennessee Democrat Andrew Johnson, and the aggressive tactics taken by white southerners against newly freed blacks, the Freedmen's Bureau, and other northerners who went South to rebuild the nation's economy and provide assistance to poor blacks. And reports of the twins themselves emphasized these feelings of anger, anxiety, and suspicion.

Their finances hurt severely by the end of the war and the emancipation of their slaves, the twins immediately began planning a tour of the northern states. The first notice appeared on August 1, 1865, in Boston and New York papers. The tour announcements themselves were innocuous; the twins, "who had been engaged in farming for some years in North Carolina," would soon be visiting northern cities. But, significantly, the announcements appeared alongside reports of intransigence among former rebels and ineptitude among northern officers in the South who allegedly had sympathies with the old Confederacy.[26]

Hard feelings still existed, and the twins felt the effects. In part, this resulted from the tone-deaf approach they took. After decades of so successfully reading public sentiment and adjusting their message accordingly, the world had changed too much for the twins to keep up. On August 2, the day after the initial announcement, the *New York Times* published a letter from the twins, dated July 25. In it, the twins reacquainted themselves with the American public, described the war's impact on their estates, and, essentially, asked for the charity of northerners:

> In former years we were received everywhere with flattering and
> substantial compliments, and after several most successful tours
> through the cities of the United States, we retired to the privacy of
> our country homes, where we had hoped to spend the remainder
> of our days in the quiet enjoyment of domestic felicity, blessed as
> we then were, with ample fortunes for ourselves and our families.
> But time has wrought a sad change. The ravages of civil war have
> swept away our fortunes, and we are again forced to appear in
> public. Remembering, as we do, with the profoundest gratitude, the
> liberality of our adopted country, we have arranged to appear on
> public exhibition in the northern cities, commencing early in August
> next, accompanied by several of our children, and we shall hope to
> meet then thousands of our old friends of *lang syne*. With sincere
> regard, we subscribe ourselves your obedient servants, Chang and
> Eng, Siamese Twins.[27]

Considering the broader context—the twins being former slaveholders from a state that had seceded over slavery and waged war against the United States; the North losing the lives of 360,000 soldiers, spending some $2.3 billion in government expenditures, and experiencing a $1.1 billion decline in consumption;[28] and now the United States embarking on a reconstruction project over a recalcitrant South—for the twins to appear hat in hand as blatantly as they did was remarkable. Of course, they also tried to obfuscate some facts and massage others. There was no mention that the fortune lost had been their slaves or that their family had just been at war with their "adopted country." And their retirement from the public stage, even from New York's exhibition halls, was less than five years old.

Perhaps the twins were unaware that the northern press had been following the Bunkers during the last year of the war. A report by a correspondent with Lee's army of northern Virginia received play in newspapers South and North. The letter, which ended with the rousing sentiment that "our army

Chang and Eng family, 1870. Ronald G. Becker Collection of Charles Eisenmann Photographs, Special Collections Research Center, Syracuse University Libraries.

is irresistible and will stand the shock" of the Union troops, described the twins' living arrangements and their physical anomaly and said the twins were "good neighbors—intelligent men and thoroughly patriotic."[29] The report left little doubt where the twins' patriotism lay. Early in 1865, with less than a month remaining in the war, a North Carolina doctor acquainted with them gave their particulars to a Philadelphia newspaper, saying that since the rebellion broke out, the twins had lived on their plantation in "quiet and harmony" and "have both dressed in the Confederate gray."[30] As for the twins' fortune, the various reports agreed that the brothers had "very wisely invested a portion of their funds in the North, so that neither emancipation nor confiscation can ruin them."[31] True or not—and the county tax records discussed earlier would not have any bearing on this, as they were county taxes levied on locally owned property—such statements damaged the credibility of the twins when paired with later declarations to the effect that they were broke.

On tour, the twins attempted to explain their position through interviews. They were aging. They each had nine children. Each had contributed a son to the rebel cause, one of whom was wounded, the other taken prisoner. They were, they said, like most southerners. "Both say they loved the old Stars and Stripes," a correspondent for the *New York Herald* reported, "but when their State seceded they considered it their duty to go with it."[32] Slavery was not mentioned, and the early battles of the postbellum era were not broached. Instead, the narrative that the twins—along with many other southerners—presented was one of sacrifice and duty, for family and for home.

In the immediate postwar period, however, such claims did not fly for many in the North. The war had cleaved a national white brotherhood in North and South, and there were those on each side who talked as if the other were an "alien race." Historian Edward J. Blum has observed that a group of northerners "maintained that southern whites were in fact not 'white' at all, but a 'race' separate from and inferior to Yankees."[33] Such claims were even easier to make about Chang and Eng, and newspapers did exactly that. "Sherman's conquering legions" had broken up the twins' plantation, one reported, depriving them of "a considerable number of slaves of about the same color as themselves."[34] Such an explicit statement of the twins' color in relation to that of their slaves was almost unprecedented, but it reflected the increasing scrutiny and animosity the twins faced as former slaveholders and Confederates. Such rhetoric was echoed in colorful but not altogether accurate—and in some places entirely inaccurate—articulations of the twins' story by northern newspapers reporting their tour. The twins had married two "ladies from Siam" and together had twenty "Siamese and Siamesses," Chang's youngest being named "Chang-hi." Though the twins had "never felt the galling chains of slavery," they turned "secesh" when they found themselves as North Carolina planters in 1860. They "bought a good many *other* colored persons"—emphasis added—who, not being bound by the same physical constraints as the twins, ran away. "Thus basely robbed of the helpless children of Africa, they fell back on their muscle." Their muscle, of course, entailed traveling the country putting their ligament on display for a "paltry" donation.[35] Chang and Eng were secessionist planters, the Bunkers were Siamese, the lot of them were colored like their slaves, and they had a history of seeking handouts.

Other indications suggested that northerners believed the twins were taking advantage of them. In July 1868, a story made the rounds that the twins were traveling to Paris to consult with a surgeon about separation. Before the journey, however, they would perform in New York. Almost immediately, the press voiced skepticism. The story had "excited public interest anew in them, and has furnished an excellent advertisement for their forthcoming exhibition," the *New York Times* commented. "Whether the story has any other foundation will be found out after one or two hundred thousand dollars has been made."[36]

Refrains of distrust reverberated in medical discussions of their bodies and their sexual relations. One acclaimed surgeon used the occasion to condemn the twins' careers and their marriages. Calling the excited speculation about the possible separation "another evidence of the lamentable ignorance of the public in medical matters," Paul F. Eve, a professor at Nashville Medical University, wrote that there "never has been a question among medical men, either in this country or in Europe, in regard to the feasibility of the separation of these two individuals." Eve, who had recently examined another instance of conjoined twins, wrote that Chang and Eng were two "distinct and segregated and perfect organizations." "Any student, who has attended a course of lectures," could use a knife to separate them.[37] We have seen that there was no such medical consensus, but as so often was the case with the Siamese twins, perception outweighed truth.

It seemed obvious to some that the twins had indeed pulled the wool over the public's eyes, just as Dan Crow and Ned Malone had done to Dr. Grabem in the "Negro Burlesque Sketch" performed on Broadway. What is more, Eve claimed, Chang and Eng also had unjustly run off with the girl, or girls, as it were: "It would appear, then, that there are no good reasons why these naturalized Asiatics should have been permitted to violate the seventh commandment, by common consent, without even a rebuke."[38] In an article purporting to explore the possibility of separation, Eve cast moral objections at the twins and their wives on two counts: the twins' race and the couples' morality, specifically the question of adultery.

In the years following the war, the twins faced a double challenge. On the one hand, their image had shifted from a union of necessity—divided they would die—to one of convenience. Duplicity, self-interest, and greed became the characteristics that representations of the twins evoked in art, politics, and even medical science. At the same time, a transformation in the racial order, replete now with "racial" hatred between northern and southern whites, similarly put the twins in a difficult position. They hoped that England would offer a fresh change, but it was not to be.

Confederates in Britain

It is not clear the extent to which the 1868–69 trip to the British Isles—they did not make it to Paris—was an opportunity to scout out medical opinions or the chance to tap a market they had not visited in more than thirty years. In their first days in Britain, a host of esteemed physicians in Edinburgh ran them through a battery of tests. This was likely a matter of course. After several decades, a new generation of doctors wanted to have a look at the famous "united twins or double monsters," as University of Edinburgh professor Sir James Y. Simpson called them.[39] The twins themselves had no desire whatsoever to be separated, Simpson wrote, and upon their return to the States in 1869, they denied having gone to Europe to be divided, calling the story an invention of Barnum.[40] But some family members did want the separation to occur if possible, Simpson wrote, because the families had been living some distance apart and, as the twins became older, the families' fears grew about what would happen to one when the other died.[41]

The trip also allowed these southerners the chance to leave behind the contentious environment they encountered in the northern states, or so they hoped. The twins remembered Britain fondly, and the two Bunker children taken along this time—Eng's daughter Kate, twenty-four years old, and Chang's daughter Nannie, twenty-one—had heard much of the British Isles and were familiar with the works of such authors as William Shakespeare, Alexander Pope, Robert Burns, and Walter Scott.[42] But Nannie was very much a southerner. Throughout the war she had exchanged letters with her older brother, Chris, following his movements and those of other young men from Mount Airy who served with him. A photo album of hers featured numerous photos of siblings, cousins, friends, and acquaintances, as well as a portrait of John Wilkes Booth.[43] Unlike her father or uncle, she had never traveled far from home or to a large city. Her diary revealed a strong appreciation of the power of nature and the supernatural and a rejection of man-made structures and order that played a foundational role in her life. In this sentiment, she was representative of a Romanticism that characterized southern thought, critical of too rapid change and of the rationality of the Enlightenment, the very rationality that underpinned scientific racism and the attempts by medical doctors to classify the twins and their children.[44]

Evident throughout Nannie's diary was a contest between nature and God, on the one side, and man, on the other. On the third night at sea, violent storms and high waves shook the ship, and passengers feared that the vessel would come apart. But Nannie "was not at all frightened at first for I knew in whose hands I was & that he could dispose of as he pleased, but after a time the vessel rocked so badly I could scarcely be in my berth." Nannie was in awe of the ocean, aware that it could call her home at any time, but glorying in its grandeur: "It is indeed a grand sight to stand on a vessel & look around and view the broad Atlantic. Watch its mountain waves as they rise in the distance, see them near you as though they could bury you in the depths beneath. Then view them sink into a great valley as if they opened to receive you but you do outride them all & look back as the white foam rises as it were in anger at their chagrin."[45]

Photograph of cousins Kate and Nannie Bunker, taken during their trip to Scotland in 1869–70. North Carolina Collection, Wilson Special Collections Library, University of North Carolina at Chapel Hill.

As the ship neared port in Liverpool, Nannie commented on the "sublime scene to gaze upon the harbors all brilliantly illuminated." This noted beauty of the city at a distance was consistent with other images in her journal, but throughout she positioned herself at odds with the corrupting influence of civilization. She created space between herself and the industrial world. Sailing to Baltimore as she left North Carolina on her way to New York, she was "astonished at the grandiur of the scenery & of the vessel. . . . [E]verything looked magnifficent to me anyway for I was brought up in the backwoods."[46] On the train from Baltimore to New York, she "sat at the window (as I presume all greenhorns do) & gazed at the cities we passed." And then, "[w]e arrived in New York & everything looked very grande to me for I had never seen a city lighted by night before."[47] Nannie admired the man-made wonders that cities were, even as she distanced herself from them. What appears to be a self-deprecating tone—she was from the "backwoods," a "greenhorn," and had never seen city lights at night—was an attempt to establish her separation from polluting influences, to dignify her pastoral, or southern, origins.[48]

Once in the Scottish countryside she reveled in its rustic beauty. "Here & there we could see the industrious farmers ploughing along with a cheerful & happy air as though he was lord of creation. Some parts of the country is perfectly level & all covered with a carpet of green grass." Man was in his natural state, and it was good. In many ways, she wrote, the countryside reminded her of home. In the English city, however, she could not wait to get away. "I shall be glad when we leave here," she wrote of Manchester. "It is so dirty and smoky & they say Liverpool is no better. In these manufacturing places it is so smoky and black one must change collars every day even if they sit in the house."[49] In the agrarian world, from which she came, farmers were lord of creation. In the industrial world, to which she went to great pains to depict herself a stranger, even those who attempted to isolate themselves were polluted all the same. By portraying herself at a distance from the manufacturing city, she created space to paint herself as more authentic—as a southerner, a farmer's daughter, and an individual.[50]

Of course, most of Nannie's time in Britain was spent in the cities. And just as her native (and idealized) Mount Airy had long been engaging in cultural and economic relations with the urbanizing North—and now, in the postbellum period, was becoming even more clearly tied to the North's industrial order, as was the rest of the South—Nannie engaged in consumerist or bourgeois activities. In Liverpool, they dined in a private room, "which I prefer to the public saloons of America," and the railcars were also different, divided as they were into separate apartments.[51] While her father and uncle took care of business of their own, she went for walks, visited historic sites, and shopped for fabric out of which to make clothes. She had her portrait taken many times at several different cities, statements of her individuality that she collected in a photo album. Many of the clothes she had made—velvet suits, silk dresses, and fancy shawls—were expensive, likely impractical for the farm.

Nannie recognized the multiple motivations that guided the choices she made, and she expressed sufficient displeasure, sometimes morosely so. If the photographer decided to stay in bed—even after ten o'clock!—she could do little but mock the "nobleman" in her diary. When she had the opportunity to explore, the images she chose to memorialize in her diary reveal something of a person who felt trapped by her circumstances. Visiting the "exceedingly small room" in which Mary, Queen of Scots, "was imprisoned & compelled to live," she looked out the window from which the infant King James VI was carried to be baptized into the Catholic faith and imagined what it would be like to fall the 250 feet to the rocks below, "instantly dashed in pieces." Another time, seeing a horse lying dead in the road, still harnessed to its cart, she wrote, "I thought it exceedingly cruel of the driver to drive a poor animal till it died but I suppose some have no thought of the service this poor animal renders them after it is old and worn out."[52] The tragic sixteenth-century monarchs—mother and child, each defining the other, whose fates were fatally interwoven—juxtaposed with a dead work-horse, all creatures trapped by the circumstances of their birth, ripped from purer and simpler lives by the whims of man, reflected Nannie's attitude toward the conditions in which she and her family found themselves and the cruel twists of fate that had similarly ripped them from the solitude of their farms.

Often, her sightseeing trips were cut short because of the demanding exhibition schedule of the twins—and herself. "For the first time in my life I was compelled to go before the public," she wrote. "I felt quite embarrassed when the hour came. It was not as I had imagined." The daily shows—often twice a day, in the afternoon and in the evening—left her feeling confined and exhausted, and the constant exposure to visiting crowds at times offended her sensibilities. "All day we were housed up receiving visitors," she wrote, "a thing exceedingly irksome to me when I think of the many beautiful things of antiquity I could see if I could go out." Her experience as a curiosity was not all bad. There was an Englishwoman from London "of a fine mind & great intelligence [who] quite fortunately for me commenced conversing with me."[53] Then there was another visitor, "an Englishman who seemed quite different from the rest with whom I had a very long conversation about the American war . . . he in the meantime being a strong southerner."[54] Just as often, however, being on exhibit sorely tested her. She was bemused when "many people flocked around us crying here are the 'Siamese Twins' and their 'Wives.'"[55] She grew indignant in Edinburgh when "one man—I will not say gentleman—asked me if my grandmother or grandfather was a negro."[56]

Intentionally or not, the inquiry about her racial heritage called into question one of the girders on which the Bunkers had built their position in southern society. While perhaps revealing British assumptions about southerners, the man's query perpetuated an assertion made in the 1864 publication *Miscegenation*, which had been published in London as well as the United States: "For three generations back, the wealthy, educated, governing class of the South have mingled their blood with the enslaved race," both the men, but also the women. "The mothers and daughters of the aristocratic slaveholders are thrilled with a strange delight by daily contact with dusky male servitors."[57] The Bunkers' position in southern society rested in part on the role the family had assumed during the antebellum period. They were masters, not "Negroes." But placing themselves daily on a public stage, inviting strangers to ask any type of question, put the twins and their children in a vulnerable position. And Nannie's reaction—"I was so angry I could scarcely speak but was compelled to say nothing"—exposes the power that racial identification exercised on her conception of herself, her family, and the place they occupied in an imagined racial hierarchy.

She recognized at some level the societal forces that constrained her life and the lives of the rest of her family, and in the end, she remained very much connected to her family—to the agenda of her father and uncle, to the wishes of her siblings and her mother. She was not a lord of creation; instead, she was a consumer of material culture, a participant in the industrial world she claimed to despise, and a loyal daughter. Whether she realized it or not, she was very much a product of a structural shift in economic and market systems, as was her family. And because of the visibility with which the Bunkers were linked with this transformation, much resentment was aimed their way.

Perhaps the twins were expecting a warm reception in Britain, due to the success of their earlier visit and the fact of their Confederate leanings. Support for the South had been especially strong among the upper classes, professionals in law and medicine, and influential newspapers such as the *London Times*, all groups with which the twins had experienced success forging connections in the United States.[58] The twins easily dismissed rumors that one had sided with the Union and the other with the Confederates: "Chang and Eng answered, laughing, that the Americans had made fun of them by inventing such tales, and that they had been, from first to last, attached to the cause of the South." Once again they were very open about the devastation the war had wrought on their fortunes; they lost their slaves, but additionally, money that they had lent before the war had been repaid during it with worthless Confederate currency, dealing the twins a double blow. This tour, they hoped, would "restore their fortunes."[59] American papers jeered at this packaging. "An ingenious admirer seeks to popularize them by announcing that 'they were slaveholders, enthusiastic southerners, and lost largely by the collapse of the South,'" a Boston paper noted, concluding sardonically, "As twin confederates . . . they have a peculiar claim upon English sympathy."[60]

Most American newspapers that followed the English press, however, focused on those stories that were critical about the twins.[61] The articulated concerns coming from London were not dissimilar to those expressed in America—race and region, public support, and the place that "monsters" ought to occupy in society. But while the last point received only little attention in the United States, it dominated reports from Britain. The twins were one of a series of "melancholy exhibitions which from time to time disgrace our civilization [by] attracting the usual gaping and unintelligent crowd," one report began. "To exhibit for shillings, and to expose to idle curiosity, the terrible physical malformations of our fellow-creatures is hardly less offensive than to make showplaces of our hospitals and lunatic asylums."[62] Closely related to this, but with significant differences, was the issue of public support. While the report quoted above centered around the humanity of placing the physically anomalous on display, others questioned whether money paid to view the twins and given as alms to *other* street beggars might be better invested on asylums. In this group of beggars were included not only the poor but, more worrisome, also those who chose to mutilate their bodies to provoke public sympathy and earn money. London's "legions of beggars"—its "parade of hideous deformity"—were a risk to the public's pocketbook, safety, and health, and giving alms simply encouraged more such behavior. "The ordinary beggars of the metropolis are an expensive pest; and the deformed mendicants are a mischievous and revolting nuisance," the report concluded. "There should be a statutory prohibition of all exhibitions of human monstrosities, including Siamese Twins."[63]

Both of these examples, it should be noted, focused on the "monstrosity" of the twins, and the context in which the twins were placed was entirely separate from their national origins or their race. The British press emphasized the twins' southern family. Some doubted whether the "family" was even real. For some, it was too "disgusting" to imagine these "human monsters" as husbands or fathers, all the more so because this "alleged fact" was designed solely to attract "the prurient curiosity of the public." "We are sorry for the hopes of any southern household which reaches to the patriarchal dimensions of two pairs of parents and eighteen children," especially in the aftermath of the American war, but the reporter simply did not believe the tale. "The two alleged daughters might be anybody's daughters," and the presence of wild-haired Zoebida, the "Circassian Beauty," who shared the stage with the Bunkers, reeked too much of the infamous Barnum humbug.[64]

A second reporter believed the family was real enough, but this belief did not stop him from being highly critical of the Bunkers on display. He mocked their southern allegiance and their story of losing their riches in the war—they "evidently thought they deserved much pity from Englishmen for the misfortune"—and expressed skepticism that they had even owned slaves. Instead, the slave imagery the reporter drew focused on the twins and their daughters on the stage. The twins' "worn and haggard looks make their unhappy predicament a condition for pity," while the show's master of ceremonies "enlarges upon their virtues and acts [before] turning at last to a girl of eighteen, one of the family who stands looking morosely, poor thing, at the floor, describing her as a slave-auctioneer would describe a slave girl at the mart."[65] The language used was not explicitly racial, but the imagery for American readers was exceedingly clear. In a postemancipation America, governed by the party of free labor, this southern family belonged to a different time. Chang's and Eng's claims to whiteness had just about expired.

Allegories of a Restored Union

Mark Twain published "Personal Habits of the Siamese Twins" in *Packard's Monthly* in 1869, and newspapers around the country reprinted the short story that summer. It took the theme of divided brothers beyond the disunion of war and made the twins an allegory for national healing. True, Twain wrote, the Siamese twins had been born "ignorant and unlettered— barbarians themselves and the offspring of barbarians, who knew not the light of philosophy and sciences." Yet they were able to overcome their differences and accept the other. "What a withering rebuke is this to our boasted civilization, with its quarrelings, its wranglings, and its separation of brothers."[66]

In Twain's story, Eng was a Baptist, Chang a Roman Catholic; Eng supported temperance reform, Chang loved his whiskey; Eng fought for the Union, Chang for the Confederacy. But through compromise, looking the other way, and forgiveness, the brothers lived together peacefully. Chang agreed to be baptized alongside his brother as long as it did not "count"; Eng got inebriated through his brother but was absolved as "physically" but not "morally" drunk; and after the two brothers took each other prisoner during the war, a jury decided they should exchange themselves for the other and be done with it. Each solution was overly simplistic and to an ideologue objectionable, but the alternative, also portrayed in Twain's story, was for the two of them to fight it out, to "beat and gouge each other without mercy," until they were senseless and disabled and had to be carried to the hospital. "There is a moral in these solemn warnings," Twain wrote, "or, at least, a warning in these solemn morals."

The "twinning" of this line—morals in warnings and warnings in morals—at once showed Twain's playfulness but also his insistence of the futility of trying to separate the self from the other. The barbarian boys got lessons in civilization and then went to war; the inseparable twins were polar opposites but found harmony and, in so doing, offered a split nation a model to follow. In accepting division, in demonizing Baptists or Catholics, abstainers or imbibers, northerners or southerners, Americans courted further disaster. In accepting compromise of seemingly absurd simplicity to the divided parties, Americans could learn something from these twins. But as literary scholar Cynthia Wu points out, the union that Twain saw in need of restoration was a white one.[67] From his use of the first-person plural in the opening—the twins' noble savagery offering a rebuke to "*our* boasted civilization"—to his straight-faced acceptance of an old joke in an offhanded postscript—"Having forgotten to mention it sooner, I will remark in conclusion that the ages of the Siamese twins are respectively fifty-one and fifty-three years"—Twain made clear where he stood, alongside Anglo-Americans, flawed and ignorant though they were. He was at once criticizing his white brothers, making fun of them, but also aligning himself with them. The Siamese twins were, after all, Siamese twins, a racial and anatomical other.

An alternative allegory of national reconciliation might have emphasized other, truer elements of the twins' postwar experience, some of which we have already covered. The twins emerged weakened, if not impoverished, by war, one better off than the other, as had the United States. Despite sectional tensions and hatred during and after the war, northern and southern middle classes restored economic and cultural relations soon after the fighting had ended. Certainly each side was vilified by the other, and in the South a violent campaign was waged against northern carpetbaggers and southern scalawags; nevertheless, the contacts established and reestablished immediately after the war opened the way for infrastructural improvements, including telegraphs and railroads, which were essential to rebuilding the nation's economy and enriching the pocketbooks of at least some Americans, north and south.[68] For Chang and Eng to improve the economic conditions of each and ensure a livelihood and future for their respective families—families that lived apart but worked together when times were rough—they followed business opportunities between the two sections, North and South, owning up to their secessionist history but embracing a united future.

The brothers also crossed the Atlantic, pursuing anew economic relations and cultural ties with Britain, just as the nation attempted to reestablish trade relations to jumpstart its war-stricken economy. The ability of the United States to recover economically from the war depended on its ability to reenter the British market, and in this it was successful despite lingering hostility in both North and South. From the 1850s to the 1870s, U.S. exports averaged $274 million per year despite an export trade during the war years that was almost nonexistent. But postwar relations were not solely economic. American and British intellectuals forged a discourse of liberal reform—democratic government, progress and justice, and universal uplift—and these themes colored the 1868–69 tour, to the twins' detriment.[69]

In 1870, Chang, Eng, and two Bunker boys traveled to Germany and then Russia. They intended to continue to Austria, Italy, Spain, and France, but the outbreak of the Franco-Prussian War sent them home instead.[70] On the voyage back to the United States, Chang suffered a stroke that paralyzed his right side, the side closest to his brother, while Eng remained in perfect health. Understandably, the public focused on Chang's affliction, but in so doing, it missed another opportunity for an alternative allegory. The twins were traveling on the same ship as Liberian president Edward James Roye. The convergence here of these free, international travelers of color, the twins being Americans from Siam, Roye a Liberian from America, resonated with contemporary discussions of slavery and emancipation, colonization and abolition, and the transatlantic world of which the United States and its peoples had long been a part. But no newspapers connected the two arrivals. If they had, there were lessons to be drawn. The twins and their sons arrived and took a room at Taylor's Hotel. President Roye arrived and found that several hotels declined to receive him or his party on account of their color, until finally they found room at a private residence. This would have been a fine opportunity to highlight the twins' privilege, to create distance between them and nonwhite peoples, if anyone had been so inclined, or to condemn the hypocrisy. But no connections were drawn.[71]

Once in America, the twins quietly returned home. While newspapers speculated about separating the two, Eng nursed his brother and tried to keep him in good spirits. "Uncle tries to cheer him up," one of Chang's daughters wrote, but her father was "low-spirited" and could "scarcely move without assistance."[72] Together, the brothers resettled into their North Carolina estates, with their families. Their attempt to rebuild their fortunes was somewhat successful. In 1870, Eng's total estate was worth $7,000, split evenly between real estate and personal estate. Chang's real estate, meanwhile, was valued at $8,000, his personal estate at $15,000. These

James Montgomery
with his father, Eng,
and Albert Bunker
with his father, Chang,
1870. North Carolina
Collection, Wilson Special
Collections Library,
University of North
Carolina at Chapel Hill.

entrepreneurs maintained their places near the top of Mount Airy's economic elite; indeed, no one in Mount Airy had a personal estate worth more than that of Chang.[73]

Eng, poorer than and tied inextricably to his ill brother, brought Chang back to good health with high spirits. Chang's right leg continued to be of little use, but the two went about their ordinary business. "Chang ties up his right or inside leg in a sling," newspapers reported, "and with the support given him by a crutch under the left shoulder, and the aid of his brother's arm, finds no difficulty in making his way around the plantation as easily as ever."[74] Together they spent time with their respective families—three days at one household, then three days at the other—being husbands to their wives and fathers to their children.

Yet, in the eyes of their American observers, things were not well. The twin households were separate; this, onlookers speculated, meant familial discord. And the twin households featured interracial marriages and mixed-race children, also a sign of disorder in an age when the word— "miscegenation"—had been spoken at last. In the antebellum South, white society tolerated relationships between white women and men of color; after the war, with black men free and voting, white men felt threatened by the illicit sex and used extraordinarily violent means to discourage what was in truth a rare practice. In the North and the West, popular representations of Chinese men wedded to white women became increasingly common, in theatrical performances, advertisements, and illustrations. One illustration, commemorating the 1869 completion of the Pacific railroad, featured a middle-class white woman in Victorian dress clasping arms with a Chinese man with queue, mustache, flowing garb, and pointed wooden shoes, standing together in front of the "Church of St. Confucius." Now that the word had been spoken for all to hear, the days of the twins being an allegory for white America were over.

CHAPTER SIX

Over Their Dead Bodies

Chang Bunker died on the morning of January 17, 1874, a Saturday, about a quarter till five. He was sixty-two years old.

His brother had little more than two hours to live, bound irrevocably to his dead twin.

In the intervening years since his stroke almost four years earlier, Chang had regained some of his strength, enough so that the twins could get around their farms, each located in rolling countryside about four miles from Mount Airy, North Carolina, and about a mile and a half apart. Nevertheless, he remained stricken on his right—the side of his body that was closest to his brother. He took to heavy drinking and stayed in poor health.

On the Monday evening before he died, at his own home, Chang came down with a deep cold characterized by a harsh cough and a rattle in his lungs. By Wednesday the cough had subsided, though his labored and loud breathing continued and he perspired heavily. On Thursday, the brothers were scheduled to travel to Eng's home, part of their long-standing habit of alternately spending three days at each household. But the weather that January was frigid, and the doctor advised him to stay indoors and not travel. His wife and brother also expressed concern. Nevertheless, despite his affliction, the freezing conditions, and Adelaide's worries, Chang left his home on Thursday, riding with his brother in an open wagon to Eng's place.

On Friday morning, Chang felt a bit better, but by evening his coughing fits had returned. After the rest of Eng's family retired upstairs for the night, the brothers remained in the downstairs quarters, a lingering effect of Chang's paralysis; he could no longer climb or descend steps easily, and so they stayed on the ground floors of their homes. On this night, Chang and Eng slept very little. Chang coughed violently and could hardly breathe when lying down. They went out on the side porch to have some water before returning to their room and building a large fire. Eng complained that he was sleepy, but Chang maintained that to lie down would kill him.

Sarah Bunker and Adelaide Bunker, c. 1860–70. North Carolina Collection, Wilson Special Collections Library, University of North Carolina at Chapel Hill.

Nevertheless, around four o'clock the two lay down again. Chang coughed and labored to breathe, and then he fell silent. At about a quarter to five, the rest of the family heard someone calling out, and Eng's fifteen-year-old son, William, went downstairs. When he lit the lamp, his father told him he felt mighty sick and asked him to check on Chang.

William did so, only to exclaim, "Uncle Chang is dead!"

This was the first that Eng knew that his partner for a lifetime was no more. "Then I am going," he replied at once.

For the next hour, Eng suffered intense pain and distress, a cold sweat covering his body. At his urging, his wife and children massaged his arms and legs. He complained of a choking sensation and asked to be raised in his bed. The only notice that he took of his dead twin was to move his body nearer to him.

Finally, he looked at Sarah. "I am dying," he told his wife of almost thirty-one years. He then went into a stupor until, some two and a half hours after his brother, he died. According to his widow, his final words were, "May the Lord have mercy on my soul!"[1]

Eng and Chang. Photograph c. 1860. Wellcome Library, London.

The deaths of Chang and Eng set into motion a series of events that called into question much that they had accomplished in their sixty-three years. The Mount Airy community with which the twins had fashioned strong, if strategic, ties seemed to turn against the family, whispering lies or half-truths to the press and looking to profit off the twins' deaths as much as it could. The medical community, with which the twins had a long relationship offering their bodies for examination in return for the free publicity that accompanied the doctor's reports, was determined to call in what it saw as the twins' final debt to science, forcing a much publicized autopsy against the families' wishes. And the twins in the end lost their struggle for whiteness as news reports made foreigners out of them and their wives, painting the Bunker family with broad strokes influenced by discourses of miscegenation and the fervent anti-Chinese sentiment that had gripped much of the country by the 1870s. In all this, of course, the twins were no longer able to answer their critics. In their stead, the Bunkers, a family wanting more than anything to be left alone, had to engage with the public and fight for its image. Even as the Bunker children were marked relentlessly by their fathers' monstrosity, they ultimately were able to humanize the twins.

Friends and Neighbors

In her synthesis of Asian American history, Sucheng Chan has argued that Asians in the United States did not receive the chance to assimilate into American society until recently. "Assimilation does not depend solely upon the predilections of the newcomers," she wrote. "It can occur only when members of the host society give immigrants a chance to become equal partners in the world they share and mutually shape."[2] But Chang and Eng lived outside the contours of Asian American history in many ways. They had come early to the United States, decades before Chinese immigrants arrived in large numbers in the 1850s. They were, of course, a centerpiece of early nineteenth-century America's market in Oriental curiosities, but they settled in the rural South, far from early communities of Chinese that developed in New York and other eastern ports. They were worldly and wealthy, and they used their business acumen and contacts to forge connections with the burgeoning middle class in the two southern communities in which they lived. It seemed that they *had* been given the chance to "become equal partners in the world they share[d] and mutually shape[d]." In response, the twins had adopted the role of well-to-do farmers, embracing American ways of life. But had the community truly accepted these strangers into their fold? Had their neighbors put on a performance of their own?

The antebellum South had been, in the words of historian Bertram Wyatt-Brown, "a world of chronic mistrust," through which the demands of honor helped all members of society navigate.[3] The Civil War, which shook the foundations of the Old South, similarly dislodged many of the social practices that governed interpersonal relations; masks of honor might have been dislodged, but this served only to bring mistrust to the surface. Upon the deaths of the families' patriarchs, the Bunkers believed they could trust only themselves. They now viewed their neighbors and friends with suspicion.

News of the deaths spread quickly, and people soon began to congregate outside the Eng family house. The size of the crowd that gathered belied any inkling that the Bunkers were just a regular family or that the twins were anything but celebrities. They were Chang and Eng, the world-famous Siamese twins, who had entertained crowds for decades by putting their conjoined bodies on display. Now, the crowds wanted one last show.

By Sunday, so many people had assembled from near and far that the family could not go on with a funeral and burial service. "There is the most awful excitement in the country that has ever been known," Chang's daughter Nannie wrote to her brother Christopher, asking that he return home from California as quickly as possible. "A crowd such as has not met for any purpose lately met there and they could not clear the room sufficiently for the familys to go in and see them." The tinsmith hired to make an extra large coffin for the brothers that could be fastened securely also commented on the size of the crowd: "It was a sight the people that was there. It was a long time before I could get my foot in at the door, so crowded. It was like a camp meeting, so many people, horses, and carriages."[4]

Both Nannie and the tinsmith voiced the families' fears: Someone might steal the twins' bodies. The Bunkers grasped quickly the spectacle that Chang's and Eng's deaths presented. The community had tolerated the mundaneness of the twins' everyday lives in Mount Airy while the brothers were breathing, but their deaths—and the potential to profit from them—proved too much; the charade could be played no longer. Their family doctor, Joseph Hollingsworth, told them that there was "no doubt" that a reward of as much as $2,000 had been offered to anyone able to snatch the bodies; the family did not know whom to trust. "Dr. Joe says their bodies would not remain in the grave three nights if they were put there, that the best friends we have can be bought (some we may think our friends may not be so)," Nannie wrote. She began to see the neighbors among whom she had lived almost her entire life as foreign to her and her family. "These Mt. Airy folks," she told her brother, only "work for each other."[5]

Within days, the family began receiving unsolicited letters from strangers seeking to buy the bodies. "Name your price," one said, promising confidentiality. And the same family doctor who warned them not to trust anyone also urged them to recognize that it would be impossible to ward off curiosity seekers; it would be no disgrace to accept any profits they could from the sale of the bodies to science. "*Some* one *would* receive something," Nannie wrote to her brother. "*Why* not their families and not strangers? Cris, this looks and seems awful to me but the Drs. put it in such force to our reason & our minds that we do not know what to do about it."[6]

The good doctor was not the family's only neighbor who worked actively to explore business opportunities in the aftermath of the twins' deaths. Members of Mount Airy's social and economic elite worked together in the weeks that followed to attain maximum profit. These included Hollingsworth's brother, William Hollingsworth, also a physician; family acquaintance Jesse Franklin Graves, a judge on the superior court circuit; and businessman and close family friend Robert S. Gilmer.

The doctors whose job it was to look after the health of the family's members were occupied with arranging for surgeons from Philadelphia to travel to Mount Airy to perform an autopsy, publicly speculating about the price the twins' bodies would fetch, and feeding the family's fears about the danger that grave robbers posed in order to buy the time necessary to get someone down to autopsy the bodies. Despite the reluctance of the wives and children, Joseph Hollingsworth persuaded the family to store the bodies carefully to preserve them for further examination. The twins were entombed in the cool and dry cellar beneath Eng's house, protected by a wooden box, the specially made tin coffin, and a layer of charcoal and guarded by family members. No doubt there truly was the danger of grave robbers, but Hollingsworth also fed the family's fears to buy the time necessary to find well-respected physicians to examine the bodies. To facilitate that, Hollingsworth traveled to Philadelphia to meet with esteemed surgeons from that city's College of Physicians. Reports following his journey stated that the wives did not want an autopsy but that the doctor's mission was to "dispose of the dead bodies . . . on the most favorable terms he could negotiate"—the numbers thrown about were $8,000 to $10,000. "Dr. Joseph Hollingsworth thinks that the families of the twins . . . will be willing to hand over the bodies if a sufficient sum is paid them."[7]

Meanwhile, his brother remained in Mount Airy trying to convince the Bunkers to agree to a postmortem. "Dr. Joe" waited in vain in Philadelphia for a letter from "Dr. Bill" conveying the family's permission that never came. Nevertheless, the Philadelphia medical community was intrigued enough to form a scientific medical commission to pursue an autopsy. A team consisting of Dr. William Pancoast, Dr. Harrison Allen, and a photographer visited the Eng household on Sunday, February 1, more than two weeks after the twins had died, and along with William Hollingsworth entered into negotiations.

Actually getting the widows to agree to give up the bodies fell to another longtime neighbor, Robert S. Gilmer. Months after the fact, Christopher Bunker complained bitterly that Gilmer, "who had . . . during life been apparently my father's and uncle's dearest friend and adviser," had taken advantage of the widows. "It was our mothers' wish that the twins should be buried, but when the man Gilmer came along . . . they could not resist his appeal."[8] (According to Nannie, Gilmer had also weakened Adelaide's resolve by suggesting that there might be issues with Chang's will, casting her claim to his estate in doubt.)[9] Although the letters to the grown sons had gone out—in addition to Chang's twenty-eight-year-old son Christopher, there were Eng's sons Decatur, twenty-six; Montgomery, twenty-five; and Patrick, twenty-three—none had returned by the time the two sides sat down on February 1, so Sarah and Adelaide had to deal with the Philadelphia commission on their own. Gilmer, who had taken care of the families' business matters when the twins went away on tour, now acted as their business agent, and Graves acted as their legal adviser.

In conference, the two sides hammered out a deal. The commission could exhume and embalm the twins' bodies, and even take them to Philadelphia to undergo an autopsy, including inspection of the ligature that joined them, providing that the brothers remained connected and all incisions to the band be made from the back, so as not to be visible from the front. This point would become significant as commentators later claimed that the family intended to exhibit the corpses and wanted to ensure that the ligament was unmarked. Critics also claimed that the families were receiving a large payment, although both sides later attested that no money was involved.[10]

The initial examination took place that day, in Eng's home. Predictably, it turned into public spectacle. Curious onlookers again crowded the home, "willing enough to give the necessary aid in exhuming the bodies," carrying the coffin to the second floor of the house and opening the tin coffin encased in a wooden box to reveal, for all to see, the dead twins. "The widows at this point entered the room, and, amid the respectful silence of all present, took a last look at the remains."[11] Finally, doctors cleared the room of all people unconnected with the examination. Photographs of the corpses were taken, plaster models were cast. Initial cuts revealed that the ligament was too complex to be studied fruitfully in this ordinary setting; further examination would have to wait for Philadelphia. On February 2, the commission left for Salem in a convoy that included a carriage carrying the doctors, a wagon containing the coffin, and two buggies with the photographers, "the whole making quite a funeral procession, which attracted the attention of the people all along the route." The following day, the bodies were shipped from Salem to Greensboro, and then on to Philadelphia, where the twins' old acquaintance Joseph Hollingsworth was waiting.[12]

In many respects, the actions of the Bunkers' neighbors and acquaintances appeared in stark contrast to the ways they behaved while the twins were still alive, but in truth the difference was one of degree, not of character. Certainly, the twins' "dearest friend" appeared to be bullying their widows, and their doctors viewed the acquisition of their corpses as an all-important step, no matter the cost. In the middle of the negotiations, for example, William Hollingsworth was quoted as saying that he "would rather have the bodies of the dead twins than the whole of Surrey County."[13] Meanwhile, the flood of onlookers on Eng's property—and in his house—in the wake of the twins' deaths signaled a lack of respect for a mourning family. But this all sounded familiar, if somewhat amplified. Curiosity seekers had regularly dropped in on Chang, Adelaide, Eng, and Sarah since the early 1840s. Robert Gilmer had handled much of the Bunkers' business and legal affairs for a quarter of a century, especially when the twins were away from home. And local medical doctors had long used their contacts with the twins to gain access to big-city contacts while caring for the twins and their families.

It was precisely these types of contacts, with this class of people, that the twins had pursued from their earliest days in North Carolina, for just this reason: the mutual benefits that each side received provided the twins with stable relationships that protected their position in Wilkes and then Surry society. In that winter of 1874, it was entirely conceivable that Gilmer, Graves, and the Hollingsworths were continuing these relations, attempting through the courses they pursued to benefit the widows and their children as much as, if not more than, themselves. Gilmer and the Hollingsworths were businessmen, and it is significant that of all the things that the tinsmith (a newcomer to Mount Airy who in his letter about the twins likely was repeating what he heard from others) might have said about the brothers, he said that "they were both real business men."[14]

Despite all this, there was one major difference from the old business days: The twins were dead. Adelaide and Sarah were left to deal with their husbands' bodies on their own. All of the grown sons were gone, and of the eldest daughters who had accompanied the twins on tours in Europe, one was dead of tuberculosis, and the other was dying. There was little indication that their former business acquaintances were looking after the widows' welfare, and the Bunker children thought this fact was clear.

Nannie Bunker protested loudly against any plan to take her father's and uncle's bodies from the home place. Chang's eldest surviving daughter objected to the denial of a proper Christian burial, and she opposed a postmortem examination. But the twins' deaths hit especially hard the young woman who, by the winter of 1873–74, knew she was "dying now of consumption," her life "nearly run out." The twenty-six-year-old faced her fate resolutely, drawing up a last will and testament on December 29, 1873. "When I am gone," she began the document that divided her modest belongings among her siblings and her only niece. She was not, however, prepared for the deaths of her father and her uncle less than three weeks later, and the public spectacle that their deaths provoked, and the final display of their bodies that the spectators appeared to demand, caused her great distress.[15] Recognizing her weakened state, the families did not want to do anything that might aggravate her condition, but ultimately, under great pressure from friends and neighbors and distinguished men from far-off places, the widows agreed to the removal of the twins' bodies to Philadelphia. As the bodies were on their way out of town, Nannie gave her reluctant assent.[16] She died a short while after, one month to the day after her father and uncle.

When Chang's eldest son, Christopher, returned from California—too late to say goodbye to his beloved sister—he was dismayed at the state of affairs he encountered and implored his cousin Decatur to return home from Missouri as quickly as possible. "The Drs come down here from Phila a purpose to give Mama and Aunt Sallie 12 or 15 thousand dollars but the Mt. Airy people met them and got all the money for their influence and Mama & Aunt Sallie did not get one cent," he wrote. "You must come or the People in Mt. Airy will soon have all you have got. . . . If you do not come you can't blame me." A *New York Herald* correspondent who made the trip to Mount Airy similarly took the pulse of the townspeople, concluding that "there is the groundwork of quite a large speculation. . . . The living twins were quite a source of profit to several of the prominent men at Mount Airy, and why not now turn the dead bodies to some account in the shape of greenbacks?"[17]

While the twins had been businessmen, their widows apparently were not. And left alone with "the Mt. Airy people," the sisters had not been able to sufficiently protect the family's interest, either in terms of money or in terms of the twins' bodies. Gilmer, Graves, the Hollingsworths, and the curiosity seekers who also perhaps hoped to collect something valuable were all talking about selling the twins or, more precisely, their bodies. This detail is key, and it points to a significant insight into the relations that they all had with the twins. The way these people responded to the twins' deaths, as well as the resonance these actions had with earlier actions, suggests that the twins' friends, acquaintances, and neighbors never viewed them as equals; rather, the twins were always a curiosity or a freak of nature, something different, something other, something alien, something that could be turned into a profit.

Medical Spectacle

Of course, to their wives, the twins had been husbands, and to the children, they had been either father or uncle. But to the medical community, the twins were monsters, and to the popular press, the whole lot appeared monstrous. This served the doctors and the press fine; it provided them with chances to make names for themselves and to write titillating stories that sold newspapers.

For the medical community, the engagement of the twins' bodies continued a relationship that had been long established. Indeed, for the Philadelphia doctors who traveled to Mount Airy and met with the widows, there was a sense of entitlement. Since their first days in the United States, the twins had used the medical community to earn legitimacy as a bona fide monstrosity—their anomaly was the real deal, in other words, and doctors proved it—and especially as a form of publicity. In 1829, medical reports by American doctors John Collins Warren, Samuel Latham Mitchill, and William Anderson were printed in newspapers and included in pamphlets to stir up business for the twins. Similar reports were published in Britain. And throughout their lives, a theme that occurred repeatedly was the twins going on tour before visiting doctors to explore the possibility of surgery to separate them—this was the last chance to see these united twins, the refrain went. So when the doctors from Philadelphia sat across the table from Sarah and Adelaide Bunker to negotiate access to the twins' bodies, part of their motivation clearly came from the belief that they, the collective medical community, had done so much for the twins and the twins' family; now it was time that the Bunkers did something for them.[18]

These sentiments were left unspoken, however. The doctors stated in their reports that they undertook the autopsy because they aspired "that the American profession might not be charged with having neglected an effort to . . . solve the mystery of their union." By 1874, in large part because of the earlier studies done upon Chang and Eng, conjoined twins had become part of a well-documented club. Dunglison's medical dictionary had given a scientific name to the twins in the classification of teratology—the study of monstrous formations, from the Greek root *teras*, or monster. Dr. George J. Fisher of New York in an article on diploteratology—the study of double monstrous formations—had just eight years before classified the twins as belonging to the third order (and least severe) of double monsters. This nomenclature is significant only in the sense that it makes clear that calling the twins monsters was not just shorthand for describing anomalous bodies; "monster" was their medical condition.[19]

It was not by chance that William H. Pancoast became the doctor most closely associated with the autopsies of Chang and Eng. Even as Joseph Hollingsworth was making his way north to try to make arrangements with the College of Physicians, Pancoast had telegraphed the mayor of Greensboro to ask him to arrange for a postmortem examination for the twins. (The mayor replied that he knew nothing of it and had no influence in the matter.) Made aware of Pancoast's interest, Hollingsworth approached the doctor upon arrival in Philadelphia, and in consultation with others it was soon agreed that Pancoast and another physician, Harrison Allen, would make the trip to North Carolina on their own funds, with the hope of being reimbursed at a later date by the College of Physicians.[20]

Pancoast was certainly among the most qualified to undertake the examination of Chang and Eng. He had previously met and conversed with the twins, and just three years before he had examined another famous pair of conjoined twins, the "Carolina Twins" Millie and Christine, sisters born to slaves in North Carolina in 1851 who were joined at the base of the spine and who, like the twins, were taken around the country and to Europe to exhibit their anomalous bodies. An ambitious man, Pancoast had served as demonstrator of anatomy at Jefferson Medical College since 1862, and he would be able to use his exposure as examiner of the Siamese twins, as well as his status as son of an eminent anatomist, to claim the position of professor of anatomy later in 1874.[21]

Just as the autopsy of the twins was instrumental in Pancoast's professional advancement, the postmortem examination was important as part of the growing professionalization of the medical field in the United States. Underlying this move was a shift from theoretical to empirical knowledge of the human body. In the early nineteenth century, physicians poked and prodded the twins' connecting band and postulated what was inside; now the opportunity to document the band's contents would prove the reputations of some of those early doctors and undermine that of others. It would also place American medical science in the forefront. Prominent physicians from around the country wrote to Pancoast that this postmortem would "attract the attention of the eminent men of European countries to such an extent that should any failure be in any way at the investigation, the surgical profession of America will be greatly censured and condemned."[22] Autopsies generally provided anatomical knowledge, and autopsies of anomalous bodies provided the necessary evidence for proclaiming what was "normal" and what was "monstrous." Indeed, the push for an increase in the number of autopsies done was part of an agenda by physicians for more actively exerting control over the lives—and deaths—of patients, and physicians argued strenuously that medical professionals be allowed to examine the dead twins. Some called on the North Carolina state legislature to hold a legal examination of the bodies but found no grounds for official interference. Others appealed unsuccessfully to the state supreme court.[23] But the pressure for advances in medical knowledge did not come solely from medical professionals, and the deaths of the twins and the very public drama that ensued over their autopsies provided Americans the chance to participate in the medical spectacle.

Newspapers almost immediately took up the call for autopsies. Rumors that the Bunker families opposed postmortem examinations alarmed many. The *New York Herald* scoffed that any suggestion that an autopsy would not be done reflected the backwardness of North Carolina. "Unless laws and usages at Mount Airey, N.C., are different from what they are in this part of the world, the burial without an autopsy was clearly illegal. Here, unless a physician can certify to the cause of death, the coroner must come in; and this seems so necessary a provision for the safety of life in civilized communities that we can scarcely believe the Old North State to be quite without it."[24] Letters to editors similarly argued that autopsies were necessary. "I trust . . . you will continue to make known the neglect of the authorities of Surrey county, North Carolina, until they are compelled to hold an autopsy," one reader wrote to the *New York Herald*. Once the Philadelphia physicians were successful in their quest to remove Chang's and Eng's bodies to the City of Brotherly Love, the *Herald* trumpeted the news, proclaiming "science triumphant," presumably a triumph over backward Mount Airy and the obstructionist and greedy Bunkers.[25]

This so-called victory for science came at a price, however. The negotiations that surrounded the dealings between the physicians and the family were well-publicized, and newspapers roundly condemned the widows for the appearance of selling their husbands' bodies (even though the family was adamant that it received nothing) and for the idea that they would take the twins' remains on a final tour for even more money. Philadelphia physicians fed these ideas, making much of the constraints that the contract forced upon them, especially the clause that forbade them from cutting open parts of the body that would be visible to the public eye—the heads and the front of the connecting ligature. "These people undoubtedly intend to make a show, and have thus bound us so that the show may not be spoiled," one of the doctors, unnamed, complained to a reporter. "The reason they consented to an investigation at all was that they believed that excitement in the scientific world would be reflected on the general public and make the show more remunerative."[26]

It is worth noting that the Bunkers were criticized when they did agree to an autopsy, just as they had faced criticism when they did not initially consent. There was very little room for the family to maneuver. They could not simply bury their dead because of some obligation they apparently had to the medical world and the fear that grave robbers would claim the bodies regardless. But they could not simply give up the bodies never to return or to return in pieces. The contract they had drawn up did not mention money; it did, however, place clear limits on what the Philadelphia physicians were able to do. The bodies were to be embalmed so as not to allow further decomposition. Doctors could examine the bodies only to settle "scientific mysteries." They could not unnecessarily mutilate the bodies; in fact, all incisions made by knife had to be able to be covered up, and there was an explicit prohibition on cutting the connecting band in the front. The autopsies were to be open only to invited physicians but closed to the general public. Photographs of the proceedings would be allowed, but no pictures were to be released to the public, and all negatives would become the property of the widows.[27]

All speculation, by medical men and the laity, was that these demands were part of a plan to put the bodies on exhibit. No one publicly considered the possibility that the family members wanted to protect their loved ones' bodies from mutilation and their memory from photographs of their eviscerated corpses. Lost in the consideration of the widows and the children as greedy schemers or helpless victims is the fact that they were not powerless. Regardless of their motives, the Bunkers were able to exercise control over the physicians' actions, an important point that we will return to later. For now, suffice it to say that the constraints placed on the physicians caused them resentment and revealed just how unique these circumstances were, for surgeons rarely needed to follow any direction but their own when engaging in postmortem examinations.

In the nineteenth century, dead bodies, like anomalous bodies, were important commodities, and the dissection of the human body that characterized postmortem examinations still was primarily associated with issues of class, race, and monstrosity. Cadavers that doctors used in training primarily came from the poor, immigrants, and African Americans whose bodies were sold after death. Grave-robbing was common, especially in the case of unusual diseases or conditions, both for dissection and for public exhibition. Autopsies that gained the most publicity—in the press, but also in attendance—were "monsters" of one sort or another.[28]

The twins, with their nonwhite, anomalous bodies, fit this bill; their autopsy, the results of which were printed widely and in very graphic detail, served further to cement their monstrosity. Up for discussion were their skin color, their genitalia and pubic hair, their Chinese ancestry, and inquiries into their sex lives with their white wives. It was discovered that they shared a liver, and the contents of the band were so complex, each body so intertwined with the other, that the doctors concluded the twins would not have survived an operation to separate them. The commission failed to settle on a certain cause of death for Chang; doctors believed that his cold was not serious enough to cause death and pointed instead to the possibility of a cerebral clot. The cause of death postulated for Eng was the fear of being attached to his deceased brother, not any actual physiological condition.[29] As Cynthia Wu notes, the general agreement that fear caused Eng's death, by the commission but also by later scholars, and the rejection of other physiological causes revealed anxieties that Americans had about the "inseparability from a weaker, parasitic other [that] signals to normatively bodied people that their individuality may not be as complete as American ideals of liberal republicanism would suggest."[30] Eng's very death was anathema to the American sense of self-determination.

The Twins and Their Families

While the scientific discourse of the 1870s used the twins' conjoined state to catalogue their monstrosity, popular discourse featured in newspapers very blatantly represented the twins and their families as monstrous too. The commonly held perception that the family had sold Chang's and Eng's bodies and planned to exhibit the corpses resulted in widespread words of condemnation. "It is a shocking thought, that of the relatives of the Siamese twins bargaining away the dead bodies of the unfortunate pair," a newspaper commented. Stories of the wives' early objections to autopsies had been made "solely to create a market for the bodies. . . . The bereaved widows are a shrewd as well as shrewish couple." "Scientifically speaking," the paper concluded, "the Siamese twins belong to the class of 'monsters.' Popularly speaking, their wives seem to belong to the same class."[31]

The *New York Sun* took aim at the twins, suggesting nothing of the Americanized mannerisms and sharp intellect on which articles had focused while they were alive. "Both were ignorant and had intelligence that scarcely rose above low cunning." In addition, "Their faces were peculiarly repelling, yellow in hue, and closely resembling those of the Chinese cigar sellers of Chatham street," referring to a part of New York City where Chinese had settled.[32] There was no attempt here to make connections between the twins and exotic Oriental origins, refined Siamese bearings, or rumors that they were in-laws to royalty. Instead, there was a particular, local context into which the paper fit the twins, one that marked them as Chinese and poor, barely able to eke out a living.[33]

The obituary repeatedly commented on the twins' "broken English," and it failed to acknowledge the twins' attempts at establishing an American identity of a certain class in other ways. It reported, falsely, that the twins had married servant girls from England—"and it is said that a Lancashire dialect still clings to them."[34] This depiction also built on a local New York context. Because of the nature of immigration from China, almost all Chinese in the United States were male; in Manhattan, of those men who married, some formed unions with English women, though Chinese-Irish marriages were far more common.[35] Even for those without knowledge of the marriage practices of Chinese in New York, however, the image carried weight. The representation of the twins' wives as English also suggested that no American women would have gone for these Chinese men. Cigar peddlers plus servant girls did not equal a southern planter family; Chinese and English certainly were not American; and if the Lancashire sisters spoke with funny accents, imagine how the Siamese twins must speak! Furthermore, the match between the grooms and the brides was not for love but for money. Indeed, according to some reports, the pairs had never met before they wed; the courting was done through an agent.[36] (Another newspaper, claiming to be correcting the record, dismissed the idea that the wives were English, stating instead that they were "North Carolina women inheriting Indian blood.")[37]

Depictions of the twins' children in other reports played more to increasingly common stereotypes of degeneration associated with miscegenation. The children were feeble and prone to illness, obituaries reported. "The girls . . . all [died] about the time they reached womanhood, with the exception of one, who is married. The male children are, also, more or less afflicted, several of them being deaf and dumb." As soon as the twins died, "the deaf-mute children of the deceased expressed their sorrow and bereavement in the most pitiful manner."[38] In truth, of the twenty-one children, two—both Chang's—were deaf. Five died before Chang and Eng, the youngest having died of burns at less than a month old,[39] and the oldest, Kate, Eng's firstborn, in 1871 at age twenty-seven, of consumption.[40] These numbers are not extraordinary, especially given that three of the children died in accidents. Child mortality records of the North Carolina planter class during the early to mid-nineteenth century suggest a death rate of

230 per 1,000; almost one in four children did not reach their fifth birthday, a rate that the Bunker children bettered.[41] Yet in the case of the Bunkers, the presence of deafness and childhood death in mixed-race children fed into prevailing stereotypes. In short, the newspaper reports attempted to fit the Bunker family—the twins, their wives, and their children—into increasingly well-defined and familiar categories of race, class, and sexuality.

The first obituaries were reprinted in many papers and influenced the ways that many others reported the battle for the twins' bodies. In these articles, the wives and children were ridiculed or condemned. "It is, perhaps, a little unreasonable to expect any high grade either of civilization or refinement on the part of two Lancashire women, low-lived enough to be willing, for a consideration, to enter upon married life under such conditions as nature had imposed upon these male Siamese," one publication opined after early reports suggested falsely that the family was trying to sell the twins' bodies. It went on to say that "the presence in their resultant families, as at present constituted, of six or eight deaf and dumb and otherwise feebly organized children in no way alters the situation materially for the better."[42] The autopsy agreement that stipulated the postmortem would not leave marks on the band was seen as evidence that the families planned to exhibit the bodies once the doctors were done. Some pointed to the autopsy as simply a way to stoke public interest, much as people had accused the twins of using the possibility of separation as a publicity tool. Reports accused the widows of being as "mercenary" as their husbands had been.[43] The twins, their wives, and their children had come under attack.

In the end, however, it was the children who, despite attempts to portray them as monsters in their own right, humanized the twins and their mothers. Much as the twins once responded promptly to a newspaper article that cast them in a negative light, the twins' children did not let the attacks on their family go unanswered. Significantly, it was the household of Chang's deaf daughter, Louisa, that struck the first blow. Her husband, Zacharias W. Haynes, wrote a rejoinder to the *Daily News* of Raleigh. Haynes established that the twins had married "ladies native of Wilkes county, N.C., and not chambermaids from England." He also defended the twins' intellect. In so doing, he acknowledged the prevailing view of education—a "liberal" education, just as the twins wanted for their children—but offered a challenge to those who thought there was only one path to wisdom. "They never spent a day in the school room for the purpose of study, yet they were educated and intelligent men. . . . They could read and write very well, and transact all of their business with facility. Their wisdom did not consist of Greek and Latin, as I presume that of the learned correspondent of the *Sun* does, but in practical, common sense."[44] Haynes set the record straight about the health of the children and then addressed the families' domestic lives.

The *Sun* correspondent had called the twins' living situation "peculiar," not because the thought of two sisters sharing their bed with two brothers seemed scandalous but because discord between the wives had forced them into separate households, quite the opposite of the affectionate families that prevailed—at least in the public imagination—in the North.[45] Haynes, however, used that same fact, that the twins' families had moved into separate dwellings, to argue that their family life was entirely normal. "Instances of two large families being brought up in the same house in perfect love, peace and harmony are very rare," he wrote, and the Bunkers were no different. Living in close quarters bred discontent, and establishing separate households had been necessary to keep relations civil.[46] Haynes's appeal operated on two levels. On the one hand, he drew on specific points of evidence that established the twins and their family members as unique individuals, in a period of increasing individualism. On the other hand, he emphasized the things they had in common, not just with their community but also with humanity.

Christopher Bunker, Chang's eldest son, provided the second example of the children humanizing their parents. Arriving home from California, he found that his father, uncle, and closest sister had died; his mother and aunt were being mocked in the press, as were his siblings and cousins; and a close family friend seemed to have betrayed them. So, in March he traveled to Philadelphia along with Eng's son Decatur to claim their fathers' bodies. While there he gave an interview to a reporter that revealed the dismay and anger that he felt. He was taking the bodies of his father and uncle back home, but to what fate he was unsure. In Mount Airy, intimate friends and neighbors would have one last chance to look on them before a religious burial. But he decried the embalming process that the physicians had used to preserve the twins' bodies. He wished instead that the bodies would naturally decay quickly, lessening their appeal to grave robbers. As it was, "they will be the same fifty years hence as they are to-day." Further, he was taking home "only the shells of our fathers," as the twins' lungs, livers, and entrails remained in the doctors' hands. "For the public comment already made, for the undue advantage taken of us, for the extent to which our own sacred and beloved dead have been paraded in false and unnatural colors in the public press, we have nothing but regret, sorrow, and tears."[47]

The sorry picture of the Bunker son inspired reflection about him and the other children, as humans and as Americans. "The public seemed to have lost sight of the children of these unfortunate parents altogether, or if they remembered their existence at all it was to view them in the light of monsters, wholly incapable of the finer feelings of humanity," one writer reflected. Forced to turn "from the scientific and sensational civilization of these times, to the consideration of their social and domestic relations," one could see in Christopher Bunker that "among the American descendants of these twins there were true American men and women, possessed in a highly sensitive degree of all our most ennobling instincts and impulses."[48]

The suggestion that it was the "ennobling instincts and impulses" that made the children "American" is ironic, of course. If anything, this study of Chang and Eng, their wives, and their children has shown how ignoble much of America was over the course of its interaction with the Bunkers. But rather than cast stones, I will say instead that it was good of the un-named writer to identify both the monstrosity and the humanity in his sub-ject and to recognize that the children's monstrosity came not from them but from the way people viewed them. If only the writer could have seen that the humanity came from this as well. These competing and comple-menting tropes of monstrosity and humanity colored representations of the twins' lives and of their deaths, just as they marked the experiences of the twins' wives and children, but they did not signify the content or composi-tion of the Bunkers as individuals.

We have seen the dangers of attaching significance to labels or, to use Christopher's word, to shells. The twins lived in a world in which Chinese could become Siamese, and Siamese, Chinese. Black men could own slaves, and slaves could have white skin. The same men could be slaves and then masters; the same men could be Asian or white, African or American In-dian. It is not that these labels were the wrong ones; it is that there were no right ones.

None of this is to say that we cannot know anything about the past or the world in which we live. Rather, it was the very pliability of the twins' identities—how they were represented, but also how they represented themselves—that allowed them to occupy seats at the table of some of the most significant occasions in the history of race in America. And it was their difference yet also their similarity—their monstrosity but also their humanity—that resulted in their being attacked by a riot in Massachusetts and being considered slaves by the Virginia state assembly during the piv-otal early years of the 1830s. They were allowed to become citizens at a time when naturalization of nonwhites was against the law, and to marry white women when sentiment in America opposed amalgamation. They became symbols of union just as that bond was breaking, then they became symbols of duplicity just as the bond was being reforged. But the twins had gotten old; their bond, which had once been so flexible, was by the end of their lives hard and stiff. And so, increasingly, were the times.

The recollection of the twins' "repelling," "yellow" faces took place in a national context as well, one that was increasingly hostile to Chinese in America. In the late 1860s, pressure came to be felt nationwide for excluding Chinese from immigrating to the United States. In the early 1870s there was anti-Chinese violence in western states. An 1875 piece of federal legislation effectively prohibited the immigration of almost all Chinese women, discouraging the permanent settlement of Chinese families in the United States; five years later, California passed a law banning miscegenation, effectively outlawing marriage for Chinese men. In 1878, a court decision formally declared that Chinese were ineligible for naturalization, and in 1882, the U.S. Congress passed the Chinese Exclusion Act, which virtually blocked the immigration of Chinese. Meanwhile, anti-Chinese violence had spread to the East Coast.[49]

The twins were marked in death by these hateful circumstances, but only briefly. If they had lived longer—especially if they had toured again, as rumors suggested they might—they may have borne the brunt of the anti-Chinese movement, being, as some apparently thought they were, the most prominent Chinese in America. And, with the stand of Christopher and Decatur against the interests that wanted to put the bodies on exhibit, the two cousins had effectively declared that they were their own men, just as their fathers had more than forty years before. Neither they nor their siblings and cousins would have to go on exhibit again. The two men were taking their fathers' bodies home, to bury on the Chang property alongside other deceased family members.

"Never," Christopher told the press, "never shall the Siamese Twins be seen again."[50]

EPILOGUE

The Past Rears Its Head

How does one negotiate a graveyard?

The tombstone at the front entrance to the cemetery at the White Plains Baptist Church, on the outskirts of Mount Airy, is large and imposing and appropriate for the historic figures whose names grace it: Eng Bunker and his wife, Sarah A. Yates, and Chang Bunker and his wife, Adelaide Yates. At the bottom of the stone, it says, "Siamese Twins Chang and Eng, Born in Siam."

The twins were moved to this site in 1917, after the death of Adelaide. It was something she had wanted, for them to be buried on the grounds of the church the Bunkers had helped establish and for which they had donated land. To stand there and meditate over these graves is to feel like a witness to the final act of a great historical drama. To go further into the graveyard, though, to leave the margins and the marked paths and tread across earth and grass, to tiptoe past graves, to pause in front of recognized names and imagine their loves and hates and passions, to walk on top of the bodies of buried strangers (of course, they are *all* strangers), to do these things seems ultimately to be a trespasser, a voyeur of deeply personal stories. Amid the order and tidy arrangement of the groomed landscape, I feel acutely out of place. The stories become jumbled, the connections illegible, the presence of the past and the permanence of death bewildering. I become disoriented, keenly aware of my profound difference, of being alive among those who are not.

Graveyards are sites of monstrous ambivalence. They are places of death and life, for the dead and the living. They are places of great disorder and order. Strangers lie side by side, and families are scattered about. Those who died more than a century ago are buried in close proximity to those who died last week. The stories they tell appear at random, and any attempt to find meaning seems futile. Imposing white stones, some new and pristine, others old and crumbling, mark the passing of individual lives, and green

193

grass creates a seamless landscape that connects these individuals together. And beneath the surface . . .

It is here, in the White Plains cemetery, on ground formerly owned by the twins, on a hill overlooking land that is still in the family's hands, that the twins, their wives, and their children seem most present, that they seem most alive.

In the Shadow of the Twins

When Christopher Wren and Stephen Decatur returned home with their fathers' bodies, there was the business of burying the twins in what was expected to be their final resting place: the front yard of Chang and Adelaide's house, a place where the family could watch over the graves and ensure they remained unmolested, a practice that was not unique to the Bunkers.[1] Gravestones marked the spot, a fence kept visitors out, and the large house overlooking the burial site contained watchful eyes. Inside Chang's home, and in the Eng household a short distance away, there were still young children to be raised. Adelaide had twelve-year-old Jesse Lafayette, eleven-year-old Margaret Elizabeth, and five-year-old Hattie Irene. Sarah was raising fourteen-year-old Rosella Virginia and eight-year-old Robert Edward.

Meanwhile, the older children were forging lives of their own. Two of Chang's daughters had actually wed during his lifetime. Victoria married Nathaniel Bolejack on her father's sixtieth birthday—May 11, 1871. She and her husband, a native of neighboring Stokes County and a student in Mount Airy, were both eighteen. Chang bought a farm for them in Stokes, about thirty miles southeast of Mount Airy, and she apparently gave her parents a granddaughter in 1872 and was pregnant with another child when her father died. By this time, however, her husband had run off and taken a good amount of money, and she had filed for divorce. (Years later, he was arrested in Florida on charges of bigamy after it turned out he married a third wife while still married to his second.)[2] In September 1873, eighteen-year-old Louisa, who was studying in Raleigh at the North Carolina Institution for the Deaf and Dumb and the Blind, married an instructor at the school, Zacharias W. Haynes, age twenty-five. Both were deaf. Together they raised nine children—none of whom had impaired hearing—and they remained married until Haynes's death in 1900. (Haynes, of course, was the son-in-law who wrote to newspapers in 1874, trying to set the record straight about the brothers' character and their wives' origins.)

In the years after 1874, all the Bunker children had to learn for themselves whom they could trust and who was trying to take advantage of them. They had to navigate terrain that had been shaped by their father and uncle before them. This meant the children were able to build on connections that had been forged by the twins, but it also meant that the young Bunkers had to overcome prejudice directed at them as a result of their "monstrous" fathers.

In the final years of Chang's and Eng's lives, some of their older sons had decided to try their luck out west. Chang's Christopher and Eng's Decatur returned to live in Mount Airy, from California and Missouri, respectively, but two more of Eng's sons, James Montgomery and Patrick Henry, remained in Missouri, soon to be joined by younger brother Frederick Marshall. Because they moved far from North Carolina—in the hopes of leaving behind the infamy of being "sons of the Siamese," according to some commentators—their experience is particularly interesting. They were not able to live in anonymity, and they were unable to use prior family connections. As early as March 1874, newspapers reported that these three had moved to Jackson County, Missouri, had purchased a "splendid" farm, and were raising a profitable crop of tobacco. These initial reports made much of the brothers' ancestry, if only to indicate that "they are not inclined to talk of their parentage."[3] But some reports did not stop there. The brothers appeared to be standoffish, living in "the utmost seclusion" and avoiding contact with neighbors, "their purpose in coming to the West to escape notoriety." It was said they were living off monthly payments coming from their family in North Carolina.[4]

Montgomery, Patrick, and Frederick did not stay in Missouri long. For reasons unknown, they picked up in 1877 and moved to Sumner County, Kansas, in 1879. Kansans were not entirely sure what to make of these brothers. The local newspaper wrote that Frederick "displays gentlemanly culture" and was "unusually intelligent," although his features were "of the Mongolian or Malayan type." Montgomery was "of ordinary intelligence only" and "has dark features like his father," another paper reported, but he was "in no way deformed." They were labeled "colored" in the 1880 federal census, which also recorded that their birthplace was Siam, and they were not categorized as "white" in the 1885 state census. But all three soon owned property in Ryan Township, and Montgomery and Patrick married fairly quickly.[5]

Despite these shared beginnings, their lives took drastically different directions. In 1886, Frederick died in Fort Smith, Arkansas, away from his

Kansas home. According to family accounts, he was killed in a barroom brawl, although there is no indication of what caused the fight, if it actually occurred.[6] Montgomery's first marriage proved contentious and short lived. Newspaper reports later claimed that he had been "forced" into marriage, and in 1885, after a year, he could not extricate himself as his wife "was determined that the son of the Siamese twins should support her and refused to agree to a divorce." Montgomery resorted to perjury to gain his divorce, traveling to another county and swearing under oath that his wife did not live in the state and could not contest the divorce. Successful, he married Anna Mears in 1886, a marriage that lasted thirty-five years—he died in 1921—but which had a rocky start. He was convicted for perjury and sentenced to two years in the state penitentiary, although he did not serve the entire sentence.[7] Patrick's marriage also ended in divorce, although in his case his wife asked for it and he agreed. "After we had six children my wife told me she wanted a divorce and the custody of all the children," he told a reporter decades later. "So I said to her, 'Well, no man ever made anything lawing with his wife, so, if your mind is set on having a divorce and the children you will want plenty to raise them with,' so I deed her the farm in Sumner county and everything on it—horses, mules, machinery, everything." The divorce was in 1891; he spent the rest of his life in poverty, eventually landing in the county poorhouse in Medicine Lodge.[8]

Of the brothers who moved west, Montgomery ultimately proved most stable and successful. By 1890, most of his legal problems were behind him, and he and his second wife were able to devote their energies to their family and farm. Together, they had six children, and in 1897, he was lauded for having one of the county's biggest wheat crops. But reminders were always there, of a past that he did not deny but also did not advertise, reminders often of a past that did not exist but which persisted in the public imagination nonetheless. A Kansas newspaper article about Chang and Eng was typical. Titled "A Forgotten Freak," the story recounted the accurate ("the father of this wonderful freak was a Chinaman and the mother a Siamese"), the contested ("they were purchased of their mother"), and the false ("they were married to mulatto sisters").[9]

In Mount Airy, much of the heavy lifting of establishing the family had already been done. Despite what the family considered the unseemly response by many town residents to Chang's and Eng's deaths, the Bunkers had property, money, and status. Several of the Bunker men ended up playing prominent roles in the community. Christopher was named postmaster of Hay Stack in Surry County in 1882, a position he held well into the twentieth century; Albert became a census enumerator for Mount Airy township in 1880; and William was elected as a delegate to the state's Republican convention in Raleigh and the national convention in Minneapolis, both in 1892.[10]

In terms of personal relationships, most of Chang's offspring—who by and large remained in North Carolina—married the sons and daughters of neighboring families, perhaps in response to Victoria's unsuccessful early marriage with Nat Bolejack, perhaps not. In 1877, Chang's oldest surviving daughter, Susan Mariana, married Squire Gordon Jones, who became their neighbor after the war. In 1882, Christopher wedded Mary Haynes, the daughter of a family that lived nearby. Later that year, Jesse married Emma Davis, Mary's first cousin. Christopher and Jesse's younger sister Margaret Elizabeth wedded Mary's younger brother Caleb Hill Haynes in 1889. But other siblings and cousins married into families whose origins were more distant and yet also experienced successful, long unions.

There are no primary-source indications that active discrimination existed against the family within Mount Airy, although Irving Wallace and Amy Wallace quote an unnamed Bunker relative who suggested otherwise. "In earlier years, many of the descendants were very defensive about the twins being their fathers or grandfathers. They were always being asked perfectly insulting questions, were openly leered at, and the like," the ancestor said. "The Bunker women especially were affected by this. Upon more than one occasion, a Bunker girl . . . found a swain had disappeared after the young man's family discovered he was courting a Bunker."[11]

In the national press, it was never difficult to find some disparaging comment about the Bunkers. Almost fifteen years after the twins' deaths, for example, a debate in the U.S. Senate over Chinese immigration provoked this response: "The assertion of Senator Stewart that the Chinese were more than a match for the Jew in commercial shrewdness and thrift has no American illustration, unless we count the children of Chang and Eng, who about ten years since sold the bicorporal 'remains' of the Siamese twins to the doctors, as Mongolians." This effort on the part of the Bunker offspring, "thrifty in bereavement and forehanded amid sorrow," was offered as proof that Americans "need not despair of becoming a homogeneous people when the Mongolian in the second generation in America has outdone the keenest Connecticut Yankee in thrift and the meanest devotee of apple jack on 'Jersey shore' in parsimony."[12] Even stories that presumed to be complimenting the Bunker offspring ultimately turned insulting. A North Carolina paper, for instance, concluded that the Bunker men were "perfectly formed" and also "nearly white."[13]

Christopher's words to the contrary, Chang and Eng never fully disappeared from the public eye. Like a monster, the past continued to rear its head, always surviving, though not in forms always recognizable. In the years and decades after their deaths, Americans remained fascinated with Chang and Eng and also with their families. Often, that awareness reflected racial discourses prominent at a particular time. The decades after the twins' deaths were characterized by the discrimination of Chinese exclusion and segregation of Jim Crow. But rhetoric on the national level that served to underscore difference was sometimes undercut by local realities.

The "Bunker" in the Bunkers

A few miles from the White Plains cemetery, on family land, there is a private cemetery that holds the body of a central actor in the historical drama—Sarah Bunker. The contrast between this site and the burial site of her husband, sister, and brother-in-law is stark. Without any signs to mark this graveyard, it remains difficult to find, and absent the landscaping and groundskeeping that more formal cemeteries enjoy, the site can be ridden with brush, leaves, and overgrowth. The stones themselves are in disrepair, the writing on many no longer legible, worn by the years and elements. The only stone whose markings can still be read belongs to Sarah.[14]

This site is not mentioned in any of the tourist literature about Mount Airy or the twins, and I only learned of it attending the 2012 iteration of the annual Bunker reunion that has occurred in the small town every July since the 1980s.[15] Explaining why Sarah's final resting place was separate from that of her husband, one descendant said she chose that burial place because of the good care her slaves had shown her during life; she hoped to repay that by remaining close to them in death.[16] An alternative account was soon offered: Sarah chose that site because she had children buried there. While perhaps more plausible, it is notable that it was the second explanation offered, not the first, and that support for each seemed to be equal. It is also notable that it was apparently necessary to correct the record, to create some distance between the family and its dead slaves.

The specter of race continues to haunt the Bunkers. Just as the twins' children were remarked to have "the countenance of their fathers," and just as Eng's sons who went west were described as looking "Mongolian or Malayan," Bunker descendants through the years struggled with the Asian part of their ancestry. A grandson of Eng, for instance "never really reconciled himself to his background," according to his daughter, who herself did not learn of her ancestry until the early 1940s when she visited relatives in Mount Airy at age nineteen. When she confronted her father with what she had learned, "he admitted that we were related to the twins but said he did not want it generally known because he thought it was terrible that he had Chinese in the family background. He considered himself a half breed."[17]

In 1952, a year after the death of the last Bunker child (Robert, son of Eng), *Life* magazine published an essay on the twins and their descendants. The reporter, who visited Mount Airy, described the eleven-year-old great-grandsons he saw working in the fields as having faces "touched with an Oriental-American blend of mischief." In general, "vigorous, brunet faces, strong black eyebrows and dark eyes, and candid expressions mark the tribe. They do not look Oriental in any slant-eyed or 'sinister' sense but most of them are very distinctive people. Other townspeople say that those with strong family marks 'look real Bunkery.'"[18] This became a self-referential term as well—at the 2012 family reunion, one descendant pointed out another as "that Bunker-looking gentleman over there"—and one that was, for some, a source of pride.

Growing up in Chang Bunker's farmhouse in the 1950s and early 1960s, in the years immediately following the *Life* correspondent's visit to Mount Airy, sisters Alex and Dottie Sink felt closely connected to their famous great-grandfather. This came, in part, from within the family. While the Sink sisters were under strict orders not to talk about their ancestry to cousins who had never been told of Chang and Eng, their father taught them to be proud of their heritage. "Daddy is the one who really placed that in our minds—that this is so exceptional what these two men did," Dottie told a journalist years later. "He is the one that planted that seed that this is something wonderful about your heritage." But the family pride also came in response to the way that town residents treated them differently. When Alex Sink went into Mount Airy as a child, strangers often approached and said to her, "'Why, you must be one of those Bunkers.' Because I had slanty eyes," she said in a 2010 interview, when she was the Democratic candidate for Florida's governor. "I would stick my chest out and say, 'Yes, I am.'"[19]

While the specter of miscegenation became very real in the case of the twins, there was one aspect that was *not* spoken about, and that was the possibility of interracial sex between Asian and black. Historians today talk about using Asians in the United States to complicate the racial binary of black and white that commonly characterizes studies of America's history. But to focus too single-mindedly on the experience of Asians, or even relations between Asian immigrants and white Americans, risks introducing a white-Asian binary that needs its own complication.[20] Bringing in the twins' slaves can serve as the complicating wrinkle. There is no evidence that such unions did take place between Chang and Eng and the women they owned, let alone evidence that any of the enslaved children among their property were the twins' own. The only things that remotely suggest this as a possibility are, one, the fact that such relations were common practice in the slave South[21] and, two, a list of names and birth years at the back of the twins' account book. On a single page, there are the names of many of Chang's and Eng's children and their birth dates; there are also the names and birth dates of some of the enslaved children among their property. Some unidentified person has scribbled in the margins of the page some annotations— "white" plus "C" or "E" are next to the names of the twins' children, and "col" (for "colored") is written next to the other names. A quick comparison of these names with what few purchase records exist shows that at least two of these people were actually bought by Chang and Eng when they were young. As for the remaining ten names, one can only speculate about what they might be doing here.[22]

In 2003, a descendant of Grace Gates, the twins' most well-known slave, attended the annual Bunker reunion hoping to find information on her own ancestry. Having traced her family through the census, Brenda Ethridge hoped to find more documentation and stories about her ancestors. While documentation was hard to come by, Bunkers were happy to share what they knew about Grace Gates, who was a wedding gift to the twins from their father-in-law and who served as nurse to the twins' children. But Ethridge's presence also raised some uneasy questions for the twins' descendants about the past. Scholar Cynthia Wu has uncovered evidence of stories passed down in the family of the twins' children playing with half brothers and half sisters who were enslaved and the attempt by some family members to pursue DNA testing to determine the validity of such anecdotes. She also details the pushback from other members of the family who worried about the turmoil the question might raise within the family and also the impact such news might have on the twins' reputation.[23]

Whether it was a source of shame or pride, something to hide or embrace, being different was something that Bunkers in Mount Airy lived with, and this difference was almost always traced to Chang and Eng and their Asian origins. Certainly, their conjoined bodies provided the exigence for their departure from Siam, fueled their international fame as performers and entertainers, offered metaphors and allegories for the political and sectional crises that plagued their adopted nation, and gave the world the phrase "Siamese twins" to refer to all conjoined twins. But their conjoined bodies were truly singular; during their lifetimes, there were only one or two other pairs of conjoined twins that commanded any public attention. In the decades after their deaths, conjoinedness became less a monstrosity and increasingly a medical condition that could be surgically "repaired." As scholar Leslie Fiedler writes, conjoined twins "have become events . . . not in the history of show biz but in that of medicine, like the beneficiaries of open heart surgery or the latest organ transplant."[24] And because most are "repaired" immediately at birth or soon thereafter, conjoined twins who remain joined are remarkably rare.

Race, though, is extraordinarily pervasive, and for that reason eminently threatening. As a cultural and social construction, it has proved malleable as the composition of America's population has undergone continual change. Despite the country's changing face, society maintains categories of difference and expects—and forces—people to act accordingly. Adopting the guise of biological truth, passing from one generation to the next through blood and genes, race has shown its ability to survive, rearing its head again and again, decade after decade, century after century. It is one thing to read Jesse Franklin Graves write in 1874 that David Yates objected in 1843 to the marriage between his daughters and Chang and Eng because of "an ineradicable prejudice against their race and nationality."[25] That was, after all, the nineteenth century. But it is something else to hear a descendant of David Yates say in 2010, "An interracial marriage today in my . . . community would be viewed much the same."[26] Looking at the ways the Bunker descendants have had to negotiate the past and grapple with the legacy of being Bunkers suggests that he is correct.

NOTES

Abbreviations

NCSA   North Carolina State Archives, Raleigh
 SHC   Southern Historical Collection, University of North Carolina, Chapel Hill

Introduction

1. "The Siamese Twins," *New York Times*, February 20, 1874; *Report of the Autopsy of the Siamese Twins*, 20; Dunglison, *Medical Lexicon*, 764; Fisher, "Diploteratology" (1866), 209, 214. Fisher's work was published in the *Transactions of the Medical Society of the State of New York* over the course of four years, from 1865 to 1868.

2. While popular memory and gossip has shaped the public's understanding of the twins, the current scholarly quest to find meaning in the lives of Chang and Eng can trace its origins to a 1964 biography written by Kay Hunter, a descendant of the British merchant who claimed to have "discovered" the twins in a Siam waterway in the 1820s. *Duet for a Lifetime*, published first in London, was a sensational account written for a popular audience; it relied on tall tales and hearsay for much of its material. But it was the first to use letters between the twins and Robert Hunter and the twins and Abel Coffin, as well as the twins' business accounts. Kay Hunter covered primarily the twins' career in show business, with particular focus on the men who managed them, including Robert Hunter, Abel Coffin, James Hale, and, incongruously, Phineas T. Barnum, who she suggests managed the twins in the late 1830s. While the brothers proved to be good businessmen, Hunter portrayed them as clear beneficiaries of their managers' largesse: "Everything was . . . accomplished with such motives of doing good that the onlooker would hesitate to suggest that anything so unpleasant as exploitation was taking place" (31). And while she did acknowledge the conflict between Coffin and the twins, her final verdict of the captain was also positive: "He reshaped the lives of two young men who . . . would have remained in poverty and obscurity on the other side of the world" (77–78).

In 1978, best-selling author Irving Wallace and his daughter Amy Wallace penned what became the most influential book in shaping public knowledge about Chang and Eng. *The Two* examined the twins as celebrities, fitting as Irving Wallace had written a number of other mass-market celebrity biographies. The focus here was on them as both public performers and private family men. *The Two* was remarkable for its exhaustive research, finding previously untapped letters, family papers, and newspaper articles, among other sources. Whereas Hunter's coverage after the twins' 1843 marriage was sketchy, the Wallaces took their detailed narrative through the rest of the twins' lives. In its narrative, *The Two* gave the twins a level of complexity that

Hunter did not, recognizing Chang and Eng as "their own men" rather than objects to be controlled by people around them. While much of the account valorized the twins, the Wallaces did not shy away from criticizing them at times. *The Two* also took almost every anecdote about the twins at face value and amplified for dramatic effect some of the tales from Kay Hunter's account. These narrative decisions by the Wallaces were significant because their work has been by far the most influential source on the twins' lives, providing meat for subsequent articles in newspapers and magazines but also for most scholarly analyses of Chang and Eng.

3. The clearest distillation of this category of academic inquiry is Jeffrey Jerome Cohen's edited volume, *Monster Theory*, published in 1996. In his introduction, Cohen proposed seven "breakable postulates" that might aid in the attempt to understand any culture through its monsters. First, monsters are the product of a particular time and place, and as a result, they are cultural constructs and projections. Second, monsters always escape death, as often as not coming back to life after being presumed dead. Third, monsters defy easy categorization, they are often hybrid, and consequently they are understood as dangerous signs of disorder. Fourth, the monster signifies difference, but a difference that is arbitrary and, perhaps, mutable. There is the sense that, but for the grace of God, we might be that monster. Fifth, the monster polices the borders of the possible; to cross demarcated lines of normative behavior risks attack from a monster or to become a monster oneself. Sixth, the fear and disgust felt for the monster is actually a kind of desire or envy of its transgressive freedom. Seventh, monsters force us to reevaluate our cultural assumptions and grapple with why we created these monsters to begin with. In one way or another, Chang and Eng as cultural constructs fit the characteristics of these monstrous categories.

In her essay "America's 'United Siamese Brothers'" in *Monster Theory*, Allison Pingree argues that "even as the *symbol* of the twins was used to support certain dominant values, their literal *bodies* presented other puzzles and contradictions for the country to solve—ones that, ironically, undermined many of those same norms" (95). Pingree focuses on two separate aspects of representations of the twins. First, she examines the ways that promotional literature paired the conjoined twins with patriotic mottos such as "United we stand" and "Union and liberty, now and forever, one and inseparable." Dueling arguments were being made using the twins' fused bodies: Unionists appropriated the bodies to urge fusion of the states, whereas others believed the twins signaled that too close a connection between the states was monstrous. Second, again looking at exhibition pamphlets, Pingree argues that representations of the twins' domestic arrangements—including their marriage to two sisters, their multiple children, and the unspoken but clear fact that sexual relations were occurring—at once served to illustrate a romantic ideal of companionate marriage while also presenting the threat of incest, adultery, and "exotic orgies of flesh" (95). In these ways the twins reflected back on the United States the greatest fears—and desires—of Americans.

The approach to monsters that Pingree takes draws closely from a related field, what is sometimes called "freak studies," and this academic field is one of the two that have given most analytic attention to Chang and Eng. A seminal text is Leslie Fiedler's *Freaks*, published in 1978, in which he reads literature and popular culture to explore the various types of "physiologically deviant humans," including giants, dwarfs, hermaphrodites, and Siamese twins (by which he means conjoined twins), and what they have meant to "normal" society. Through its freaks, Fiedler concludes, society can define what it means to be "fully human" (347). In discussing "Siamese twins," he uses Hunter's book and some publicity literature to place Chang and Eng within the larger history of conjoined twins. Whereas conjoined twins challenge our individuality and the uniqueness of our consciousness, often necessitating "enemy" twin brothers who are distinctly separate (a pattern that representations of the twins fall into), Chang and Eng have become the most popular conjoined twins because, through their longevity and their fecundity, they suggest a happy ending.

While Fiedler concerns himself with various forms of anomalous bodies, Robert Bogdan focuses on the performances that enable the social construction of freaks. In other words, "the onstage freak is something else off stage. 'Freak' is a frame of mind, a set of practices, a way of thinking about and presenting people" (3). By focusing on the period from 1840 to 1940, the height of freak-show popularity, Bogdan is able to trace the mistreatment of some people but also the opportunities for fame, fortune, and enhanced social status. Bogdan identifies two modes of presentation, the exotic, in which the freak was different and inferior, and the aggrandized, in which the freak was upstanding and high status. Drawing from Hunter and the Wallaces, he uses Chang and Eng particularly well to illustrate these ways to present freaks, as the twins performed both roles at different points in their careers.

Unlike these approaches to Chang and Eng, which see their conjoined state as the primary avenue for analysis (with very little if any consideration of secondary approaches), I see their "physiological deviance" play a dominant role at two precise moments in their lives in America: when they first arrive, in 1829, and when they die, in 1874. Even then, their race and national origins play very significant roles in how the public makes sense of them. While their conjoinedness is the curiosity that draws attention, their race is the major factor behind the fear and concern felt by many about their presence and influence, at least as it is articulated.

The major influences to my study of Chang and Eng and their worlds come from the field of Asian American studies. The twins were, after all, the most well-known Asians in America in the nineteenth century. Most influential, and most extensive in its coverage of the twins and the larger nineteenth century about which my own project is concerned, is John Kuo Wei Tchen's 1999 monograph, *New York before Chinatown*. Building off the insights of Edward Said, Tchen uncovers a uniquely American form of Orientalism. In the process, he extends the narrative of Asian American history back to the nation's founding, in the guise of a vibrant discourse about China and Chinese people and a healthy trade in Chinese goods, and he demonstrates the central position that Asia occupied in American political thought. He also shows the ways that Orientalist discourses influenced the everyday lives of Chinese traders and sailors living in New York City in the mid-nineteenth century. Chang and Eng are just two of many cultural figures that appear in this book. They illustrate a "commercial Orientalism" that arose in the 1820s and 1830s, in which Chinese culture and, increasingly, people were commodified as part of an emerging urban culture.

Robert G. Lee's *Orientals*, a 1999 study of Asian American stereotypes in popular culture from the 1850s to the 1990s, addresses similar processes of oppositional representation. Lee identifies six dominant stereotypes: pollutant, coolie, deviant, yellow peril, model minority, and gook. Racist anti-Asian representations in a wide range of cultural forms, including songs, minstrel shows, museum exhibits, pulp fiction, and Hollywood films, helped create a "white" American identity, even among recent immigrants from Europe. In the antebellum context, Chang, Eng, and their mixed-race children became a prime example of Asian as "pollutant," a threat to the white republic, "symbolic of the collapse of racial, class, and sexual order" (32).

Similarly placing a brief discussion of Chang and Eng within a larger consideration of American history, Gary Y. Okihiro's *Common Ground*, published in 2001, uses the Asian American subject as a third figure in an attempt to destabilize entrenched binaries in U.S. history such as west versus east, white versus black, man versus woman, and heterosexual versus homosexual. Arguing that these paradigmatic pairs at once work to naturalize dualisms and create hierarchies of superiority and inferiority, Okihiro places Asian American experiences in the foreground to show that "those categories of geographies, race, gender, and sexuality are constructions of the human imagination" (134). Okihiro limits his discussion of the twins to illustrate the constraints of idealized manhood and womanhood, but we can extrapolate this illustration to other social categories. As Asians in America, Chang and Eng were in between multiple categories. As a result, the brothers exposed the limits of these categories if not calling into question their very legitimacy.

Cynthia Wu's 2012 book, *Chang and Eng Reconnected*, successfully spans the fields of Asian American studies and disability studies. A scholar of American studies, Wu undertakes a rich theoretical reading of a wide range of cultural texts, ranging from the mid-nineteenth-century exhibition pamphlets and doctors' reports that I include in my source base to novels, films, museum exhibits, and family reunions of the very recent past. Wu's book is not a biography of Chang and Eng but an analysis of the discourse of remembrance, commemoration, appropriation, and ridicule that has characterized cultural productions about the "Original Siamese Twins." Looking at the debates over individuality and interdependence that have surrounded discussions about the twins since 1829, Wu argues that the conjoined brothers have posed a challenge to American national identity, which has celebrated individualism. "The conjoined physical body, which wavers between unity and plurality, becomes a gold standard of sorts among literary and visual metaphors when debating the particulars of an idealized national community," she writes (3), and she shows the ways that Americans have used the twins to grapple with the tensions that exist between imagined group identities and idealized individualism.

The promotional text on the back cover of Wu's book claims that *Chang and Eng Reconnected* is a welcome change from "the generally more narrowly historically focused work on the Bunkers," but as this review of the scholarly literature on Chang and Eng shows, in fact there has not been any work of historical scholarship that has examined in depth the lives of Chang and Eng and their families in the context of nineteenth-century history and historiography. (The work that comes closest to having done this is *New York before Chinatown*.) There has not been any history that examines rigorously or systematically extant archival, demographic, and popular sources to see what the lived experiences and discursive representations of Chang and Eng can tell us about the United States of the nineteenth century. The present book is an attempt to fill that gap.

4. Bragg, "Planet of the Normates," 180. The essay under discussion was Pingree, "America's 'United Siamese Brothers.'"

5. Jackson, "Diploteratology" (1868), 276.

6. See Rotundo, *American Manhood*; Mintz and Kellogg, *Domestic Revolutions*; Hodes, *White Women, Black Men*; and Lui, *The Chinatown Trunk Mystery*.

7. The definition comes from Omi and Winant, *Racial Formation in the United States*.

8. Baynton, "Disability and the Justification of Inequality in American History."

9. As Chapter 2 shows, racial epithets such as "nigger" were used in reference to the twins. For example, see "The Lynnfield Battle," *Columbian Centinel*, August 17, 1831.

10. Said, *Orientalism*; Tchen, *New York before Chinatown*; Lee, *Orientals*.

11. Joan W. Scott writes that historicizing experience "entails focusing on processes of identity production, insisting on the discursive nature of 'experience' and on the politics of its construction. Experience is at once always already an interpretation *and* something that needs to be interpreted. . . . Experience is, in this approach, not the origin of our explanation, but that which we want to explain." See Scott, "The Evidence of Experience," 797.

12. I am thinking especially of Spivak, "The Rani of Sirmur" and "Can the Subaltern Speak?" Alcoff also cautions against putting words in the mouths of silenced actors in "The Problem of Speaking for Others." Liebersohn unhelpfully dismisses this point of view as "radical agnosticism" in *The Travelers' World*, 140–42, arguing that the belief we can know nothing about subaltern peoples does more to perpetuate long-standing stereotypes. While in theory I lean more toward Spivak, in practice I appear to have landed alongside Liebersohn.

Chapter One

1. Abel Coffin to Susan Coffin, June 28, 1829, Twins Papers, NCSA; House of Commons, *Minutes of Evidence Taken*, 203; Tomlin, "Missionary Journals and Letters," 58–63.

2. Abel Coffin to Susan Coffin, August 2, 1829, Twins Papers, NCSA.

3. The article, credited to the *Daily Boston Advertiser* and John Collins Warren, was reprinted in a number of newspapers, such as the *Aurora & Pennsylvania Gazette* (Philadelphia), August 27, 1829; the *New York Spectator*, August 28, 1829; and the *Washington Daily National Intelligencer*, August 29, 1829. Similar accounts appeared later that year in two medical journals. See Warren, "An Account of the Siamese Twin Brothers," and "The Siamese Brothers."

4. [Hale], *A Few Particulars concerning Chang-Eng*, 6, and Hale, *An Historical Account of the Siamese Twin Brothers*, 7.

5. On U.S. commercial and cultural influence in Southeast Asia, see Lord, "Missionaries, Thai, and Diplomats"; Gould, "American Imperialism in Southeast Asia before 1898"; and Spector, "The American Image of Southeast Asia."

6. In *Orientalism*, cultural theorist Edward W. Said provided the framework for understanding this type of work. "People, places, and experiences can always be described by a book, so much so that the book (or text) acquires a greater authority, and use, even

than the actuality it describes," Said wrote. "Such texts can *create* not only knowledge but also the very reality they appear to describe" (93–94).

While Said focused on the English and French traditions in the Near East, historian John Kuo Wei Tchen extended the concept of Orientalism to the early United States and the lives of Chinese living in New York City in *New York before Chinatown*. By historicizing varieties of Orientalism in the United States, Tchen showed how representations of China and Chinese at different times served the interests of cultural, commercial, and political elites and how actual Chinese living in the United States had no place in public discourse and, eventually, were excluded from the nation. Such exclusion would be symbolic, on the one hand, as Asian Americans by the late twentieth century became subject to a "perpetual foreigner" paradigm in which they were always regarded as recent immigrants and thus as foreigners. Exclusion was also literal; the Chinese Exclusion Act of 1882 prohibited the immigration of the vast majority of Chinese men (women had already been prohibited from coming to the United States under the Page Act of 1875). The Naturalization Act of 1790, limiting naturalization to "free white persons," was also used to exclude many Asians from U.S. citizenship.

7. One nineteenth-century American traveler to Siam pursued the question and came up with nothing. Two Thai researchers make reference to a royal record produced in the 1850s but appear not to have uncovered any other documentary evidence. See Feudge, "The Siamese Twins in Their Own Land," 383; Chintaphamitchakun, *Khukan nirandon*; and Niransuksiri, *Faet Sayam In-Chan*.

8. *Boston Patriot and Mercantile Advertiser*, August 17, 1829. Other reports, however, suggested that their mother was unsure of the date and that perhaps their birth was in late 1811 or early 1812. The records of Siam's King Phra Nangklao, often referred to in English as Rama III, report the birth as occurring in the year of the monkey, in the fourth year of the reign of King Phra Phuttaloetla, or Rama II, in the Chulasakarat (or "Lesser Era") year of 1190, which corresponded to the Christian era year of 1812. These records, which were compiled as late as the 1850s, reported on the departure of the twins from Siam in 1829. The attempt to pinpoint a specific date, while fun, might also be dismissed as much ado about nothing. After all, they were born, they survived, and they eventually caught the public's attention—how important is their birth date? And yet, as the next chapter shows, their specific age would become important as they reached the age of majority and began to break the bonds of servitude that linked them to Abel Coffin. See *Chotmaihet Ratchakan thi 3*, vol. 3.

9. For example, see Hale, *An Historical Account of the Siamese Twin Brothers*, 7.

10. This nomenclature did not obtain while they were actually in Siam. Later claims suggested that the brothers were known to their neighbors as the "Chinese Twins." Notably, these names did not represent the correct Siamese (or Chinese) pronunciation of their names, which were In arĭd Chun, a fact that, curiously, made it into several newspaper articles, as well as the exhibition pamphlets published about them, and yet which, despite this public acknowledgment, did not influence the decision to call them "Chang" and "Eng" in public. On the market in Oriental curiosities, see Tchen, *New York before Chinatown*.

11. Moor, *Notices of the Indian Archipelago and Adjacent Countries*, 191.

12. For a discussion of Siam's relations with the West, see Vella, *Siam under Rama III*, 115–40.

13. Memorial from R. Hunter to Lord Ellenborough, April 24, 1844, *The Burney Papers*, vol. 4, pt. 2, 129; Vella, *Siam under Rama III*, 126, 128–30; Bristowe, "Robert Hunter in Siam"; Plainoi, *Chao tang chat nai prawattisat Thai*, 135–42. Henry Burney's reports from Siam reveal the role Hunter played, both as a liaison between the British and Siamese governments and as a source of information for the British on their prospects in Siam. See Burney, Report, December 2, 1826, *The Burney Papers*, vol. 2, pt. 4, 36–37, 45. Hunter occupies a prominent place in the missionary accounts in Farrington, *Early Missionaries in Bangkok*. By the mid-1830s, Hunter's favored position as middleman became increasingly tenuous—the Siamese began viewing him more as a competitor—and in 1844 the king expelled him from the country.

14. Bolton, "Statement of the Principal Circumstances respecting the United Siamese Twins," 177; Warren, "An Account of the Siamese Twin Brothers." The accounts made no distinction between the monarch at the time of the twins' birth, Phra Phuttaloetla—known by Westerners today as Rama II—and the monarch at the time of the twins' departure, Phra Nangklao, or Rama III, referring simply to a generic "king of Siam."

15. "Spice Trade," *Daily National Journal*, November 3, 1824; House of Commons, *Minutes of Evidence Taken*, 185, 358; Tomlin, "Missionary Journals and Letters," 20–21, 26, 29, 40. Coffin did not leave any documentation attesting to his experience, but the first pamphlets published to coincide with the exhibition of the twins in 1830 and 1831 do include these images and more to represent the twins' homeland. Although these early pamphlets were officially authored by Hale, Tchen calls them the twins' story as told by Coffin.

16. Hale, *An Historical Account of the Siamese Twin Brothers*, 4, 5; Said, *Orientalism*, 93–94.

17. Hale, "A Few Facts concerning Them by a Correspondent Who Knew Them Intimately," *Brooklyn Eagle*, February 16, 1874.

18. *Boston Patriot and Mercantile Advertiser*, August 17, 1829; John Collins Warren, "Some Account of the Siamese Boys," *Boston Daily Advertiser*, reprinted in the *Aurora & Pennsylvania Gazette* (Philadelphia), August 27, 1829; *Baltimore Patriot*, August 27, 1829; and *New York Spectator*, August 28, 1829, among others.

19. The 1836 exhibition pamphlet, "published under their own direction," said they were "born of Chinese parents." An 1853 account said their mother was Siamese. Jesse Franklin Graves, who knew the twins and who is said to have based his biography largely on what the twins told him, simply says that their mother had a Chinese father and was "of lighter complexion than most Siamese women." Of the twentieth-century biographers and historians, those who identified the mother as part Siamese included the Wallaces and Bhamorabutr. Those who identified the mother as part Malay included Hunter, Tchen, and Niransuksiri. It is not clear where the Malay line originated. Chapter 2 explores the ways in which the twins presented their story. See [Hale], *A Few Particulars concerning Chang-Eng*, 4; *An Account of Chang and Eng*, 13; Graves, "The Siamese Twins," 1; Wallace and Wallace, *The Two*, 15; Bhamorabutr, *The Story of American Missionaries*, 10; Hunter, *Duet for a Lifetime*, 13; Tchen, *New York before Chinatown*, 134; Niransuksiri, *Faet Sayam In-Chan*, 5.

20. "The Siamese Boys," *Rhode Island American*, September 4, 1829; Felix Pascalis, "The Siamese Boys—Homo Duplex," *Morning Courier and New-York Enquirer*, September 22, 1829; Warren, "Some Account of the Siamese Boys," *Boston Daily Advertiser*; "The Siamese Boys," *Rhode Island American*, September 15, 1829.

21. And beyond: Scholars have similarly focused on the twins' racial origins. American studies scholar Robert G. Lee labeled the twins "ethnically Chinese" without discussion in his treatment of the "Heathen Chinee," and historian Tchen made the twins an important part of his research on Chinese in America in the nineteenth century. See Lee, *Orientals*, 30–33, and in addition to Tchen's *New York before Chinatown*, see also his "Staging Orientalism and Occidentalism." For another example, see McCunn, "Chinese in the Civil War," which includes two of the twins' sons among the "ten who served."

22. I am in conversation here with the work of Greta Ai-Yu Niu, who interrogates the apparent need of scholars today to specify the twins' ethnicity, if only to minimize its significance. "I want to turn away from the question of whether the twins are Chinese or Siamese to examine the assumptions behind the question," Niu writes. "Attempts to erase their history of 'confused,' or 'impure' ethnicity points to the place of ethnic labels in contemporary cultural scholarship, for example, notions of authenticity that arise in conjunction with border crossing." This criticism of scholarship's attempt to label the twins as one or the other is apt and appears to be a nod toward a framework that recognizes, if not embraces, hybridity. But as I show, the attempt to label the twins either/or is not in any way limited to scholarship of the late twentieth century. "Sinification" of the twins, if we want to call it that, prevailed from their first weeks in the United States. See Niu, "People of the Pagus," 32–36.

23. Vella, *Siam under Rama III*, 26–27; Wyatt, *Thailand*, 123–28, 135; Lysa, *Thailand in the Nineteenth Century*, 46–48.

24. Terwiel, *Through Travellers' Eyes*, 224–33; Tomlin, "Missionary Journals and Letters," 62–63.

25. "Siam," *The Missionary Herald*, December 1844.

26. Eoseewong, *Pen and Sail*, 77–80.

27. Eoseewong makes this argument, as does Skinner, *Chinese Society in Thailand*.

28. Tejapira argues this in "Pigtail."

29. Cushman, "The Chinese in Thailand."

30. Finlayson, *The Mission to Siam and Hue*, 166–67; Gutzlaff, "Journal of Three Voyages along the Coast of China," 72.

31. Finlayson, *The Mission to Siam and Hue*, 227.

32. Ibid., 224, 227–28.

33. Ibid., 108–9, 230.

34. For an introduction to the European roots of these sciences, as well as excerpts from leading practitioners, see Taylor and Shuttleworth, *Embodied Selves*. Davies, *Phrenology, Fad and Science*, offers a survey of America's infatuation with phrenology. Tchen considers the science's specific implications for Chinese in the United States in *New York before Chinatown*, 148–51.

35. Crawfurd, *Journal of an Embassy*, 310–11, 340. The illustration faces page 311.

36. "The Siamese Boys," *The Youth's Companion*, September 9, 1829.

37. Warren, "Some Account of the Siamese Boys," *Boston Daily Advertiser*; "The Siamese Youths," *London Literary Gazette*, November 28, 1829; "Sir Astley Cooper and the Siamese Youths," *London Morning Herald*, November 25, 1829, republished in the *New-York Spectator*, January 19, 1830, among others.

38. Crawfurd, *History of the Indian Archipelago*, 205; "The Siamese Boys," *The Youth's Companion*, September 9, 1829.

39. Warren, "Some Account of the Siamese Boys," *Boston Daily Advertiser*.

40. "The Siamese Youths," *Aurora & Pennsylvania Gazette* (Philadelphia), August 31, 1829; Letter from Cotton Mather to the Royal Society, October 15, 1713, in Silverman, *Selected Letters of Cotton Mather*, 132; Wish, *The Diary of Samuel Sewell*, 135–36; Warren, "An Account of the Siamese Twin Brothers," 256; "The Siamese Brothers," *Boston Medical and Surgical Journal*, September 1, 1829; "The Siamese Boys," *Saturday Evening Post*, October 10, 1829.

41. *Bangor (ME) Register*, October 29, 1829; "Another Account of United Twins in the East," *Edinburgh Journal of Science* (1830): 374–75.

42. "The Siamese Brothers," *Boston Medical and Surgical Journal*, September 1, 1829; "The Siamese Boys," *Saturday Evening Post*, October 10, 1829; "A Tour," *Western Monthly Review*, December 1829.

43. Newspapers around the country reprinted the first report in the *Boston Patriot and Mercantile Advertiser*, August 17, 1829. See also "Remarkable Natural Curiosity," *New-Bedford (MA) Mercury*, August 21, 1829; Warren, "Some Account of the Siamese Boys"; "The Siamese Brothers," *Boston Medical and Surgical Journal*, September 1, 1829; "A Tour," *Western Monthly Review*, December 1829; "The Siamese Boys," *Rhode Island Journal*, September 15, 1829; "From Late London Papers," *New York Spectator*, January 19, 1830, citing a November 25, 1829, report from the *London Morning Herald*.

44. *Boston Patriot and Mercantile Advertiser*, August 17, 1829; "Remarkable Natural Curiosity," *New-Bedford (MA) Mercury*, August 21, 1829; "The Siamese Boys," *Youth's Companion*, September 9, 1829; "A Tour," *Western Monthly Review*, December 1829.

45. "From Late London Papers," *New York Spectator*, January 19, 1830, citing a November 25, 1829, report from the *London Morning Herald*; Warren, "Some Account of the Siamese Boys"; "The Siamese Brothers," *Boston Medical and Surgical Journal*, September 1, 1829.

46. Samuel L. Mitchill and William Anderson, "The Siamese Boys," *New York Spectator*, September 29, 1829; Bolton, "Statement of the Principal Circumstances respecting the United Siamese Twins," 185; Warren, "Some Account of the Siamese Boys."

47. Bolton, "Statement of the Principal Circumstances respecting the United Siamese Twins," 180–82.

48. Mitchill and Anderson, "The Siamese Boys," *New York Spectator*, September 29, 1829.

49. Warren, "An Account of the Siamese Twin Brothers," 256.

50. Mitchill and Anderson, "The Siamese Boys," *New York Spectator*, September 29, 1829. Mitchill was assisted in his examination by New York physician William Anderson.

51. Felix Pascalis, "The Siamese Boys—Homo Duplex," *Morning Courier and New-York Enquirer*, October 3, 1829; Mitchill and Anderson, "The Siamese Boys," *New York*

Spectator, September 29, 1829; Hale, *An Historical Account of the Siamese Twin Brothers*, 15–16.

52. "The Siamese and Sir Astley," *Boston Medical and Surgical Journal*, February 9, 1830, 830.

53. "From Late London Papers," *New York Spectator*, January 19, 1830, originally published in *London Morning Herald*, November 25, 1829.

54. Ibid.

55. Cited in Tchen, *New York before Chinatown*, 109; Mitchill and Anderson, "The Siamese Boys," *New York Spectator*, September 29, 1829.

56. Many newspaper reports made much of the fact that the twins were studying English and picking it up quickly. One telling revision in the exhibition pamphlets: The earliest edition of the England exhibition pamphlet says that while they have acquired enough English to understand all that is said to them, they can speak only a little and are as yet too bashful to try their language skills out with strangers (*Account of the Siamese Twin Brothers from Actual Observations*, 1829, 7–8). Months later, a revised seventh edition of the pamphlet claims that they can "converse with tolerable fluency" (*An Historical Account of the Siamese Twin Brothers*, 1830, 7).

57. See, for instance, Bolton, "Statement of the Principal Circumstances respecting the United Siamese Twins," 184.

58. "The Siamese Brothers," *Boston Medical and Surgical Journal*, 460; "Anecdotes of the Siamese Youths," *Albion*, February 13, 1840.

59. Warren, "Some Account of the Siamese Boys"; "The Siamese Youth," *Lynn Mirror and Mechanics Magazine*, August 29, 1829; "The Siamese Brothers," *Boston Medical and Surgical Journal*, September 1, 1829; "The Siamese Boys," *Youth's Companion*, September 9, 1829; "A Tour," *Western Monthly Review*, December 1829.

60. "From Late London Papers," *New York Spectator*, January 19, 1830.

61. "A Tour," *Western Monthly Review*, December 1829; Bolton, "Statement of the Principal Circumstances respecting the United Siamese Twins"; "From Late London Papers," *New York Spectator*, January 19, 1830.

62. Warren, "Some Account of the Siamese Boys."

63. "A Tour," *Western Monthly Review*, December 1829.

64. See, for example, Felix Pascalis, "The Siamese Boys—Homo Duplex," *Morning Courier and New-York Enquirer*, September 22, 1829.

65. "Anecdotes of the Siamese Youths," *Albion*, February 13, 1830. Published initially in the British *Literary Gazette*, widely republished in the United States.

66. "The Siamese Twins," *Christian Watchman* 12 (December 9, 1831), 198.

67. "Double, Double, Toil and Trouble," reprinted in the *Aurora & Pennsylvania Gazette* (Philadelphia), September 8, 1829, and the *Salem Observer*, September 9, 1829.

68. I elaborate on these themes in subsequent chapters. For an exploration of the twins as metaphor for American ideals of both domesticity and union, see Pingree, "America's 'United Siamese Brothers.'"

69. [Tucker], "The Siamese Twins," *Virginia Literary Museum*, February 3, 1830, 529. In 1836, Tucker had the chance to perform his experiment on the twins. He concluded that his hypothesis was correct, that between these two brothers who had

shared the same experiences their entire lives there existed marked differences in personality and intellectual character. "Eng exhibits in his answers a more comprehensive and accurate memory, an acuter discrimination, and greater powers of reflection than his brother," Tucker wrote. This observation "seems sufficient to show that there was a difference in their original cerebral organization." See "On the Siamese Twins," 256.

70. "A Tour," *Western Monthly Review*, December 1829.

71. Slack, "The Siamese Boys, or a Lusus Naturae," *Rhode Island American*, September 15, 1829.

72. See, for instance, Pingree, "America's 'United Siamese Brothers.'" Most commonly, these uses described the political world and some sort of political deal that had been made.

73. Bradley journal, November 21, 1835, vol. 5 (July 1835–July 1836), Dan Beach Bradley Papers, Oberlin College Special Collections.

74. Said, *Orientalism*, 93–94.

Chapter Two

1. Harris to William Davis, April 11, 1832, Twins Papers, NCSA.

2. Virginia General Assembly, *Acts Passed at a General Assembly*, 4–5.

3. "Memorial of Chang and Eng, known as the Siamese Twin Brothers," Virginia General Assembly Legislative Petitions, Miscellaneous, March 12, 1832, Reel 236, Box 298, Folder 48, State Library of Virginia.

4. Ibid. For one example of the rowdy and potentially subversive nature of public performances at this same period, see Johnson, *Sam Patch, the Famous Jumper*.

5. Wiltse, *David Walker's Appeal*, 30. The most thorough discussion of Walker's *Appeal* and its connections with moral universalism and moral reform is Hinks, *To Awaken My Afflicted Brethren*.

6. On the slavery debate of 1831–32, see Freehling, *Drift toward Dissolution*, and Shade, *Democratizing the Old Dominion*, 191–224.

7. Harris to Davis, April 11, 1832, Twins Papers, NCSA.

8. Warren, "Some Account of the Siamese Boys," first published in the *Boston Daily Advertiser*, and Warren, "An Account of the Siamese Twin Brothers."

9. "The Siamese Twins," *Mechanics Free Press* (Philadelphia), March 12, 1831, and April 9, 1831; "Commercial," *Virginia Free Press* (Charlestown), March 10, 1831, reprinted from the *Philadelphia Gazette*; [Classified advertisement], *Baltimore Patriot*, April 25, 1831; "Siamese United Twin Brothers," *Baltimore Patriot*, May 10, 1831; "Siamese Twins," *Connecticut Courant*, June 21, 1831.

10. Hunter apparently sold his interest in the twins after the England tour.

11. Slack, "The Siamese Boys, or a Lusus Naturae," *Rhode Island American*, September 15, 1829; "The Siamese Twins," *Christian Watchman* 12 (December 9, 1831), 198; "Siamese Twins," *Baltimore Patriot*, May 7, 1831.

12. Unless otherwise noted, the following discussion is based on this *New York Constellation* article, reprinted in the *Macon Telegraph*, June 25, 1831.

13. Scholars of Asian America have shown how Orientalist discourse has commonly transformed Asians and Asian Americans into children who need the guidance

of mature white Americans. Studies that have applied this insight to the twins include Tchen, *New York before Chinatown*; Lee, *Orientals*; and Okihiro, *Common Ground*.

14. "Very Much Alike," *Atkinson's Saturday Evening Post*, July 9, 1831; *Republican Star*, November 29, 1831; "To Correspondents," *Ariel* 5 (April 30, 1831), 16.

15. Hale to Susan A. Coffin, July 24, 1831, Hale and Coffin Papers, Clements Library Special Collections, University of Michigan.

16. The earliest report apparently was in the *Salem Mercury*, which I have not located. On August 4, 1831, the *Essex Register* of Salem, Massachusetts, and the *Boston Patriot and Mercantile Advertiser* each published accounts informed by the *Mercury* report.

17. "Commonwealth vs. Chang and Eng," *Boston Patriot and Mercantile Advertiser*, August 4, 1831, and "Siamese Twins," *Essex Register* (Salem, MA), August 4, 1831.

18. *Essex Democrat*, August 5, 1831, and *Lynn Mirror*, August 6, 1831, both of Lynn, Massachusetts; "Siamese Twins," *Connecticut Mirror*, August 13, 1831.

19. Harris to Davis, January 7, 1832, Twins Papers, NCSA.

20. Harris to Davis, April 11, 1832, Twins Papers, NCSA; photocopy of the contract reproduced from the *Winston-Salem Journal*, August 6, 1977, Twins Papers, NCSA. Contrary to the reference to "parents," the twins' father died in 1819. Their mother did take another husband, though it is not clear when.

21. Wallace and Wallace, *The Two*, 44; Harris to Davis, April 11, 1832, Twins Papers, NCSA. Of course, the question might still remain in some minds, *Didn't* their mother sell them? After all, she did receive money and sent her sons off with the man who paid for them. While I see this more as the twins and their family entering into a contract and receiving a signing bonus, so to speak, some of my readers have seen this as a clear example of buying and selling. Historian Benjamin Reiss shows that there is room for distinction, however. Does the proprietor own the person or simply the rights to exhibit that person? Writing about the exhibition of Joice Heth, an elderly black slave woman placed on exhibit by P. T. Barnum in 1835 as the former nurse to George Washington, Reiss argues that if Barnum was not "exactly her owner," then he was "for a time certainly her master." The point I am attempting to make here, though, is that regardless of whether the twins' mother sold them or not, it pained them to have people believe she did; they did not think this was an appropriate topic for public discourse. This viewpoint may have been entirely self-interested; they did not want people to think of them as having been bought and sold, either for the shame of it or for the complications such a perception held for their legal and social status. For whatever reason, they felt this topic should be off-limits. See Reiss, *The Showman and the Slave*, 23–27.

22. This "Letter from the Siamese Twins" was dated February 1, 1832, and signed "your absent Chang Eng." It was reprinted in the *Workingman's Advocate*, March 10, 1832, and the *Providence Patriot*, March 24, 1832.

23. "To the Public," *Essex Register*, August 15, 1831; "Siamese Twins," *Connecticut Mirror*, August 13, 1831; *Salem (MA) Gazette*, October 25, 1831; Hale to Harris, September 14, 1831, Chatham Papers, NCSA; *New London (CT) Gazette*, August 31, 1831; *New York Spectator*, August 30, 1831; Cutter, *Historic Homes and Places*, 665.

24. "To the Public," *Essex Register*, August 15, 1831; Vinton, *The Vinton Memorial*, 231–32.

25. Cutter, *Historic Homes and Places*, 665.

26. "To the Public," *Essex Register*, August 15, 1831.

27. "Siamese Twins," *New-York Commercial Advertiser*, May 27, 1831, emphasis in original; letter to the editor, *New-York Commercial Advertiser*, May 31, 1831, emphasis in original; "Peale's Museum," *New-York Commercial Advertiser*, June 1, 1831; "Hale vs. Howe," *Boston Courier*, June 3, 1832.

28. Hale to Davis, September 7, 1831, Twins Papers, NCSA.

29. Hale to Harris, March 18, 1832, Chatham Papers, NCSA.

30. Felix Pascalis, "The Siamese Boys—Homo Duplex," *Morning Courier and New-York Enquirer*, September 22, 1829; reprinted as "Siamese Twins," *Bristol Mercury*, May 10, 1831.

31. Abel Coffin to Susan Coffin, January 8, 1831, September 2, 1831, and October 25, 1831, Twins Papers, NCSA.

32. Abel Coffin to Susan Coffin, January 8, 1831; Chang Eng to Davis, July 4, 1832, both in Twins Papers, NCSA.

33. *New-York Constellation*'s "Dialogue between the Siamese Twins and a Visitor," reprinted in the *Macon Telegraph*, June 25, 1831, and "Letter from the Siamese Twins," reprinted in the *Workingman's Advocate*, March 10, 1832, and the *Providence Patriot*, March 24, 1832; Chang Eng to William Davis, July 4, 1832, Twins Papers, NCSA.

34. Bhabha, "Of Mimicry and Man."

35. "Siamese Twins," *Essex Register*, August 4, 1831.

36. "The Lynnfield Battle," *Columbian Centinel*, August 17, 1831.

37. Ibid.

38. I wonder if James Hale wrote the report. Although it does refer to "Mr. Hale" in the third person and disavows any close tie to the twins, it is decidedly favorable to their cause, it engages in hyperbole that is not uncommon in Hale's writing, and its use of the "battle" at Lynnfield resembles a turn of phrase later used by Hale in reference to the incident. There are other reasons to suggest that he did not write it, however. First, although he was quick to respond to stories painting the twins in a bad light, and he would do this for the rest of his life, he usually signed his own name. Second, the final paragraph—which I have not yet discussed—presents a caricature of the twins that would have been out of character for Hale.

39. Abel Coffin to Susan Coffin, September 2, 1831, Twins Papers, NCSA; Owen, "Letter No. 16, to Amos Gilbert," *Free Enquirer*, April 14, 1832; *Boston Investigator*, July 27, 1832.

40. On "Negrophobia," see Richards, *"Gentlemen of Property and Standing,"* 30–43. My discussion is also informed by Grimsted, *American Mobbing*, and Melish, *Disowning Slavery*.

41. On this episode, see Cohen, "Passing the Torch," 572, 579.

42. See testimony and cross-examination of Elbridge Gerry and Edward Phelps, *Trial of John R. Buzzell*, 30–32, and *The Charlestown Convent*, 39. The latter book notes that Gerry "described [the proceedings on the night of the fire] a little more methodically than most of the witnesses who were called to the stand were able to do" (39).

43. Cohen, "Passing the Torch," 532.

44. The only reproduction of the entire article that I have seen appeared in the *Baltimore Patriot*, August 20, 1831.

45. See, for example, the *Daily National Intelligencer* (Washington, DC), August 22, 1831; *Maryland Gazette* (Annapolis), August 25, 1831; *Dover (NH) Gazette and Strafford Advertiser*, August 30, 1831; *Raleigh Register and North-Carolina Gazette*, September 1, 1831; *Connecticut Mirror* (Hartford), September 3, 1831; and the *Liberator* (Boston), September 3, 1831.

46. "Siamese Logic," *Atkinson's Saturday Evening Post*, August 27, 1831.

47. The initial article in the *Exeter News Letter* was reprinted in the *Globe* of Washington, DC, October 10, 1831; the *Rhode-Island American* of Providence, October 14, 1831; and the *Virginia Free Press and Farmers' Repository* of Charlestown, October 20, 1831, among others.

48. "An Expostulary Ode to the Siamese Twins," *Philadelphia Album and Ladies' Literary Portfolio* 7 (December 7, 1833), 392. For reports of the Ohio incident, information from the *Warren (OH) News Letter*, July 2, 1833, was reproduced in the *Globe* (Washington, DC), July 9, 1833; the *Salem (MA) Gazette*, July 16, 1833; and the *Lynchburg Virginian*, July 18, 1833, among others.

49. The initial report was published in the *Athenian*; reprints appeared in the *Boston Courier*, November 21, 1833; *Atkinson's Saturday Evening Post*, November 23, 1833; the *Vermont Patriot and State Gazette* (Montpelier), November 26, 1833; and the *Fayetteville (NC) Observer*, December 3, 1833, among others.

50. Harris, "The Siamese Twins, from the Florence Gazette," *Morning Chronicle* (London, England), December 24, 1833.

51. Ibid.

52. Ibid. While other reports clearly took information from this letter, none included the attempts at negotiation that occurred before the fight actually broke out, instead skipping from the initial challenge directly to the fight.

53. Historians have written about ritualized violence in the South—dueling—in great depth. See Greenberg, *Honor and Slavery*, 51–86; Wyatt-Brown, *Southern Honor*, 349–61; and Gorn, "Gouge and Bite."

54. The relationship between Chang, Eng, Hale, and Harris, on the one hand, and Susan Coffin, on the other, deserves more consideration than I have room for here. Just as I argue that race played a tremendous role in marginalizing or diminishing the impact of the twins' voice, gender certainly had an impact on the ways in which these four men dealt with Abel Coffin's wife and how she dealt with them. As the following analysis will show, the twins made several attempts to make rational arguments to Susan Coffin on a variety of subjects, and she apparently either ignored or slighted them. I focus my analysis on the twins' reaction to this, how they understood her perceived rejection. In short, there appears to be a gendered perception of irrationality on the parts of Chang, Eng, Hale, and even Harris. The question that would reward consideration—but which is not asked here—is, What constraints did Susan Coffin believe she was acting under? As the wife of a sea captain, she certainly was accustomed to handling the family's business while he was away. But had these responsibilities in the past required her to manage personnel of any sort? After all, attempting to oversee a touring troupe full of strong characters is quite different from managing a household.

55. Chang Eng to Susan Coffin, December 22, 1831; Harris to Davis, January 8, 1832; Harris to Davis, January 16, 1832, all in Twins Papers, NCSA. Mrs. Coffin also instructed Harris not to pay them unless he absolutely had to.

56. Harris to Davis, January 9, 1832; Harris to Davis, January 16, 1832; Harris to Davis, April 11, 1832, all in Twins Papers, NCSA. Letters signed by the twins might have been addressed to Mrs. Coffin or Davis. Per his contract, and likely in response to the fallout between Hale and Mrs. Coffin, letters from Harris were always to Davis. Similarly, all letters from Newburyport, of which we have none but to which Harris and the twins constantly referred, were supposed to be from Davis to Harris. During this period, Susan Coffin was not writing letters to her husband, or perhaps I should say he was not receiving any. In letters to her from Surabaya in present-day Indonesia, Captain Coffin asked again and again why she had not written. There is the possibility that letters from her were not making it to him. See Correspondence from Abel Coffin to Susan Coffin, 1831–1832, Twins Papers, NCSA.

57. Harris to Davis, December 6, 1831; Chang Eng to Susan Coffin, December 22, 1831; Hale to Harris and the Siamese Twins, March 18, 1832; Abel Coffin to Susan Coffin, September 2, 1831, and March 21, 1832, all in Twins Papers, NCSA.

58. Harris to Davis, April 11, 1832; Harris to Davis, April 30, 1832, both in Twins Papers, NCSA.

59. Chang Eng to Davis, May 29, 1832, Twins Papers, NCSA.

60. Chang Eng to Davis, May 29, June 15, July 4, and July 11, 1832, Twins Papers, NCSA.

61. Chang Eng to Davis, June 15 and July 11, 1832, Twins Papers, NCSA.

62. Chang Eng to Davis, July 11, 1832, Twins Papers, NCSA. The emphasis is in the original, as is the repetition of the phrase "Gentleman from Newbury Port," suggesting irony on the part of the twins. The ledger to which they refer is unaccounted for.

63. Chang Eng to Davis, July 11, 1832, Twins Papers, NCSA.

64. Chang Eng to Davis, July 4, 1832, Twins Papers, NCSA.

65. Harris to Davis, July 1832, Twins Papers, NCSA.

66. Hale to Harris and Chang-Eng, November 4, 1832, Chatham Papers, NCSA; Abel Coffin to Susan Coffin, October 5, 1832, Twins Papers, NCSA.

67. Hale to Harris and Chang-Eng, November 4, 1832, Chatham Papers, NCSA. Hale did not believe Coffin's story. "It *cannot* have been so, for he is *yet alive*," he wrote; in other words, if the captain had engaged the twins in a physical contest, the twins would have won, easily. Emphasis in original.

68. Abel Coffin to Susan Coffin, October 5, 1832, Twins Papers, NCSA.

69. "The Siamese Twins," *Salem (MA) Gazette*, March 5, 1833.

70. Owen, "Letter No. 16," *Free Enquirer*, April 14, 1832. See also the *Boston Investigator*, July 27, 1832.

71. Hone, *Diary of Philip Hone*, March 15, 1831, 28; Feudge, "The Siamese Twins in Their Own Land," 382; "The State Journal and Siamese Twins," *Vermont Patriot and State Gazette* (Montpelier), August 17, 1835; S. D. Bumpass to Frances Bumpass, August 23, 1847, Bumpass Family Papers, SHC.

72. "The New Year," *Western Monthly Magazine* 3 (January 1834), 46; *New Hampshire Sentinel* (Keene), September 11, 1834.

73. Hale to Chang Eng and Harris, May 17, 1833, Chatham Papers, NCSA.

74. Hale to Harris and Chang-Eng, November 14, 1832, Chatham Papers, NCSA, emphasis in original.

75. Hale to Chang Eng and Harris, May 17, 1833, Chatham Papers, NCSA.

76. Hale, *An Historical Account of the Siamese Twin Brothers*, 8; Tchen, *New York before Chinatown*, 109–10.

77. [Hale], *A Few Particulars concerning Chang-Eng*, 1.

78. Ibid., 1–7.

79. Ibid., 7, 11.

80. Pingree argues that these exhibition booklets, which juxtaposed the parlance of the day, referring to the twins as "united brothers" or "united twins," with the symbolism of the American eagle with an "E Pluribus Unum" banner in its beak, were playing to political concerns of the period. "Even as the twins' bond was appropriated by a unionist enterprise that urged fusion of the states, it also posed an alternative interpretation—that connecting the states too closely was 'monstrous' and excessive." See Pingree, "America's 'United Siamese Brothers,'" 94–95.

81. See the *New-Bedford (MA) Mercury*, March 16, 1838; *Pennsylvania Inquirer* (Philadelphia), April 10, 1838; and *Daily National Intelligencer* (Washington, DC), May 1, 1838, for excerpts of Ruschenberger's *Voyage Round the World*. See also Smithies, *Two Yankee Diplomats in 1830s Siam*, 125–227.

82. *New Bern Spectator*, November 30, 1838; *Pittsfield (MA) Sun*, December 27, 1838; "The Captives of the Amistad," *Emancipator* (New York), October 3, 1839, quoting the *Connecticut Observer* of September 28, 1839.

83. Wu, *Chang and Eng Reconnected*, 30.

Chapter Three

1. See Mitchell, *Diary of a Geological Tour*, for a discussion of Wilkes County's landscape. The 1840 census provides information on the agriculture products grown in the county. For a discussion of the anxieties of Wilkes's pioneering generation, see Shrader, "William Lenoir, 1751–1839," 206–8.

2. Joan E. Cashin has dealt with both Wilkes County and the larger seaboard context in *A Family Venture*.

3. Brown, "The Emergence of Urban Society"; Melish, *Disowning Slavery*; Takaki, *Iron Cages*.

4. In addition to the twins and Harris, the traveling party by this time included a man named George Prendergast, who handled day-to-day affairs, and Peter Marsh. For their troubles, Prendergast earned eighteen dollars per month and Marsh earned sixteen. Harris, the business manager, earned fifty dollars each month, the same payment he had received from the Coffins. These payments stopped once the twins settled in North Carolina, and Prendergast and Marsh disappeared from the historical record. See An Account of Money Expended by Chang-Eng, Chang and Eng Bunker Papers, SHC.

5. Interestingly, the twins met with a Raleigh attorney for a "legal opinion" on December 24, 1838. Such a consultation was very rare, even unique. The meeting

could have been about anything, about any minutiae concerning exhibition in North Carolina, for instance. But given that the twins had not engaged a lawyer (on the books) anywhere else in their travels, including earlier visits to North Carolina, and given their retirement six months later, it is reasonable to guess that they were planning ahead and inquiring about such things as the legal logistics of landownership and citizenship in the state. An Account of Money Expended by Chang-Eng and Account of Money Received by Chang-Eng, 1833–1839, both in Chang and Eng Bunker Papers, SHC.

6. Moreheid, *Lives, Adventures, Anecdotes, Amusements, and Domestic Habits*, 14; Graves, "The Siamese Twins," 13; Dugger, *Romance of the Siamese Twins*, 12.

7. For a discussion of the "Rip Van Winkle" state, as well as an attempt to place the state in a larger context, see Lefler and Newsome, *North Carolina*. As for the South, the perspective offered here is a nod toward approaches taken by James Oakes, John C. Inscoe, and Jonathan Daniel Wells, each of whom has done much to place the South squarely in the nation's emerging capitalist economy. See Oakes, *The Ruling Race*; Inscoe, *Mountain Masters*; and Wells, *Origins of the Southern Middle Class*. For a different interpretation that posits a precapitalist South dominated by a prebourgeois slaveholding class, see Genovese, *The Political Economy of Slavery*.

8. Dugger, *Romance of the Siamese Twins*, 8. Two points about this specific encounter between Chang and Eng and Calloway are clearly wrong. First, in spring 1839, when Dugger claims the meeting took place, the twins were on tour in Georgia and North Carolina, not in New York. Second, he claims the twins were on exhibit at Barnum's Museum, which had not yet opened. In the spring of 1837, the twins did receive visitors at Peale's Museum in New York for several months.

9. *Carolina Watchman* (Salisbury, NC), December 24, 1842; M.L.F. [Martha Lenoir Finley] to Caroline L. Gordon, December 18, 1842, Gordon-Hackett Papers, SHC; Robert C. Martin to Chang and Eng Bunker, January 27, 1848, Chang and Eng Bunker Papers, SHC.

10. See M.L.F. to Caroline L. Gordon, December 18, 1842, Gordon-Hackett Papers, SHC; Powell, *Dictionary of North Carolina Biography*, 307–8; James Gwyn to Mary Ann Gwyn, July 21, 1839, Gwyn Papers, SHC.

11. On the Lenoirs, see Shrader, "William Lenoir, 1751–1839," and the entry for Thomas Lenoir in the 1840 U.S. Federal Census, Stewart's District, Wilkes County, NC. (Unless otherwise noted, population schedules were accessed through Ancestry.com.)

12. On the decision to settle in Wilkes, Graves writes that "partly from their [the twins'] own inclination and partly at the insistence of their old and long tried friend, the Doctor [Harris], it was determined they would spend an indefinite time in that retreat." Graves, "The Siamese Twins," 13.

13. On court bonds, see Wilkes County Criminal Action Papers, NCSA; correspondence between James Gwyn and Charles Harris mentions such other notable county residents as General Horton, P. J. L. Finley, J. L. Bryan, Major Little Hickerson, Colonel Mitchell, and the Reverend Colby Sparks. See letters of December 19, 1843, October 18, 1844, and December 20 [no year], Gwyn Papers, SHC. On his appointment as postmaster, see Hale to Harris, May 12, 1843, Chatham Papers, NCSA. Hale also entered the postal business, campaigning for cheaper postage. In the 1840s, he formed a letter

delivery company that competed directly with the U.S. government. The United States took him to court and won, but it also lowered its postal rates.

14. Chang-Eng, Declaration for Naturalization, Superior Court, Fall Term 1839, Siamese Twins Papers, NCSA. The Wilkes County Superior Court Minute Docket, 1830–1849, NCSA, has entries for both the twins' and Harris's applications. In this docket, the (single) entry for the twins immediately precedes that of Harris; their proceedings are dated simply "October 1839" and "Fall Term 1839," whereas Harris's bears the date of October 12, 1839. The October 12 entry in their expense account does list a fee paid to Colonel Mitchell, who served as the twins' attorney in Wilkes County in other matters, which suggests they did take this step at the same time as Harris. A newspaper account reported that the twins made their application on a Saturday, which corresponds to the Harris application (see "The Siamese Twins," *Carolina Watchman* [Salisbury, NC], November 1, 1839).

15. Tchen, *New York before Chinatown*, 76, 230.

16. My discussion of wealth or economic standing relies heavily on slaveholding data. The practical reason for this is simply that the most complete source of data for this period, the 1840 federal census, offers a wealth of information with respect to the slaveholdings of individual households but nothing with respect to individual land-holdings or other sources of personal wealth. Unlike the 1850 or 1860 census, the 1840 census lists only the name of the head of household and offers the number of people living in each household, categorized by sex, race, and status (free or slave). For a lengthy discussion of slaveholding as a marker of economic success, see Cashin, *A Family Venture*, 123.

17. 1840 U.S. Federal Census, Stewart's District, Wilkes County, NC. In 1841, much of this district became part of the new Caldwell County, which the state carved from southwestern Wilkes County and northern Burke County. While this had an impact on aggregate measures of the wealth of Wilkes County in later years, in practice many of the commercial and personal relationships continued, certainly throughout the period under consideration here.

In the 1840 census, districts took their name from the person charged with collecting data for that district, and not from any name related to place or geography. (The exception is Wilkesboro.) In this census, Wilkes County had sixteen districts, with a total population of 12,577, and 1,965 households. Districts ranged in population size from 354 (Wilkesboro) to 1,214 (Wheeler's District, west of Wilkesboro). I can only approximate the actual locations of most of these districts, either using geographic notations made in the margins of the census data or cross-listing census records with county tax records, which included more elaborate descriptions of property location.

18. 1840 U.S. Federal Census, Martin's District, Wilkes County, NC; Wilkes County Tax List, no district, no date, 1841–1848, NCSA.

19. It is possible I am making too much of these family connections. The concentration of slaveholdings among a handful of families such as these is more evidence of the wealth of their forebears rather than a conglomerate at this point in 1840. After all, it was the very breakup of larger land- and slaveholdings among offspring that resulted in smaller and poorer farms in North Carolina during this period and the migration of

large numbers to the Old Southwest, as Cashin has shown. Nevertheless, these numbers do put the district's slaveholdings in a clearer perspective.

20. Baugus's categorization as an agriculturalist is more evidence of the shortcomings of census data. He, as well as others—including the twins—clearly engaged in various forms of commerce, although the census is silent on these. The only person involved in commerce according to the census is the district's namesake, Joseph Spicer. Over time and in different documents, the name "Baugus" has alternatively been spelled "Bauguss" and "Bauguess."

21. Graves says that the twins' hunting and fishing excursions introduced them to the area, but, as does any assertion that sport attracted them, this conclusion begs the question, Why this spot in particular? As the twins' exhibition booklets and their expense accounts make clear, Chang and Eng regularly visited natural wonders—such as New York's Niagara Falls and Virginia's Natural Bridge—when their travels brought them into the vicinity.

22. Caleb Martin to Chang Eng the Siamese Twin Brothers, Wilkes County Record of Deeds, vol. 23, p. 490, NCSA.

23. See Account of Money Expended, General store account book, circa 1840, Chang and Eng Bunker Papers, SHC; Chang-Eng to Robert Hunter, November 15, 1842, published in Hunter, *Duet for a Lifetime*, 80.

24. Graves, "The Siamese Twins," 14; Account of Money Expended, Chang and Eng Bunker Papers, SHC; Wilkes County Tax Lists, 1778–1888, Caudill's District, no date, NCSA.

25. "The Siamese Twins," *Carolina Watchman* (Salisbury, NC), November 1, 1839. The *Fayetteville (NC) Observer*, November 6, 1839, reprinted most of the *Watchman* article. Charles Harris, James Hale, or the twins were apparently in communication also with the *New York Gazette*, which became the source for other reports. See *North American* (Philadelphia), November 9, 1839; *Connecticut Courant* (Hartford), November 16, 1839; *Virginia Free Press* (Charlestown), November 21, 1839; and *Indiana Journal* (Indianapolis), November 23, 1839, among others. The *Transcript* (Boston) called the twins "happy as lords," as reported by the *Liberator* (Boston), July 24, 1840, and *Fayetteville (NC) Observer*, July 29, 1840. I intend this list of newspapers, carrying for the most part the same information, to illustrate the scope of interest. In this story and in others afterward, papers around the country followed the twins' lives closely, even after they had retired from the public eye.

26. "Double Farmers," *New-Yorker*, November 23, 1839; *Haverville (MA) Gazette*, July 25, 1840; "A Knotty Question in Prospective," *Vermont Patriot* (Montpelier), December 30, 1839, reprinting an article from the *Philadelphia Gazette*; *New Hampshire Sentinel* (Keene), July 22, 1840.

27. As Graves posits in "The Siamese Twins," 13.

28. As Wallace and Wallace suggest, misreading Graves, in *The Two*, 166.

29. See Graves, "The Siamese Twins," 14, and Wallace and Wallace, *The Two*, 166–68. To illustrate this encounter, however, the Wallaces offer an extended repartee between the twins and the sisters taken from Dugger's *Romance of the Siamese Twins*, another misreading. Dugger placed the initial meeting at an exhibition of the twins in Wilkesboro (8–10). The frequent misreading of Dugger, Graves, and other sources

by the Wallaces provides a vivid illustration of why *The Two*, in every sense a popular biography whose purpose is to narrate a lively story, needs to be read with caution, the very impressive research that the book features notwithstanding.

30. North Carolina General Assembly, *Laws of the State of North Carolina*, 33. The impetus behind this legislation is not clear—it certainly had nothing to do with the twins' decision to settle in the state that same year—and it served only to reinforce regulations that were already on the books. A 1741 statute fined any white man or woman who married "an Indian, negro, mustee or mulatto man or woman, or any person of mixed race to the third generation." A second 1741 statute forbade any minister or justice of the peace from performing any such marriage. See North Carolina General Assembly, *Revised Statutes*, 386–87.

31. *Carolina Watchman* (Salisbury, NC), April 3, 1840; *Raleigh Register*, February 9, 1841; *Fayetteville (NC) Observer*, February 15, 1843; M.L.F. to Caroline L. Gordon, December 18, 1842, Gordon-Hackett Papers, SHC; James Gwyn to Mary Ann Gwyn, September 26, 1841, Gwyn Papers, SHC.

32. Charles Harris, Marriage Bond, October, 31, 1839, Wilkes County Marriage Bonds, NCSA; Johnson, *Ante-Bellum North Carolina*, 203–4. For specific examples in just a short span of time, see proceedings against Taylor Burris and Sarah Benge/Burris and against John and Nancy Gilreath/Whittington, Wilkes County Criminal Action Papers, 1841–42, Folder: Criminal—1842 (folders 2–4), NCSA.

33. This does not rule out the possibility of a miscarriage, a stillbirth, or a child who died in infancy. Almost three years passed between the marriage and the firstborn child, perhaps an indication of one of these occurrences. On bastardy, see Johnson, *Ante-Bellum North Carolina*, 657–58. For the act, see North Carolina General Assembly, *Laws of the State of North Carolina*, 33. For deliberations on this act and one bill that did not pass, see General Assembly Session Records, Nov. 1838–Jan. 1839, House Bills, Dec. 4–14, 1838, and House Bills, Dec. 15–21, 1838, NCSA.

34. Carpenter, *John Yates (1712–1779) and His Descendants to 1989*. Bunker family records are consistent on these dates. Census data taken in 1850 and afterward are much more elastic. The 1850 census, for instance, lists Sarah as 27 and Adelaide as 22; in 1860, Sarah was 40, Adelaide 37; in 1870, Sarah was 47 and Adelaide was 43; in 1880, Sarah was 56 and Adelaide was 57.

35. Wilkes County Tax Lists, 1829, Call's District, NCSA; David Yates entries in the 1830 U.S. Federal Census, Wilkes County, NC, and the 1840 U.S. Federal Census, Shumate's District, Wilkes County, NC.

36. Wilkes County Criminal Action Papers, 1838–1840, Folder: Criminal—1840 (folder 2), NCSA.

37. For the bastardy case against Alston Yates (sometimes spelled "Austen"), see Wilkes County Bastardy Bonds and records, 1840 folder, and Wilkes County Criminal Action Papers, 1841–1842, Folder: Criminal—1841 (folders 1, 2, and 3), NCSA; 1840 U.S. Federal Census, Shumate's District, Wilkes County, NC.

38. As historian Victoria E. Bynum writes, an indictment for fornication and adultery "might simply reflect feuding among members of a community. Many people routinely used the courts to punish and embarrass each other." See Bynum, *Unruly Women*, 98. I have examined fornication and adultery cases from 1835 through 1844.

To place the quantity of Wilkes cases in context, for this ten-year period, I have identified thirty-four cases in the criminal action papers. For the ten-year period from 1850 to 1860, Bynum's study of sexual misconduct in three Piedmont counties identified twenty-one such cases in Granville County, forty-three in Orange County, and five in Montgomery County. (There are problems with making these comparisons between different periods of time.)

I must emphasize that my interest is not in "actual" incidents of illicit sex; rather I am reading the criminal action papers to get a sense for *how* these cases played out. Who was being charged? Who was making these charges? Who was called to testify, for prosecution and for defense? What did this information suggest about community dynamics? My exploration into the roles that accusations of illicit sex played in community dynamics suggests two relevant points. First, allegations of adultery and fornication and bastardy allowed community members to pursue grievances, often against their neighbors, that might have nothing to do with sex. Second, allegations of illicit sex, or relationships that were contested as illegitimate, often were accompanied by violence, sometimes neighbor against neighbor, sometimes against body, sometimes against property.

39. Wilkes County Criminal Action Papers, 1841–1842, Folder: Criminal—1841 (folder 1), NCSA; Wilkes County School Census, 1841, NCSA.

40. Bolton, "Statement of the Principal Circumstances respecting the United Siamese Twins," 184–85; Tucker, "On the Siamese Twins," 250–54; Sophonia Robinson to Chang and Eng, September 15, 1831, Siamese Twins Collection, Mount Airy Museum of Regional History. I have not found any other information about Robinson.

41. *Virginia Free Press* (Charlestown), November 27, 1834; *New Hampshire Sentinel* (Keene), December 18, 1834; *Virginia Free Press*, January 5, 1837; *Fayetteville (NC) Observer*, February 9, 1837; *New Hampshire Sentinel* (Keene), February 2, 1837; "A Word or Two with Chang, the Siamese Twin," *London Dispatch*, March 12, 1837.

42. The *New York Mirror* and the *Boston Post* apparently offered the details. Newspapers that picked up these stories included the *Mississippian*, June 8, 1838, and the *Macon Georgia Telegraph*, July 23, 1838. For a discussion of Afong Moy, see Tchen, *New York before Chinatown*, 101–6.

43. Graves, "The Siamese Twins," 17; Tchen, *New York before Chinatown*; *Liverpool Mercury*, January 22, 1830; *New York Spectator*, November 28, 1833; *Virginia Free Press*, December 5, 1833. Okihiro's *Common Ground* introduces the themes of attraction and repulsion with respect to the twins, and Tchen's *New York before Chinatown* explicates America's consumption of "Oriental" goods and bodies.

44. This speculation was published in the *Arkansas Gazette* (Little Rock), December 18, 1833.

45. Printed in the *Whig* (Jonesborough, TN), October 21, 1840; *Cleveland Daily Herald*, November 24, 1840; *Virginia Free Press* (Charlestown), November 26, 1840.

46. Reports of their naturalization and purchase of a farm began in the *Carolina Watchman* (Salisbury, NC), November 1, 1839, and spread rapidly to newspapers around the country.

47. *New England Weekly Review* (Hartford, CT), January 30, 1841, citing the *Baltimore Clipper*. It is also possible that this tale of unrequited love was true. Later reports

relate a similar story about this period in time, complete with names and other details. For example, see *Greenville (SC) Mountaineer*, July 14, 1848.

48. Letter, Chang-Eng to Robert Hunter, November 15, 1842, published in Hunter, *Duet for a Lifetime*, 80.

49. Hodes has made a useful distinction between "toleration" and "tolerance": "*tolerance* implies a liberal spirit toward those of a different mind; *toleration* by contrast suggests a measure of forbearance for that which is not approved." She applies the latter term to describe the attitudes of southern whites toward sexual relationships between white women and black men in the antebellum South. See *White Women, Black Men*, 3.

50. The discussion here will *not* answer two questions, primarily of individual motive, that observers then and now have found so compelling: Why did Chang and Eng choose these two women? And why did Adelaide and Sarah marry these two men? Unlike the attempt to reclaim the "voice" of the twins, in which the challenge for historians is gauging the reliability of sources that claim to speak for the twins, the obstacle here is the utter lack of evidence that allows us to get inside the heads of the brothers or the sisters. In no extant document do Chang or Eng discuss their selection of mates or their marriage. Sarah and Adelaide do not appear in the historical record until their weddings, and they remain almost entirely voiceless the remainder of their lives.

51. See Graves, "The Siamese Twins," and Dugger, *Romance of the Siamese Twins*.

52. Hunter, *Duet for a Lifetime*, 81–87; the quotations are on pages 85 and 86.

53. Joffre Bunker eventually donated his collection to the Southern Historical Collection at the University of North Carolina at Chapel Hill. The possibility that the story did come from a family member, perhaps as oral history passed along from generation to generation, would not preclude its being apocryphal; long after the twins' deaths, newspaper interviews with some of their children include demonstrably false claims about Chang and Eng. See, for example, "Siamese Twin's Son Dependent," Clippings Folder, in Chang and Eng Bunker Papers, SHC, and Dugger, *Romance of the Siamese Twins*, 13. I have searched published reports from the twins' deaths in 1874 to 1964 and have found no such tale, although I cannot rule out the possibility that this story originated in a press account.

54. Wallace and Wallace, *The Two*, 173.

55. Although Hunter does not reference Graves's biography, some similarities lead me to believe it influenced her account. It is possible that Graves's manuscript influenced the story told to her by relatives.

56. Graves, "The Siamese Twins," 17. The finding guide at the North Carolina State Archives suggests that this biography was "as told to" Graves by the twins. The Wallaces share this assumption. It is only prudent, however, to note that Graves wrote the biography shortly after the twins' death, in 1874, a time when there was a very different racial landscape from that of the 1840s.

57. Okihiro, *Common Ground*, 74; Pingree, "America's 'United Siamese Brothers'"; Clark and Myser, "Being Humaned."

58. Hodes has written about the shortcomings of legal evidence when it comes to documenting hints of sexual improprieties across racial lines. See Hodes, *White Women, Black Men*, 11–14.

59. Wilkes County Marriage Bonds, NCSA; Marriage License and Certificate, private collection.

60. Moreheid, *Lives, Adventures, Anecdotes, Amusements, and Domestic Habits*, 23. The name of the officiating clergy published here is James L. Davis and not Colby Sparks. This discrepancy is noteworthy and a bit puzzling because of the lengths to which the twins and the Yates family went to ensure that the wedding appeared legitimate, meeting all the necessary forms that such a ceremony should take.

61. *Carolina Watchman* (Salisbury, NC), April 29, 1843; *Louisville Journal*, as quoted in the *Milwaukee Sentinel*, May 27, 1843; *Constitution* (Middletown, CT), May 3, 1843, quoting the *New York Express; Vermont Gazette* (Bennington), May 3, 1843, quoting the *New York Commercial*.

62. "Recent Southern Scenes," *Emancipator and Free American*, May 18, 1843; "Marriage Extraordinary," *Liberator*, May 12, 1843.

63. See Walters, "The Erotic South."

64. For the argument that "Negrophobia" and the fear of amalgamation fueled anti-abolitionist sentiment—and riots—see Richards, *"Gentlemen of Property and Standing,"* 30–32, 40–46, and Lemire, *"Miscegenation,"* 55–70, 87–99. Linda Kerber makes the argument that the amalgamation rhetoric masked economic fears in "Abolitionists and Amalgamators."

65. Lemire, *"Miscegenation,"* 82–83; Walters, "The Erotic South," 181, 186; Allen, *The American Prejudice against Color.*

66. *Weekly Raleigh Register and North Carolina Gazette*, October 11, 1844, citing the South Carolina *Spartan.*

67. *New-York Spectator*, August 29, 1829, citing the *Boston Daily Advertiser.*

68. Wyatt-Brown, *Southern Honor*, 440–53; quotations on 440, 447.

69. Hale to Harris, May 12, 1843, emphasis in original; Hale to Harris, July 27, 1843, both in Chatham Papers, NCSA.

70. "The Siamese Twins at Home," *Trumpet and Universalist Magazine*, November 2, 1850.

71. His abuse of her would escalate and eventually lead Letha to initiate divorce proceedings, highly unusual in the mid-nineteenth century. See Letha Baugus v. Samuel Baugus, Wilkes County Divorce Records, 1820–1912, NCSA.

72. Wallace and Wallace, *The Two*, 175.

73. A. F. Hackett to R. F. Hackett, October 20, 1844, Gordon-Hackett Papers, SHC.

74. In the only 1844 communication between the two men, Hale let Harris know that he was not the only one having difficulty with the twins. "From all I can learn, they have ceased corresponding with *all* their former friends," Hale wrote, including their close acquaintance Fred Bunker, whose last name they adopted. Hale to Harris, March 14, 1844, Chatham Papers, NCSA.

Chapter Four

1. *Raleigh Register*, April 13, 1853.

2. "An Inquiry," *National Era*, January 18, 1855.

3. The quotation marks around "Asian" and "American" are meant, first, to signify that these are contested terms; there is not now, nor has there ever been, a single definition for either of these terms on which everyone can agree.

4. Lord, "Missionaries, Thai, and Diplomats"; Bhongbhibhat, Reynolds, and Polpatpicharn, *The Eagle and the Elephant*, 7–23; Bhamorabutr, *The Story of American Missionaries*.

5. "Siamese Mission: Extract from the Journal of the Rev. W. P. Buell," *Christian Advocate and Journal* 19 (April 2, 1845), 135; "Siam: Missionary Excursion of Mr. Hemenway," *Missionary Herald* 40 (December 1844), 401–3.

6. See, for example, a letter from the Reverend Samuel R. House in Siam to the Twins in North Carolina, dated January 29, 1849, and reproduced in Graves, "The Siamese Twins." This information is consistent with other documents. For instance, the contract between Chang and Eng and Robert Hunter was signed by the twins in Chinese characters, but playful banter in letters between the twins and James W. Hale is written in transliterated Siamese.

7. "Siam: Missionary Excursion of Mr. Hemenway," *Missionary Herald* 40 (December 1844), 403.

8. "Siamese Mission: Extract from the Journal of the Rev. W. P. Buell," *Christian Advocate and Journal* 19 (April 2, 1845), 135; "Siam: Missionary Excursion of Mr. Hemenway," *Missionary Herald* 40 (December 1844), 403.

9. Cohen, *Chinese in the Post–Civil War South*, 1–16.

10. Chang & Eng Bunkers from Wm. Rawley & Wife, March 1, 1845, Surry County Record of Deed, 1839–1847, v. 4, pp. 295–96, NCSA; Chang & Eng Bunkers from T. F. Prather, September 29, 1845, Surry County Record of Deed, 1839–1847, v. 4, pp. 305–6, NCSA. Surry County Land Entry Book, March 12, 1850, p. 123, entry no. 2487, NCSA, has the reference to the "Sime twins."

11. Versions of the *Biblical Recorder* and *Southerner* reports appeared in newspers across the country. For the former, these included the *Boston Recorder*, September 30, 1847; *New York Evangelist*, October 14, 1847; *Southern Patriot* (Charleston, SC), October 23, 1847; *Cleveland Herald*, November 2, 1847; and *Greenville (SC) Mountaineer*, November 19, 1847, among others. For the latter, these included the *Raleigh Register*, May 24, 1848; *Greenville (SC) Mountaineer*, June 2, 1848; *Boston Daily Atlas*, August 17, 1848; and *Cleveland Herald*, August 30, 1848, among others.

12. "The Siamese Twins [from the Richmond *Southerner*]," *Raleigh Register*, May 24, 1848; "From the *Raleigh N.C. Standard*," *Greenville (SC) Mountaineer*, February 7, 1845; "The Siamese Twins," *Boston Daily Atlas*, December 9, 1852.

13. Moreheid, *Lives, Adventures, Anecdotes, Amusements, and Domestic Habits*. The author's name and the place of publication of this booklet similarly served to make the production appear more southern. Barclay, working out of Philadelphia, made a name chronicling famous people and extraordinary events through publications that featured fictitious authors and a local place of publication to lend immediacy to his reports. In this case, Raleigh was readily familiar to a wider reading public as the capital of North Carolina, the state in which the twins had settled, and the author's name, written as "Hon. J.N. Moreheid," bore a strong resemblance to the state's former governor, John M. Morehead. There is nothing to indicate that the former governor, though a Whig

from Guilford County, actually wrote about or was acquainted with the twins. On Barclay, see McDade, "Lurid Literature of the Last Century."

14. On the purifying role that wives were seen to play, see Wells, *Origins of the Southern Middle Class*, 76–80.

15. For descriptions of Sarah and Adelaide, see versions of the *Biblical Recorder* and *Southerner* articles reprinted in "The Siamese Twins," *Raleigh Register*, May 24, 1848; "The Siamese Twins at Home," *Trumpet and Universalist Magazine*, November 2, 1850; "The Siamese Twins," *Boston Recorder*, September 30, 1847; and "The Siamese Twins," *Boston Investigator*, July 5, 1848.

16. "The Siamese Twins at Home," *Trumpet and Universalist Magazine*, November 2, 1850; "The Siamese Twins," *Boston Recorder*, September 30, 1847. The intent here is to show how Americans read about and understood the matches; there is no indication whatsoever that this is representative of what actually happened. It is worth noting that these accounts differ from that given by Graves in his unpublished biography. Graves presents it as a given that each twin was attracted to the sister he ended up with; the great concern was that Sarah did not immediately reciprocate these feelings. Dugger's account features mutual attractions between the eventual couples from the first time they met.

17. 1850 U.S. Federal Census, Surry County, NC, retrieved from Historical Census Browser, University of Virginia, Geospatial and Statistical Data Center, http://mapserver.lib.virginia.edu. On entrepreneurial slave society in northwestern North Carolina, see Inscoe, *Mountain Masters*, 37–44, 65–68.

18. "The Siamese Twins," *Greenville (SC) Mountaineer*, July 14, 1848; "The Siamese Twins," *Raleigh Register*, May 24, 1848; "The Siamese Twins," *Greensborough Patriot*, October 16, 1852; *Milwaukee Sentinel and Gazette*, May 18, 1849; "The Siamese Twins," *New Hampshire Sentinel* (Keene), May 24, 1849, citing the *Daily Mail*.

19. "The Siamese Twins: Visit of Chang and Eng to the Herald Establishment," *New York Herald*, April 11, 1853.

20. Tchen, *New York before Chinatown*, 141; Byrne, *Becoming Bourgeois*, 33–36; Rawley to Chang and Eng, April 30, 1849; Gilmer to Chang and Eng, May 13, 1853; Banner to Chang and Eng, June 23, 1853; Gilmer to Chang and Eng, November 13, 1853, all in Chang and Eng Bunker Papers, SHC.

21. On the new sensibilities for southern middle-class women and the critique of extravagance, see Wells, *Origins of the Southern Middle Class*, 76–80. A progressive model of nineteenth-century southern religion, at least among Virginia's Baptist and Methodist churches, is put forward in Schweiger, *The Gospel Working Up*; quotation on 84.

22. See the *Biblical Recorder* report that was reprinted in the *Boston Recorder*, September 30, 1847, and *New York Evangelist*, October 14, 1847; S. D. Bumpass to Francis Bumpass, August 23, 1847, Bumpass Family Papers, SHC.

23. This Richmond *Southerner* report was reprinted in the *Greenville (SC) Mountaineer*, July 14, 1848.

24. "The Siamese Twins at Home," *Trumpet and Universalist Magazine*, November 2, 1850.

25. "Siam," *Christian Examiner* 66 (March 1859): 237; "Commercial Troubles with China—Trade with Eastern Nations," *New York Herald*, December 28, 1855.

26. Howes and Smith to Chang and Eng, December 24, 1852, private collection.

27. See, for example, Wallace and Wallace, *The Two*, and Hunter, *Duet for a Lifetime*.

28. Compare *An Account of Chang and Eng*, 11–12, with Crawfurd, *Journal of an Embassy*, 450, 454.

29. Compare *An Account of Chang and Eng*, 14–15, with Crawfurd, *Journal of an Embassy*, 327–28.

30. Compare *An Account of Chang and Eng*, 15–16, with Crawfurd, *Journal of an Embassy*, 336–37.

31. Compare *An Account of Chang and Eng*, 18, with Crawfurd, *Journal of an Embassy*, 332.

32. On disease, funeral rites, and mourning rituals, compare *An Account of Chang and Eng*, 18–19, with *A Few Particulars concerning Chang-Eng*, 4, and *An Account of Chang and Eng*, 19–20, 23–24, with Crawfurd, *Journal of an Embassy*, 321–22. On Siamese superstition, compare *An Account of Chang and Eng*, 24–28, with Crawfurd, *Journal of an Embassy*, 378–79, 390–93.

33. It perhaps should be noted explicitly that none of this acknowledges Crawfurd or his journal. There is one extended quoted passage citing Crawfurd that appears later on, a description of Hue that "will convey an excellent idea of the town as it was when visited by the twins" (*An Account of Chang and Eng*, 50–54), as well as one other reference to Crawfurd, which I consider presently.

34. Compare *An Account of Chang and Eng*, 29–30, with Crawfurd, *Journal of an Embassy*, 78–79. If the twins actually did make this voyage, they would have approached Bangkok from the same direction, most likely along the same waterway.

35. Compare *An Account of Chang and Eng*, 30–33, with Crawfurd, *Journal of an Embassy*, 90–99. Unlike earlier comparisons, this section is largely rewritten and condensed rather than copied.

36. *An Account of Chang and Eng*, 39.

37. Compare *An Account of Chang and Eng*, 40–55, with Crawfurd, *Journal of an Embassy*, 151–55, 213–50. Again, this section is largely rewritten and condensed.

38. Crawfurd, *Journal of an Embassy*, 450.

39. *An Account of Chang and Eng*, 12. The braided hairstyle was understood to symbolize submission to the Qing emperor.

40. Crawfurd, *Journal of an Embassy*, 454.

41. *An Account of Chang and Eng*, 13.

42. Tchen, *New York before Chinatown*, 21–24.

43. Tchen calls these impulses "commercial Orientalism" and "political Orientalism," respectively.

44. Miller, *The Unwelcome Immigrant*, 113–41, has a lengthy discussion of the Taiping Rebellion's impact on the way that Americans saw the Chinese. As one example of the prejudicial views Americans had of Chinese, Miller quotes at length a critical newspaper editor from Boston: "It is time for those who have derived their stereotype cut in geographies, in which an oblique eyed, mild looking individual, with shaven poll, lengthy queue and voluminous breeches, is presented hawking about 'rats and puppies for pies' to turn to more reliable sources for information" (118). See also Cohen, *America's Response to China*, 15–23, 32.

45. [Palmer], "The Chinaman." The book under review was Mackie, *Life of Tai-Ping-Wang*, which says nothing about the Siamese twins.

46. [Palmer], "The Chinaman," 338–39.

47. Some newspaper articles that made reference to the twins' slaves during this period include "The Siamese Twins at Home," *Trumpet and Universalist Magazine*, November 2, 1850; "The Siamese Twins," *Boston Daily Atlas*, December 9, 1852; and "The Siamese Twins," *New York Herald*, April 11, 1853.

48. Vella, *Siam under Rama III*, 25–26.

49. See An Account of Money Expended by Chang-Eng, Chang and Eng Bunker Papers, SHC.

50. Other people of non-European descent pursued a similar path. In Georgia and North Carolina, Cherokee men had been encouraged by the federal government during the late eighteenth century to demonstrate their masculinity through the ownership of land and slaves. In so doing, the Cherokee gradually replaced a more fluid understanding of slavery with a racial attitude toward blacks that had been influenced by white Americans. See Miles, *Ties That Bind*, 34–36.

51. Chang & Eng Bunkers from T. F. Prather and Chang & Eng Bunkers from William Marsh, Surry County Record of Deed, 1839–1847, vol. 4, pp. 304–6, 530, NCSA; *Raleigh Register and North-Carolina Gazette*, May 24, 1848, the *Arkansas State Democrat* (Little Rock), June 16, 1848, and the *Greenville (SC) Mountaineer*, July 14, 1848; Graves, "The Siamese Twins"; *New York Herald*, April 11, 1853; Surry County Record of Deed, 1856–1869, vol. 10, pp. 223–24, NCSA. See also the single entry for Chang and Eng Bunker in the 1850 Federal U.S. Census Slave Schedule, Stewart's Creek District, Surry County, NC, and the separate entries in the 1860 Federal U.S. Census Slave Schedule for Eng Bunker, Dobson District, Surry County, NC, and Chang Bunker, Dobson District, Surry County, NC. (Unless otherwise indicated, census slave schedules were accessed through Ancestry.com.) The 1860 slave schedule lists Eng with eighteen slaves and Chang with fourteen. Two flags are raised by this discussion of the twins' slaveholdings. The first is the relative youth of their slaves, which I will discuss presently. The second is the rapid increase in their numbers, combined with the fact that there are so few records of purchase. Only four can be accounted for in the county purchase records, though this may simply suggest that the twins did not register their purchases. Another possible explanation for the growth in population is natural increase.

52. Graves, "The Siamese Twins"; U.S Census of 1860, Agricultural Schedule, North Carolina, Surry County, Hollow Springs District, pp. 31–32, lines 33–34, farms of Eng Bunker and Chang Bunker, on microfilm at NCSA.

53. Graves, "The Siamese Twins"; "Surry County," *Greensborough Patriot*, October 16, 1852; "The Siamese Twins," *New York Daily Times*, November 24, 1852; "The Siamese Twins," *North American and U.S. Gazette*, November 25, 1852; *Boston Daily Atlas*, November 22, 1852; *Liberator*, November 26, 1852. For a discussion of the ideology of paternalism and the issue of brutality against slaves, see Genovese, *Roll, Jordan, Roll*, 3–7, 40–43. In *A Family Venture*, Cashin examines paternalism and includes consideration of Wilkes County, the North Carolina county in which the twins first settled.

54. *Greensborough Patriot*, November 20, 1852; *An Account of Chang and Eng*, 87; *New York Herald*, April 13, 1853. Despite such public relations efforts, however, the

twins' reputation as hard masters would persist until the end of slavery. One visitor in 1860 noted, "They . . . have quite a number of very likely negroes, and are said to be rather hard masters." James C. Pass to Mary E. Ireland, August 19, 1860, Croom Collection, East Carolina University, Greenville, NC.

55. Chang and Eng to Wives and Children, October 11, 1853; Chang and Eng to Sarah Bunker, December 8, 1853; Chang and Eng to Wives and Children, February 13, 1854; Adelaide Bunker to Husbands and Children, February 20, 1854; Chang and Eng to Wives and Children, March 11, 1854, all in private collection. These quotations are rendered as their authors wrote them.

56. These concerns have similarly characterized historiography of the 1850s. Holt, in *The Political Crisis of the 1850s*, for instance, argues that "ethnocultural" issues such as temperance and nativism undermined the second party system, and Gienapp, in *The Origins of the Republican Party*, points to similar issues underlying the origins of the Republican Party. Anbinder, *Nativism and Slavery*, meanwhile, argues that slavery, and not ethnocultural concerns, was the fundamental concern of the day, explaining the Know-Nothings' brief history.

Although Jacobson's *Whiteness of a Different Color* gives short shrift to the 1850s, his treatment of nativism in the mid- to late nineteenth century offers a theoretical framework for understanding the process of racial formation that takes place. Aarim-Heriot focuses specifically on the shifting meanings attached to Chinese and African Americans in *Chinese Immigrants, African Americans, and Racial Anxiety*.

57. Foner, *Free Soil, Free Labor, Free Men*, 232–37.

58. Stuart Creighton Miller makes clear that anti-Chinese sentiment was a product of a larger national discourse, not merely the result of racists in California. Focusing on New York City, Tchen makes similar claims. The numbers of Chinese to California come from Coolidge, *Chinese Immigration*, 498. The German and Irish immigration numbers come from *Congressional Globe*, 33rd Cong., 2nd sess. (Jan. 15, 1855), 95, and (Dec. 18, 1854), 51. On the anti-Chinese sentiment of the California Know-Nothings, see Aarim-Heriot, *Chinese Immigrants, African Americans, and Racial Anxiety*, 51–52.

59. *Richmond Dispatch*, May 12, 1853. For a discussion of coolieism, see Jung, *Coolies and Cane*, 11–33; Aarim-Heriot, *Chinese Immigrants, African Americans, and Racial Anxiety*, 30–31; and Cohen, *Chinese in the Post–Civil War South*, 22–45.

60. "Slavery in China, from the *Anti-Slavery Reporter*," *Frederick Douglass' Paper*, April 14, 1854; "Canton Correspondence," *National Era*, May 8, 1856. See also "Extension of Slave Territory," *National Era*, March 11, 1847.

61. Aarim-Heriot, *Chinese Immigrants, African Americans, and Racial Anxiety*, 30–42, see p. 60 for the Lippincott quotation; "Rapid Strides toward Slavery," *Liberator*, December 15, 1854.

62. "Slavery in California," *National Era*, February 10, 1859; "An Inquiry," *National Era*, January 18, 1855.

63. "The United States of the United Races," *National Era*, September 15, 1853. The author signs his name "E."

64. J. W. Steffy, "A Few Facts from a Plain Man," *National Era*, December 28, 1854; "The Chinese and the Times," *Golden Hills' News* (San Francisco), June 10, 1854, reprinted in Odo, *The Columbia Documentary History*, 22–23.

65. The qualifier "native-born" is significant here. Many early histories of anti-Chinese sentiment identify European immigrants—Irish, especially—at the root of the movement. Irish immigrants certainly played a role, but responsibility can be spread among native-born Americans as well. See Saxton, *Rise and Fall of the White Republic*.

66. Lee, *Orientals*, 42. Biographical information on Helper can be found in Frederickson, *The Arrogance of Race*, 28–53.

67. Helper, *The Land of Gold*, 47, 86, 96.

68. Lee, *Orientals*, 42.

69. The letter was reprinted widely. See "Siamese Twins," *Daily National Intelligencer* (Washington, DC), December 6, 1850; *Daily Scioto Gazette* (Chillicothe, OH), December 9, 1850; *Boston Daily Atlas*, December 10, 1850; and "Siamese Twins," *Raleigh Register*, December 11, 1850. As always, whether the letter truly came from Chang and Eng is up for question. Of the four sons named, one is misnamed. Instead of James Montgomery, the letter identifies a "James Madison." Rather than ruling out the possibility of having come from the twins, the mistake may also have been an editorial change by the newspaper, which published the letter as an extract.

70. Hale to Harris, March 14, 1844, Chatham Papers, NCSA. For examples of the *Spartan* report, see the *Southern Patriot* (Charleston, SC), November 14, 1844, and the *Newport (RI) Mercury*, November 16, 1844. For the *Southerner* report, see "The Siamese Twins," *Boston Investigator*, July 5, 1848.

71. This *South Carolina Spartan* article was reprinted widely. See "The Siamese Twins," *Weekly Raleigh Register*, October 11, 1844; "The Siamese Twins," *Greenville (SC) Mountaineer*, October 25, 1843; "Siamese Twins," *North American and Daily Advertiser* (Philadelphia), November 7, 1844; "The Siamese Twins," *Boston Daily Atlas*, November 8, 1844; "The Siamese Twins," *Cleveland Herald*, November 11, 1844; "Theatricals &c.," *New York Herald*, November 15, 1844; and "The Siamese Twins, Their Wives, and Babies," *Southern Patriot* (Charleston, SC), November 15, 1844, among many others.

72. "Birth," *Boston Daily Atlas*, May 9, 1844.

73. Versions of this article, from the Richmond *Southerner*, were also reprinted widely. See, for example, the *Boston Daily Atlas*, August 17, 1848, and the *Mississippi Free Trader and Natchez Gazette*, October 12, 1848.

74. "The Siamese Twins," *New York Herald*, May 4, 1849; *Greensborough Patriot*, October 16, 1852; James C. Pass to Mary E. Ireland, August 19, 1860, Croom Collection, East Carolina University, Greenville, NC; *Raleigh Register*, April 13, 1853.

75. *An Account of Chang and Eng*, vi, 79; Graves, "The Siamese Twins," 22–23; Wallace and Wallace, *The Two*, 199–200; *Greensborough Patriot*, October 16, 1852. On education among the southern elite and middle class, see Censer, *North Carolina Planters*, 42–65, and Wells, *Origins of the Southern Middle Class*, 10–11.

76. The former version of the *Southerner* profile was reprinted in the *Boston Investigator*, July 5, 1848; *Boston Daily Atlas*, August 17, 1848; and *Cleveland Herald*, August 30, 1848. The latter version of the *Southerner* interview was reprinted in the *Greenville (SC) Mountaineer*, July 14, 1848.

77. "Miscegenation," the term most commonly associated with the mixing or interbreeding of different races, would not enter the lexicon until the very end of 1863, in

the middle of the American Civil War, as part of a propaganda ploy asserting that the Republican Party favored interracial marriages. See Lemire, *"Miscegenation,"* 116–17.

78. Nott, *Two Lectures*.

79. *Raleigh Register*, April 13, 1853; "The Siamese Twins at Home," *Trumpet and Universalist Magazine*, November 2, 1850; "The Siamese Twins," *Youth's Companion*, May 5, 1853.

80. Chang and Eng to Sarah, December 8, 1853, private collection. Copy in possession of the author.

81. Chang and Eng to Wives and Children, October 11, 1853; Adelaide to Husbands and Children, February 20, 1854; Chang and Eng to Wives and Children, March 11, 1854, all in private collection. Copies in possession of the author.

82. *New York Daily Times*, April 19, 1853.

83. Latham was speaking on a bill to establish a line of mail steamships between San Francisco and Shanghai. See Latham, *Speech of Hon. Milton S. Latham*, 14.

84. "Movements of the Prince," *New York Times*, October 15, 1860; "Some of Uncle Sam's Passengers," *Daily Evening Bulletin*, December 6, 1860; "The Next Steamer," *Daily Alta California*, December 5, 1860; "Chang and Eng," *Sacramento Daily Union*, November 28, 1860; [Letter from Patrick or Montgomery Bunker to his brothers and sisters], San Francisco, December 10, 1860, Chang and Eng Bunker Papers, SHC. For more details on the twins' trip to California, see Wallace and Wallace, *The Two*, 220–34.

85. The 1850 number comes from the "U.S. Census Commissioner's Report," *Daily Alta California*, April 18, 1851. The actual returns for the city for 1850 were destroyed in a fire. See also Chen, *Chinese San Francisco*, 55.

86. "John Learns Christian Ways," *Daily Evening Bulletin*, December 13, 1860. See also "The Abolishment of the Chinese School," *Daily Alta California*, January 3, 1860; "The Chinese School to Be Continued," *Daily Evening Bulletin*, January 4, 1860; and X, "Information as to the Chinamen in California—The So-Called 'Coolies,'" letter to the editor, *Daily Evening Bulletin*, February 25, 1860.

87. For examples of the commercial argument, see Cosmopolite, "The Chinese Question," letter to the editor, *Daily Evening Bulletin*, February 1, 1860; Merchant, "The Chinese Question Further Discussed," letter to the editor, *Daily Evening Bulletin*, February 8, 1860.

88. See, for example, Cosmopolite, "The Chinese Question," letter to the editor, *Daily Evening Bulletin*, February 1, 1860; Cosmos, "A Miner's Views on the Chinese Question," letter to the editor, *Daily Evening Bulletin*, February 24, 1860, which argues against the Chinese but concedes ground on the question of rice agriculture in the swamps; and Merchant, "The Chinese Question: 'Merchant' in Answer to 'Cosmos,'" letter to the editor, *Daily Evening Bulletin*, February 28, 1860.

89. Cosmos, "A Miner's Views on the Chinese Question," letter to the editor, *Daily Evening Bulletin*, February 24, 1860; Fair-Play, "The Chinese Question," letter to the editor, *Daily Evening Bulletin*, February 3, 1860; "The Chinese Laboring Class—What Is to Be Done with Evil?" *Daily Evening Bulletin*, February 27, 1860.

90. "Who Is White?," *The Leisure Hour: A Family Journal of Instruction and Recreation* 4 (February 1, 1855), 80; "The Naturalization Laws—How They Bear upon

the Chinese-Education in California," *New York Daily Times*, October 3, 1854; "White Chinese Baby Deserted," *Daily Evening Bulletin*, January 6, 1860.

91. The *Oriental*, quoted in "The Chinese in California," *New York Daily Times*, March 7, 1855; "The Chinese and the Times," *Golden Hills' News*, June 10, 1854, reprinted in Odo, *The Columbia Documentary History*, 24–25.

92. "Chinamen on the Pacific, and Negroes on the Atlantic," *Daily Evening Bulletin*, June 7, 1860.

93. "The Siamese Twins," *Daily Evening Bulletin*, December 7, 1860; "The Siamese Twins," *Daily Alta California*, December 10, 1860; "The Siamese Twins," *Daily Evening Bulletin*, December 13, 1860; "The Siamese Twins," *Daily Evening Bulletin*, December 11, 1860; "Siamese Twins," *Sacramento Daily Union*, December 22, 1860.

94. "The Siamese Twins," *Daily Alta California*, December 15, 1860.

95. Reports of the twins' faith had appeared since their first arrival in 1829. Most recently, in early 1860, reports of Chang's wife being baptized at a Surry County revival and of Chang's and Eng's nod toward Christianity made the rounds of the national press, including California. See *Daily Evening Bulletin*, March 21, 1860.

96. "The Siamese Twins," *Daily Evening Bulletin*, December 11, 1860; Lee, *Orientals*, 43–50.

97. For the date the twins left San Francisco, see [Advertisement], *Daily Alta California*, February 5–9, 1861.

Chapter Five

1. Pingree, "America's 'United Siamese Brothers,'" 94–95; Hale, *An Historical Account of the Siamese Twin Brothers*; [Hale], *A Few Particulars concerning Chang-Eng*.

2. The item was reprinted in such diverse locations as *Lowell (MA) Daily Citizen and News*, July 30, 1860; *Daily Cleveland Herald*, August 4, 1860; *Fayetteville (NC) Observer*, August 6, 1860; *Milwaukee Daily Sentinel*, August 8, 1860; and *Charleston (SC) Courier*, August 11, 1860.

3. "The Siamese Twins," *Fayetteville (NC) Observer*, August 16, 1860.

4. This story first published in the *New York Tribune* was widely reprinted in such papers as *Boston Daily Advertiser*, November 13, 1860; *Lowell (MA) Daily Citizen and News*, November 14, 1860; *Chicago Tribune*, November 16, 1860; and *Milwaukee Daily Sentinel*, November 17, 1860.

5. "A Forcible Comparison," *Fayetteville (NC) Observer*, April 4, 1860.

6. McPherson, *Battle Cry of Freedom*, 290–92.

7. "The Latest Report of Chang and Eng," *Daily Missouri Republican*, January 30, 1861. Italics in the original.

8. See Chapter 4.

9. "The Latest Report of Chang and Eng," *Daily Missouri Republican*, January 30, 1861. Italics in the original.

10. Inscoe, *Mountain Masters*, 250–51, quotation on 257; Lefler and Newsome, *North Carolina*, 447–50.

11. Separate entries for Eng Bunker and Chang Bunker in the 1860 U.S. Federal Census, Mount Airy District, Surry County, NC, and the 1860 U.S. Federal Census Slave

Schedule, Dobson District, Surry County, NC. (Unless otherwise noted, population and slave schedules were accessed through Ancestry.com.)

12. U.S Census of 1860, Agricultural Schedule, North Carolina, Surry County, Hollow Springs District, pp. 31–32, lines 33–34, farms of Eng Bunker and Chang Bunker, on microfilm at NCSA.

13. Surry County List of Taxables, 1862–1865, NCSA. The numbers that follow are taken from this source.

14. Wallace and Wallace, *The Two*, 330–31.

15. Virginia Dept. of Confederate Military Records, Cavalry unit records, 37th Battalion, Co. I, C. W. Bunker and D. C. Bunker, State Government Records Collection, State Library of Virginia, Richmond, VA. On Christopher Bunker's experience at Camp Chase, see C. W. Bunker to Father, Mother, et al., October 12, 1864, Christopher Wren Bunker Papers, SCH. For a description of the action he saw and news about Surry County men serving with him, see letters from C. W. Bunker to Nancy Bunker, Christopher Wren Bunker Papers, SHC.

16. Bettie Dobson to Mary Dobson, Mount Airy, NC, February 6, 1865, and April 6, 1865, Dobson Family Papers, SHC. On Stoneman's raid, see Barrett, *The Civil War in North Carolina*, 350–53.

17. On the experience of newly emancipated African Americans, see Foner, *Reconstruction*, 77–123; Litwack, *Been in the Storm*; and Hunter, *To 'Joy My Freedom*, 20–43.

18. Joseph Banner to Pocahontas Galloway, Surry County Negro Cohabitation Certificates, 1866, NCSA; Henry Banner to Caroline Bunker, March 8, 1868, and Thomas Davis to Betty Bunker, August 9, 1868, Surry County Marriage Register (Negro), 1867–1878, NCSA; entry for Eng Bunker, 1870 U.S. Federal Census, Mount Airy Township, Surry County, NC.

19. Surry County List of Taxables, 1862–1865, NCSA.

20. "The Siamese Twins," *New York Times*, October 6, 1864.

21. Sumner's Faneuil Hall speech was published in full in many papers. See, for example, "Union Men in Council," *Boston Daily Advertiser*, September 29, 1864; "Speech of Hon. Charles Sumner," *Liberator*, October 7, 1864; and "The War a Failure(?)," *Vermont Watchman and State Journal*, October 14, 1864.

22. "In General," *Boston Daily Advertiser*, November 5, 1864.

23. "The Political 'Siamese' Twins: The Offspring of Chicago Miscegenation" (New York: Courier and Ives, 1864), American Antiquarian Society, Worcester, MA.

24. [Croly and Wakeman], *Miscegenation*. Although the publication of the political pamphlet is often listed with an 1864 publication date, Lemire notes that the pamphlet title was entered for copyright in late December 1863. See Lemire, *"Miscegenation,"* 116–44, and 173–74, n. 8.

25. The Irish became increasingly "white" in the postbellum years—in large part by positioning themselves against blacks and Chinese—and either disappeared from these works or became the hypocritical persecutor, replaced in some popular representations by American Indians.

26. See "The Siamese Twins" and "The Pardoned Rebels in North Carolina," *Boston Daily Advertiser*, August 1, 1865, and "The Siamese Twins," "Difficulties in the

Shenandoah Valley," and "Government Appointments in the South," *New York Times*, August 1, 1865.

27. "The Siamese Twins Again," letter to the editor, *New York Times*, August 2, 1865.

28. The economic costs come from Goldin and Lewis, "The Economic Costs." In comparison, the South lost at least 260,000 lives, and southern governments spent $1 billion on the war and experienced a decline in consumption of $6 billion. On top of that, Goldin and Lewis estimate the physical destruction of the South at $1.5 billion. In all, they calculate the total per capita cost of the war at $670,000 for the South and $199,000 for the North.

29. "From North Carolina and Virginia," *Macon Daily Telegraph*, May 10, 1864. The story was reprinted in whole or in part in other newspapers, including the *Daily South Carolinian*, May 15, 1864; *Milwaukee Daily Sentinel*, June 13, 1864; *Daily Cleveland Herald*, June 17, 1864; *Daily Evening Bulletin* (San Francisco), July 9, 1864; *Brooklyn Eagle*, July 23, 1864; and *The Congregationalist* (Boston), August 12, 1864.

30. "A Curious Story [from the Philadelphia Ledger]," *Brooklyn Eagle*, March 16, 1865; "The Siamese Twins," *New Haven Daily Palladium*, March 17, 1865; "The Siamese Twins," *New York Times*, March 19, 1865; "The Siamese Twins," *Chicago Tribune*, March 22, 1865. All except the *Times* cite the Philadelphia paper.

31. The quote comes from "The Siamese Twins," *Wisconsin State Register*, April 1, 1865, but the Philadelphia report also mentioned the presence of northern investments.

32. Reprinted as "The Siamese Twins," *Woonsocket Patriot and Rhode Island State Register*, August 11, 1865.

33. Blum, *Reforging the White Republic*, 5, 22.

34. "The Siamese Twins," *Wisconsin State Register*, April 1, 1865. It is important not to place too much credence in the accuracy of what articles said and rather to read them as examples of what people were hearing and saying about the twins. For instance, this last article also stated that the twins had always been Union men, contradicting most everything else that was written during the period and in the years after.

35. "The Siamese Twins," *Daily Cleveland Herald*, February 19, 1866, from the *New Haven Palladium*.

36. "Minor Topics," *New York Times*, August 11, 1868.

37. Eve, "The Siamese Twins."

38. Ibid.

39. Simpson, "A Lecture on the Siamese," 139–41.

40. "News by the Mails," *Boston Daily Advertiser*, August 12, 1869; "By Telegraph and Mail," *North American and U.S. Gazette* (Philadelphia), August 13, 1869.

41. Simpson, "A Lecture on the Siamese," 141.

42. Graves, "The Siamese Twins"; Nannie Bunker diary, December 27, 1868, and January 19, 1869, Twins Papers, NCSA.

43. See Christopher Wren Bunker Papers, SHC, and Nannie Bunker album, Twins Papers, NCSA.

44. My understanding of southern Romanticism is informed by O'Brien, *Rethinking the South*, 5–6, 38–56.

45. Nannie Bunker diary, December 7, 1868, Twins Papers, NCSA. What remains of the diary is limited. The typescript version at the North Carolina State Archives

mentions pages in the original ripped out. As it is, December 1868 is covered fairly well, and January 1869 has a couple of entries, as does May 1869.

46. Ibid., December 1, 1868. I have rendered the spelling here and elsewhere as it is in the journal.

47. Ibid., December 2, 1868.

48. The Romantic South "was a provincial culture anxious to invent and legitimate itself," O'Brien has written. "To call it provincial is not to insult, for any Romantic sensibility honored itself by the adjective. The indigenous always mattered. The attraction of Romanticism was precisely the dignity it gave to the local." See O'Brien, *Rethinking the South*, 50–51.

49. Nannie Bunker diary, May 30, 1869, Twins Papers, NCSA.

50. In this analysis, I am assuming—correctly, I believe—that the diary was meant to be read by others, even if only family. According to the typescript, Nannie's brothers later went in and added their own entries, and Jesse Franklin Graves's biography of Chang and Eng quotes from this diary. There is also the possibility that she intended the journal to be published. Her cousin Kate also kept a detailed journal of the British Isles and hoped her manuscript would reach a London publisher, though no one knows the fate of the document. As for Nannie's journal, in some instances there are what appear to be rough entries followed by polished versions of the same entry.

51. Nannie Bunker diary, December 19–20, 1868, Twins Papers, NCSA.

52. Ibid., December 21–29, 1868.

53. Ibid., December 27, 1868.

54. Ibid., January 19, 1869.

55. Ibid., December 2, 1868.

56. Ibid., December 26, 1868.

57. [Croly and Wakeman], *Miscegenation*, 52, 54.

58. See Butler, *Critical Americans*, 74–86, and Blackett, *Divided Hearts*.

59. "The Siamese Twins," *Echo*, February 13, 1869, reproduced in a London pamphlet, *The Siamese Twins, Chang and Eng*, 27, Siamese Twins Collection, Mount Airy Museum of Regional History.

60. "Summary of European News," *Boston Daily Advertiser*, March 2, 1869.

61. As part of my project to understand the twins' significance in the U.S. context, the following discussion considers only those news stories from London that were reported by American newspapers. Attention to the British context of the 1868–69 tour would repay further study, but it falls outside the scope of the current effort.

62. "Chang and Eng Not in Favor," *Milwaukee Daily Sentinel*, March 13, 1869.

63. "London Beggars," *Daily Evening Bulletin* (San Francisco), August 7, 1869.

64. "The Siamese Twins," *Brooklyn Eagle*, March 15, 1869.

65. "London," *Chicago Tribune*, March 6, 1869.

66. "Personal Habits of the Siamese Twins" was first published in *Packard's Monthly* in 1869 and then after the twins' death in *Sketches New and Old*. My discussion here of the story as an allegory of the nation's disunion and restoration is informed primarily by Wu, "The Siamese Twins in Late-Nineteenth-Century Narratives." Conjoined twins appear in other of Twain's works, most famously *The Tragedy of Pudd'nhead Wilson* and *The Comedy of Those Extraordinary Twins*, both published in 1894. Both featured Italian twins.

67. Wu, "The Siamese Twins in Late-Nineteenth-Century Narratives," 40.

68. Wells, *Origins of the Southern Middle Class*, 231–33; Foner, *Reconstruction*, 137–38, 294–97, 325–26, 395.

69. LaFeber, *The New Empire*, 1–2, 9–10; Sexton, "Toward a Synthesis," 61; Butler, *Critical Americans*, 128–74.

70. There is very little documentation about this trip. Eng brought along his son Montgomery, twenty-two, and Chang brought Albert, thirteen. A few newspapers noted that the twins were in Berlin (see "Summary of European News," *Boston Daily Advertiser*, March 19, 1870, and "Persons and Things," *Milwaukee Daily Sentinel*, April 6, 1870). The dearth of information may represent a lack of interest on the part of American editors or their lack of access to news. Graves offers some details of the trip, presumably derived from conversations with the family if not with Montgomery and Albert themselves. See Graves, "The Siamese Twins," 37.

71. "The Siamese Twins," *New York Times*, August 14, 1870; "The Siamese Twins," *Chicago Tribune*, December 3, 1870 (from the *New York Sun*); "Discrimination on Account of Color in Liberia," *New York Herald*, August 17, 1870.

72. "In General," *Boston Daily Advertiser*, October 25, 1870, citing a story in the *Lancet*.

73. 1870 U.S. Federal Census, Mount Airy Township, Surry County, NC.

74. "The Siamese Twins," *Chicago Tribune*, December 3, 1870; "The Siamese Twins," *Daily Cleveland Herald*, December 5, 1870; "The Siamese Twins," *Georgia Weekly Telegraph* (Macon), December 6, 1870, all citing the *New York Sun*.

Chapter Six

1. Chang's and Eng's death scene is based on a letter from Nannie Bunker to Christopher Bunker, January 19, 1874, Twins Collection, NCSA; *Report of the Autopsy of the Siamese Twins*, 8–9, 17; and Allen, *Report of an Autopsy*, 3–5.

2. Chan, *Asian Americans*, xiv. Ronald Takaki argues that systems of discrimination and exploitation have kept Asian Americans perpetual strangers. See Takaki, *Strangers from a Different Shore*, 3–18.

3. Wyatt-Brown, *Southern Honor*, xv.

4. Nannie Bunker to Christopher Bunker, January 19, 1874, Twins Collection, NCSA; Augustus Rich to Jacob Rich, January 19, 1874, Chang and Eng Bunker Papers, SHC. These quotations and others are rendered as their authors wrote them.

5. Nannie Bunker to Christopher Bunker, January 19, 1874, Twins Collection, NCSA.

6. Ibid.

7. "Siamese Twins—Medical Opinions," *Daily Evening Bulletin* (San Francisco), January 26, 1874; "The Negotiations for the Bodies of the Siamese Twins," *Brooklyn Daily Eagle*, January 27, 1874.

8. "The Last of Chang and Eng," *New York Herald*, March 31, 1874.

9. Nannie Bunker to Christopher Bunker, January 19, 1874, Twins Collection, NCSA. Nothing came of this concern.

10. *Report of the Autopsy of the Siamese Twins*, 12.

11. Ibid., 13.

12. "The Dead Twins," *Brooklyn Daily Eagle*, February 6, 1874.

13. "The Siamese Twins," *New York Herald*, January 25, 1874.

14. Augustus Rich to Jacob Rich, January 19, 1874, Chang and Eng Bunker Papers, SHC.

15. Wallace and Wallace, *The Two*, 296–97; "The Siamese Twins," *New York Herald*, January 24, 1874; N. A. Bunker will, Surry County Record of Wills, 1867–1916, vol. 6, p. 61.

16. Rozell Horton to Mrs. Kang and Ang [*sic*], January 29, 1874, Chang and Eng Bunker Papers, SHC; Nannie Bunker to Christopher Bunker, January 19, 1874, Twins Collection, NCSA; "The Siamese Twins," *New York Herald*, January 24, 1874; "The Siamese Twins," *New York Herald*, January 25, 1874; "Chang and Eng," *New York Herald*, February 5, 1874.

17. Christopher Bunker to Stephen Decatur Bunker, February 25, 1874, private collection; "The Siamese Twins," *New York Herald*, January 25, 1874.

18. Medical professionals and freak-show entrepreneurs had placed dead bodies on public display—including public autopsies—before. Among the most prominent examples are Sara Baartman, the "Hottentot Venus," whose remains were placed on display at France's National Museum of Natural History in Paris, and Joice Heth, the enslaved woman advertised by P. T. Barnum as George Washington's 161-year-old nurse. Barnum charged a fifty-cent admission to her autopsy at New York's City Saloon. See Qureshi, "Displaying Sara Baartman," and Reiss, *The Showman and the Slave*, 126–58.

19. *Report of the Autopsy of the Siamese Twins*, 19–20.

20. Ibid., 10–11.

21. Pancoast, "The Carolina Twins," 43–57; "By Mail and Telegraph," *New York Times*, April 8, 1874.

22. "The Dead Siamese Twins to be Surrendered to Science," *Baltimore Sun*, January 29, 1874.

23. *Boston Daily Globe*, January 30, 1874; "The Siamese Twins," *New York Herald*, January 29, 1874.

24. "The Siamese Twins," *New York Herald*, January 22, 1874.

25. "The Siamese Twins," *New York Herald*, January 26, 1874; "Chang and Eng," *New York Herald*, February 5, 1874.

26. "The Siamese Twins," *New York Tribune*, February 13, 1874.

27. Specific details of the contract, which was never published in full and which does not appear to be extant, come from published reports from newspapers covering the autopsies. See "Eng and Chang," *New York Herald*, February 10, 1874; "The Siamese Twins," *New York Tribune*, February 10, 1874; and "The Siamese Twins," *New York Times*, February 12, 1874.

28. Sappol, *Traffic of Dead Bodies*, 85–88; Wu, *Chang and Eng Reconnected*, 37–46.

29. *Report of the Autopsy of the Siamese Twins*, 31–32.

30. Wu, *Chang and Eng Reconnected*, 75. These anxieties reflected the same thinking that underlay earlier parallels drawn between the twins' union and the national union, comparisons that were rendered superfluous after the Civil War.

31. *Boston Daily Globe*, January 26, 1874, and February 16, 1874.

32. "The Dead Siamese Twins," *New York Sun*, January 21, 1874. Many newspapers reprinted this obituary. As we will see, this account influenced the ways that many other papers reported the ensuing battle over the twins' bodies.

33. Tchen, *New York before Chinatown*, 74–77; "The Dead Siamese Twins," *New York Sun*, January 21, 1874.

34. "The Dead Siamese Twins," *New York Sun*, January 21, 1874.

35. See Tchen, *New York before Chinatown*, 75–79, 159–63, and Lui, *The Chinatown Trunk Mystery*, 154–56.

36. "Death of the Siamese Twins," *Frank Leslie's Illustrated Newspaper*, February 7, 1874.

37. "The Negotiations for the Bodies of the Siamese Twins," *Brooklyn Daily Eagle*, January 27, 1874.

38. "Obituary, The Siamese Twins," *Boston Daily Advertiser*, January 21, 1874; *Wilmington (NC) Morning Star*, January 23, 1874; *Hillsborough (NC) Recorder*, January 28, 1874.

39. Another daughter was scalded to death by boiling water at age two, and there is the family book entry that suggests that a son, Columbus, also died from burns at a young age, although very few published accounts include mention of him. Households often kept open fires for cooking or heating, and apparently accidents involving these fireplaces or the water, stews, or soups cooking on them were not rare.

40. There is the possibility that another child was stillborn to Adelaide and Chang. Sarah Bunker said as much in her statement to the commission. The autopsy section on the children contains other factual errors, so perhaps Sarah misspoke, misremembered, or was misquoted. See *Report of the Autopsy of the Siamese Twins*, 17.

41. Censer, *North Carolina Planters*, 28.

42. *The Congregationalist* (Boston), January 29, 1874.

43. "Chang and Eng," *New York Herald*, February 14, 1874; "Mrs. Chang and Mrs. Eng," *Inter Ocean* (Chicago), February 20, 1874.

44. Letter to the editor, *Raleigh Daily News*, February 15, 1874. The author is identified only as "Z.W.H."

45. *Wilmington (NC) Morning Star*, January 23, 1874.

46. Letter to the editor, *Raleigh Daily News*, February 15, 1874.

47. "Chang and Eng," *New York Herald*, March 23, 1874.

48. "A Sad Sequel," *Daily Arkansas Gazette*, April 11, 1874. The provenance of this essay is not at all clear.

49. See Takaki, *Strangers from a Different Shore*, and Tchen, *New York before Chinatown*, 252–53.

50. "Chang and Eng," *New York Herald*, March 23, 1874.

Epilogue

1. Sappol, *Traffic of Dead Bodies*, 13–14.

2. Indexed Register of Marriages, Surry County, North Carolina, NCSA; Bryant, *The Connected Bunkers*, 499; "A Case of Bigamy," *News and Observer*, August 15, 1895.

3. "Jottings," *Emporia (KS) News*, March 6, 1874; "In General," *Boston Daily Advertiser*, August 14, 1876.

4. "Sons of the Siamese," *Milwaukee Daily Sentinel*, September 9, 1876.

5. "A Famous Family," *Sumner County Press*, August 28, 1879; "Son of the Siamese Twins," *Chicago Daily Tribune*, February 10, 1888; "Personal," *Boston Daily Advertiser*, August 5, 1879.

6. Family accounts can be found in Bryant, *The Connected Bunkers*, 299, and Wallace and Wallace, *The Two*, 331. These accounts must be taken with a grain of salt. For one, they claim that Frederick was killed in St. Louis, a detail explained perhaps because a St. Louis paper reported his death (without giving any details). But we should also read this report with some skepticism; for one, it said that Frederick was the eldest son of Chang. See "Death of Chang's Son," *St. Louis Globe*, October 26, 1886.

7. "Son of the Siamese Twins," *Chicago Daily Tribune*, February 10, 1888; "Kansas State News," *Barton County Democrat* (Great Bend, KS), March 22, 1888.

8. "Son Describes Home Life of Original 'Siamese Twins,'" *Durham Sun*, ca. 1926, reprinted in Bryant, *The Connected Bunkers*, 16. Eng's son William Oliver lived briefly in Missouri around 1880, and Chang's son Jesse Lafayette spent a year or two in Kansas in the mid-1880s. Both returned to Mount Airy and spent the rest of their lives there.

9. "Son of Siamese," *Wichita (KS) Daily Eagle*, September 4, 1897; "Success of a Son of Siamese Twins," *Milwaukee Journal*, September 4, 1897; "A Forgotten Freak," *Atchison (KS) Champion*, April 26, 1890.

10. *Record of Appointment of Postmasters, 1832–1971*, National Archives Microfilm Publication M841, roll 95, volume 49, pages 336-37; 1880 United States Census, Mount Airy Township, Surry County, NC; *Wichita Daily Eagle*, May 13, 1892; and "News and Comments," *Fayetteville (NC) Observer*, August 24, 1893.

11. Wallace and Wallace, *The Two*, 334.

12. *Morning Oregonian*, January 1, 1888.

13. "News and Items," *Fayetteville (NC) Observer*, August 24, 1888.

14. Bryant, *The Connected Bunkers*, 245–46; Niransuksiri, *Faet Sayam In-Chan*, 357.

15. While descendants of Eng and Sarah began coming together in the 1980s, it was not until 1990 that members from Chang and Adelaide's side of the family joined the reunion. The twins have thousands of descendants scattered across the United States—the greatest proportion still live in North Carolina—and the annual reunion usually attracts at least a hundred. In 2001, Eng's great-granddaughter Jessie Bunker Bryant published the first attempt at a comprehensive genealogy, *The Connected Bunkers*. Cynthia Wu has provided the type of ethnographic study of the annual reunion that it deserves in *Chang and Eng Reconnected*, 145–69.

16. This is also the version that is told in Josh Gibson's 2008 documentary film on the twins, *The Siamese Connection*.

17. The interview was with June Klemmer Ellison; her father was Napoleon B. Bunker, son of William Oliver Bunker. It would have been about 1941–42 when Ellison discovered her ancestry and confronted her father. The clipping that featured the interview was reproduced without publication information in Bryant, *The Connected Bunkers*, 76.

18. Archie Robertson, "Chang-Eng's American Heritage," *Life*, August 11, 1952, 70.

19. Adam C. Smith, "Celebrity Runs in Sink's Family," *Tampa Bay Times*, September 26, 2010. Before her unsuccessful gubernatorial campaign, Sink was a banking executive, serving as president of NationsBank Florida.

20. Okihiro's *Common Ground* called for the use of Asian American history to complicate simplistic black-white binaries, and a number of scholars have answered this call. See, for example, Jung, *Coolies and Cane*, and Kim, "Racial Triangulation."

21. Hodes, *White Women, Black Men*; Ball, *Slaves in the Family*; Faust, *James Henry Hammond and the Old South*.

22. An Account of Monies Expended by Chang-Eng, Chang and Eng Bunker Papers, SHC.

23. Wu, *Chang and Eng Reconnected*, 163–66.

24. Fiedler, *Freaks*, 197.

25. Graves, "The Siamese Twins."

26. Gibson, *The Siamese Connection*.

BIBLIOGRAPHY

Archival and Other Primary Sources
MANUSCRIPT COLLECTIONS

Clements Library Special Collections, University of Michigan, Ann Arbor
    James W. Hale and Susan A. Coffin Papers
East Carolina University, Greenville, NC
    Elizabeth Rudder Fearington Croom Collection
Mount Airy Museum of Regional History, Mount Airy, NC
    Siamese Twins Collection
North Carolina State Archives, Raleigh
    Thurmond Chatham Papers
    Siamese Twins Collection
    Siamese Twins Papers
Oberlin College Special Collections, Oberlin, OH
    Dan Beach Bradley Papers
Southern Historical Collection, University of North Carolina, Chapel Hill
    Bumpass Family Papers
    Chang and Eng Bunker Papers
    Christopher Wren Bunker Papers
    Dobson Family Papers
    Gordon-Hackett Papers
    James Gwyn Papers

GOVERNMENT DOCUMENTS

North Carolina General Assembly Records, North Carolina State Archives
Surry County records, North Carolina State Archives
U.S. Census reports, 1840–1870, North Carolina State Archives
Virginia Dept. of Confederate Military Records, State Library of Virginia, Richmond, VA
Virginia General Assembly Legislative Petitions, State Library of Virginia, Richmond, VA
Wilkes County records, North Carolina State Archives

PUBLISHED BOOKS AND ARTICLES

An Account of Chang and Eng, the World Renowned Siamese Twins. New York: T. W.
    Strong, 1853.
Allen, Harrison. *Report of an Autopsy on the Bodies of Chang and Eng Bunker, Com-*
    monly Known as "The Siamese Twins." Philadelphia: Collins, 1875.

Allen, William G. *The American Prejudice against Color: An Authentic Narrative Showing How Easily the Country Got into an Uproar.* London: W. and F. G. Cash, 1853.

Bolton, George Buckley. "Statement of the Principal Circumstances respecting the United Siamese Twins Now Exhibiting in London." *Philosophical Transactions of the Royal Society of London* 29 (1830): 177–86.

The Burney Papers. 5 vols. Bangkok: Committee of Vajiranana National Library, 1910–14.

The Charlestown Convent: Its Destruction by a Mob. Boston: Patrick Donahoe, 1870.

Chotmaihet Ratchakan thi 3, Vol. 3. Bangkok: Khana Kammakan Chaloem Phrakiat 200 Pi Phrabat Somdet Phra Nangklao Chaoyuhua, 2530 (1987).

Crawfurd, John. *History of the Indian Archipelago, Containing an Account of the Manners, Arts, Languages, Religions, Institutions, and Commerce of Its Inhabitants.* Edinburgh: A. Constable, 1820.

———. *Journal of an Embassy to the Courts of Siam and Cochin China.* Singapore: Oxford University Press, 1987 (1828).

[Croly, David Goodman, and George Wakeman]. *Miscegenation: The Theory of the Blending of the Races, Applied to the American White Man and Negro.* New York: Dexter, Hamilton, 1863–64.

Dunglison, Robley. *Medical Lexicon: A Dictionary of Medical Science.* 6th ed. Philadelphia: Lea and Blanchard, 1846.

Eve, Paul F. "The Siamese Twins: Can They Be Safely Separated?" *Richmond and Louisville Medical Journal* 6 (October 1868): 367–70.

Farrington, Anthony, ed. *Early Missionaries in Bangkok: The Journals of Tomlin, Gutzlaff and Abeel, 1828–1832.* Bangkok: White Lotus Press, 2001.

Feudge, Fannie Roper. "The Siamese Twins in Their Own Land." *Lippincott's Magazine of Popular Literature and Science* 13 (March 1874): 382–84.

Finlayson, George. *The Mission to Siam and Hue.* Singapore: Oxford University Press, 1988 (1826).

Fisher, George J. "Diploteratology: An Essay on Compound Human Monsters." *Transactions of the Medical Society of the State of New York* (1866): 207–96.

———. "Diploteratology: An Essay on Compound Human Monsters." *Transactions of the Medical Society of the State of New York* (1868): 276–307.

Graves, Jesse Franklin. "The Siamese Twins as Told by Judge Jesse Franklin Graves." Unpublished manuscript, North Carolina State Archives, n.d.

Gutzlaff, Karl. "Journal of Three Voyages along the Coast of China." In *Early Missionaries in Bangkok: The Journals of Tomlin, Gutzlaff and Abeel, 1828–1832*, edited by Anthony Farrington, 65–90. Bangkok: White Lotus Press, 2001.

[Hale, James W.] *A Few Particulars concerning Chang-Eng, the United Siamese Brothers, Published under Their Own Direction.* New York: J. M. Elliott, 1836.

Hale, James W. *An Historical Account of the Siamese Twin Brothers, from Actual Observations.* New York: Elliott and Palmer, 1831.

Helper, Hinton R. *The Land of Gold: Reality versus Fiction.* Baltimore: Henry Thomas, 1855.

Hone, Philip. *The Diary of Philip Hone, 1828–1851.* New York: Dodd, Mead, 1927.

House of Commons. *Minutes of Evidence Taken before the Select Committee of the House of Commons Appointed to Enquire into the Present State of the Affairs of the East-India Company.* London: Parbury, Allen, 1830.

Latham, Milton S. *Speech of Hon. Milton S. Latham, of California.* Washington, DC: Congressional Globe Office, 1855.

Mackie, J. Milton. *Life of Tai-Ping-Wang: Chief of the Chinese Insurrection.* New York: Dix, Edwards, 1857.

Mitchell, Elisha. *Diary of a Geological Tour by Dr. Elisha Mitchell in 1827 and 1828, with Introduction and Notes by Dr. Kemp P. Battle, LL.D.* James Sprunt Historical Monograph, No. 6. Chapel Hill: University of North Carolina Press, 1905.

Moor, J. H. *Notices of the Indian Archipelago and Adjacent Countries: Being a Collection of Papers relating to Borneo, Celebes, Bali, Java, Sumatra, Nias, the Philippine Islands, Sulus, Siam, Cochin China, Malayan Peninsula, &c.* London: Frank Cass, 1968 (1st ed. 1837).

Moreheid, J. N. *Lives, Adventures, Anecdotes, Amusements, and Domestic Habits of the Siamese Twins.* Raleigh: E. E. Barclay, 1850.

North Carolina General Assembly. *Laws of the State of North Carolina, Passed by the General Assembly at the Session of 1838–1839.* Raleigh: J. Gales and Son, 1839.

———. *Revised Statutes of the State of North Carolina, Passed by the General Assembly at the Session of 1836–1837.* Raleigh: Turner and Hughes, 1837.

Nott, Josiah C. *Two Lectures on the Natural History of the Caucasian and Negro Races.* Mobile, AL: Dade and Thompson, 1844.

[Palmer, J. W.] "The Chinaman: Domestic, Scholastic, Iconoclastic, and Imperial." *Putnam's Monthly Magazine of American Literature, Science, and Art* 9 (April 1857): 337–51.

Pancoast, William H. "The Carolina Twins." *Photographic Review of Medicine and Surgery* 1 (1870–71): 43–57.

Report of the Autopsy of the Siamese Twins: Together with Other Interesting Information concerning Their Life. Philadelphia: J. B. Lippincott, 1874.

Ruschenberger, William S. W. *A Voyage Round the World, Including an Embassy to Muscat and Siam, in 1835, 1836, and 1837.* Philadelphia: Carey, Lea, and Blanchard, 1838.

The Siamese Twins, Chang and Eng: A Biographical Sketch. London: W. Last, 1869.

Silverman, Kenneth, ed. *Selected Letters of Cotton Mather.* Baton Rouge: Louisiana State University Press, 1971.

Simpson, James Y. "A Lecture on the Siamese and Other Viable United Twins." *British Medical Journal* 1 (February 1869): 139–41.

Smithies, Michael, ed. *Two Yankee Diplomats in 1830s Siam.* Bangkok: Orchid Press, 2002.

Tomlin, Jacob. "Missionary Journals and Letters." In *Early Missionaries in Bangkok: The Journals of Tomlin, Gutzlaff and Abeel, 1828–1832,* edited by Anthony Farrington, 1–64. Bangkok: White Lotus Press, 2001.

Trial of John R. Buzzell, before the Supreme Judicial Court of Massachusetts, for Arson and Burglary, in the Ursuline Convent at Charlestown. Boston: Russell, Odiorne, and Metcalf, 1834.

Tucker, George. "On the Siamese Twins." In *Essays, Moral and Metaphysical,* 246–56. 1860. Reprinted, Bristol, England: Thoemmes Continuum, 2004.

Twain, Mark. "Personal Habits of the Siamese Twins." In *Sketches New and Old*, 208–12. Hartford, CT: American Publishing, 1875.

Virginia General Assembly. *Acts Passed at a General Assembly of the Commonwealth of Virginia*. Richmond: Thomas Ritchie, 1832.

Warren, John Collins. "An Account of the Siamese Twin Brothers United Together from Their Birth." *American Journal of the Medical Sciences* 5 (November 1829): 254–56.

———. "The Siamese Brothers." *Boston Medical and Surgical Journal* 2 (September 1829): 459–62.

White, Charles. *Siamese Twins: A Negro Burlesque Sketch*. New York: DeWitt Publishing House, ca. 1874.

Wiltse, Charles M., ed. *David Walker's Appeal to the Colored Citizens of the World, but in Particular, and Very Expressly, to Those of the United States of America*. New York: Hill and Wang, 1965.

Wish, Harvey, ed. *The Diary of Samuel Sewell*. New York: G. P. Putnam's Sons, 1967.

Secondary Sources

Aarim-Heriot, Najia. *Chinese Immigrants, African Americans, and Racial Anxiety in the United States, 1848–82*. Urbana: University of Illinois Press, 2003.

Alcoff, Linda. "The Problem of Speaking for Others." *Cultural Critique* 20 (Winter 1991–92): 5–32.

Anbinder, Tyler. *Nativism and Slavery: The Northern Know-Nothings and the Politics of the 1850s*. New York: Oxford University Press, 1992.

Ball, Edward. *Slaves in the Family*. New York: Farrar, Straus, and Giroux, 1998.

Barrett, John G. *The Civil War in North Carolina*. Chapel Hill: University of North Carolina Press, 1963.

Baynton, Douglas C. "Disability and the Justification of Inequality in American History." In *The New Disability History: American Perspectives*, edited by Paul K. Longmore and Lauri Umansky, 33–57. New York: New York University Press, 2001.

Bhabha, Homi. "Of Mimicry and Man: The Ambivalence of Colonial Discourse." *October* 28 (Spring 1984): 125–33.

Bhamorabutr, Abha. *The Story of American Missionaries*. Bangkok: Department of Corrections Press, 1981.

Bhongbhibhat, Vimol, Bruce Reynolds, and Sukhon Polpatpicharn, eds. *The Eagle and the Elephant: 150 Years of Thai-American Relations*. Bangkok: United Publishing, 1982.

Blackett, R. J. M. *Divided Hearts: Britain and the American Civil War*. Baton Rouge: Louisiana State University Press, 2001.

Blum, Edward J. *Reforging the White Republic: Race, Religion, and American Nationalism, 1865–1898*. Baton Rouge: Louisiana State University Press, 2005.

Bogdan, Robert. *Freak Show: Presenting Human Oddities for Amusement and Profit*. Chicago: University of Chicago Press, 1988.

Bragg, Lois. "Planet of the Normates." *American Anthropologist* 100 (March 1998): 177–80.

Bristowe, W. S. "Robert Hunter in Siam." *History Today* 24 (February 1974): 88–95.

Brown, Richard D. "The Emergence of Urban Society in Rural Massachusetts, 1760–1820." *Journal of American History* 61 (June 1974): 29–51.

Bryant, Jessie Bunker. *The Connected Bunkers: Descendants of the Siamese Twins Eng and Chang Bunker*. Winston-Salem, NC: Jostens Graphics, 2001.

Butler, Leslie. *Critical Americans: Victorian Intellectuals and Transatlantic Liberal Reform*. Chapel Hill: University of North Carolina Press, 2007.

Bynum, Victoria E. *Unruly Women: The Politics of Social and Sexual Control in the Old South*. Chapel Hill: University of North Carolina Press, 1992.

Byrne, Frank J. *Becoming Bourgeois: Merchant Culture in the South, 1820–1865*. Lexington: University of Kentucky Press, 2006.

Carpenter, Evelyn Yates. *John Yates (1712–1779) and His Descendants to 1989: Includes the History and Genealogy of John Yates*. Clarksville, TN: Jostens Printing and Pub. Division, 1989.

Cashin, Joan E. *A Family Venture: Men and Women on the Southern Frontier*. Baltimore: Johns Hopkins University Press, 1991.

Censer, Jane Turner. *North Carolina Planters and Their Children, 1800–1860*. Baton Rouge: Louisiana State University Press, 1984.

Chan, Sucheng. *Asian Americans: An Interpretive History*. Boston: Twayne Publishers, 1991.

Chen, Yong. *Chinese San Francisco, 1850–1943: A Trans-Pacific Community*. Stanford, CA: Stanford University Press, 2000.

Chintaphamitchakun, Ariya. *Khukan nirandon: Eng & Chang Bunker*. Krung Thep: Kantana Publishing, 2546 [2003].

Clark, David L., and Catherine Myser. "Being Humaned: Medical Documentaries and the Hyperrealization of Conjoined Twins." In *Freakery: Cultural Spectacles of the Extraordinary Body*, edited by Rosemarie Garland Thomson, 338–55. New York: New York University Press, 1996.

Cohen, Daniel A. "Passing the Torch: Boston Firemen, 'Tea Party' Patriots, and the Burning of the Charlestown Convent." *Journal of the Early Republic* 24 (Winter 2004): 527–86.

Cohen, Jeffrey Jerome. "Monster Culture (Seven Theses)." In *Monster Theory: Reading Culture*, edited by Jeffrey Jerome Cohen, 3–25. Minneapolis: University of Minnesota Press, 1996.

Cohen, Lucy. *Chinese in the Post–Civil War South: A People without a History*. Baton Rouge: Louisiana State University Press, 1984.

Cohen, Warren I. *America's Response to China: A History of Sino-American Relations*. 4th ed. New York: Columbia University Press, 2000.

Coolidge, Mary Roberts. *Chinese Immigration*. New York: Henry Holt, 1909.

Cushman, Jennifer Wayne. "The Chinese in Thailand." In *The Ethnic Chinese in the ASEAN States: Bibliographical Essays*, edited by Leo Suryadinata, 221–59. Singapore: Institute of Southeast Asian Studies, 1989.

Cutter, William Richard, ed. *Historic Homes and Places and Genealogical and Personal Memoirs relating to the Families of Middlesex County, Massachusetts*. Vol. 2. New York: Lewis Historical Publishing, 1908.

Davies, John D. *Phrenology, Fad and Science: A 19th-Century American Crusade*. New Haven, CT: Yale University Press, 1955.

Dugger, Shepherd M. *Romance of the Siamese Twins, and Other Sketches*. Burnsville, NC: Edwards Printing, 1936.

Eoseewong, Nidhi. *Pen and Sail: Literature and History in Early Bangkok*. Edited by Chris Baker and Ben Anderson. Seattle: University of Washington Press, 2006.

Faust, Drew Gilpin. *James Henry Hammond and the Old South: A Design for Mastery*. Baton Rouge: Louisiana State University Press, 1982.

Fiedler, Leslie. *Freaks: Myths and Images of the Secret Self*. New York: Simon and Schuster, 1978.

Foner, Eric. *Free Soil, Free Labor, Free Men: The Ideology of the Republican Party before the Civil War*. New York: Oxford University Press, 1970.

——. *Reconstruction: America's Unfinished Revolution, 1863-1877*. New York: Harper and Row, 1988.

Frederickson, George M. *The Arrogance of Race: Historical Perspectives on Slavery, Racism, and Social Inequality*. Middletown, CT: Wesleyan University Press, 1988.

Freehling, Alison Goodyear. *Drift toward Dissolution: The Virginia Slavery Debate of 1831-1832*. Baton Rouge: Louisiana State University Press, 1982.

Genovese, Eugene D. *The Political Economy of Slavery*. New York: Pantheon Books, 1965.

——. *Roll, Jordan, Roll: The World the Slaves Made*. New York: Pantheon Books, 1974.

Gibson, Josh, dir. *The Siamese Connection*. Durham, NC: Hard Light, 2008. DVD.

Gienapp, William E. *The Origins of the Republican Party, 1852-1856*. New York: Oxford University Press, 1987.

Goldin, Claudia, and Frank Lewis. "The Economic Costs of the American Civil War: Estimates and Implications." *Journal of Economic History* 35 (June 1975): 299–326.

Gorn, Elliott J. "Gouge and Bite, Pull Hair and Scratch": The Social Significance of Fighting in the Southern Backcountry." *American Historical Review* 90 (February 1985): 18–43.

Gould, James W. "American Imperialism in Southeast Asia before 1898." *Journal of Southeast Asian Studies* 3 (September 1972): 306–14.

Greenberg, Kenneth S. *Honor and Slavery: Lies, Duels, Noses, Masks, Dressing as a Woman, Gifts, Strangers, Humanitarianism, Death, Slave Rebellions, the Proslavery Argument, Baseball, Hunting, and Gambling in the Old South*. Princeton, NJ: Princeton University Press, 1996.

Grimsted, David. *American Mobbing, 1828-1861: Toward Civil War*. New York: Oxford University Press, 1998.

Hinks, Peter P. *To Awaken My Afflicted Brethren: David Walker and the Problem of Antebellum Slave Resistance*. University Park: Pennsylvania State University Press, 1997.

Hodes, Martha. *White Women, Black Men: Illicit Sex in the Nineteenth-Century South*. New Haven, CT: Yale University Press, 1997.

Holt, Michael F. *The Political Crisis of the 1850s*. New York: Wiley, 1978.

Hunter, Kay. *Duet for a Lifetime: The Story of the Original Siamese Twins*. New York: Coward-McCann, 1964.

Hunter, Tera. *To 'Joy My Freedom: Southern Black Women's Lives and Labors after the Civil War*. Cambridge, MA: Harvard University Press, 1997.

Inscoe, John C. *Mountain Masters, Slavery, and the Sectional Crisis in Western North Carolina*. Knoxville: University of Tennessee Press, 1989.

Jacobson, Matthew Frye. *Whiteness of a Different Color: European Immigrants and the Alchemy of Race*. Cambridge, MA: Harvard University Press, 1998.

Johnson, Guion Griffis. *Ante-Bellum North Carolina: A Social History*. Chapel Hill: University of North Carolina Press, 1937.

Johnson, Paul E. *Sam Patch, the Famous Jumper*. New York: Hill and Wang, 2003.

Jung, Moon Ho. *Coolies and Cane: Race, Labor, and Sugar in the Age of Emancipation*. Baltimore: Johns Hopkins University Press, 2006.

Kerber, Linda. "Abolitionists and Amalgamators: The New York City Race Riots of 1834." *New York History* 48 (January 1967): 28–39.

Kim, Claire Jean. "The Racial Triangulation of Asian Americans." *Politics and Society* 27 (March 1999): 105–38.

LaFeber, Walter. *The New Empire: An Interpretation of American Expansion, 1860–1898*. Ithaca, NY: Cornell University Press, 1963.

Lee, Robert G. *Orientals: Asian Americans in Popular Culture*. Philadelphia: Temple University Press, 1999.

Lefler, Hugh Talmage, and Albert Ray Newsome. *North Carolina: The History of a Southern State*. Chapel Hill: University of North Carolina Press, 1973.

Lemire, Elise. *"Miscegenation": Making Race in America*. Philadelphia: University of Pennsylvania Press, 2002.

Liebersohn, Harry. *The Travelers' World: Europe to the Pacific*. Cambridge, MA: Harvard University Press, 2006.

Litwack, Leon. *Been in the Storm So Long: The Aftermath of Slavery*. New York: Knopf, 1979.

Lord, Donald C. "Missionaries, Thai, and Diplomats." *Pacific Historical Review* 35 (November 1966): 413–31.

Lui, Mary Ting Yi. *The Chinatown Trunk Mystery: Murder, Miscegenation, and Other Dangerous Encounters in Turn-of-the-Century New York*. Princeton, NJ: Princeton University Press, 2005.

Lysa, Hong. *Thailand in the Nineteenth Century: Evolution of the Economy and Society*. Singapore: Institute of Southeast Asian Studies, 1984.

McCunn, Ruthanne Lum. "Chinese in the Civil War: Ten Who Served." *Chinese America, History and Perspectives* (1996): 149–81.

McDade, Thomas M. "Lurid Literature of the Last Century: The Publications of E. E. Barclay." *Pennsylvania Magazine of History and Biography* 80 (October 1956): 452–64.

McPherson, James. *Battle Cry of Freedom: The Civil War Era*. New York: Oxford University Press, 1988.

Melish, Joanne Pope. *Disowning Slavery: Gradual Emancipation and "Race" in New England, 1780–1860*. Ithaca, NY: Cornell University Press, 1998.

Miles, Tiya. *Ties That Bind: The Story of an Afro-Cherokee Family in Slavery and Freedom*. Berkeley: University of California Press, 2005.

Miller, Stuart Creighton. *The Unwelcome Immigrant: The American Image of the Chinese, 1785–1882*. Berkeley: University of California Press, 1969.

Mintz, Steven, and Susan Kellogg. *Domestic Revolutions: A Social History of American Family Life*. New York: Free Press, 1988.

Niransuksiri, Wilat. *Faet Sayam In-Chan khon khu su chiwit*. Krung Thep: Samnakphim Matichon, 2549 [2006].

Niu, Greta Ai-Yu. "People of the Pagus: Orientalized Bodies and Migration in an Asian Pacific Rim." Ph.D. diss., Duke University, 1998.

Oakes, James. *The Ruling Race: A History of American Slaveholders*. New York: Knopf, 1982.

O'Brien, Michael. *Rethinking the South: Essays in Intellectual History*. Baltimore: Johns Hopkins University Press, 1988.

Odo, Franklin, ed. *The Columbia Documentary History of the Asian American Experience*. New York: Columbia University Press, 2002.

Okihiro, Gary Y. *Common Ground: Reimagining American History*. Princeton, NJ: Princeton University Press, 2001.

Omi, Michael, and Howard Winant. *Racial Formation in the United States: From the 1960s to the 1980s*. New York: Routledge, 1986.

Pingree, Allison. "America's 'United Siamese Brothers': Chang and Eng and Nineteenth-Century Ideologies of Democracy and Domesticity." In *Monster Theory: Reading Culture*, edited by Jeffrey Jerome Cohen, 92–114. Minneapolis: University of Minnesota Press, 1996.

Plainoi, Sombat. *Chao tang chat nai prawattisat Thai*. Phranakhon: Ruamsan, 2505 [1962].

Powell, William S., ed. *Dictionary of North Carolina Biography*. Vol. 1, *A–C*. Chapel Hill: University of North Carolina Press, 1979.

Qureshi, Sadiah. "Displaying Sara Baartman, the 'Hottentot Venus.'" *History of Science* 42 (June 2004): 233–57.

Reiss, Benjamin. *The Showman and the Slave: Race, Death, and Memory in Barnum's America*. Cambridge, MA: Harvard University Press, 2001.

Richards, Leonard L. *"Gentlemen of Property and Standing": Anti-Abolition Mobs in Jacksonian America*. New York: Oxford University Press, 1970.

Rotundo, E. Anthony. *American Manhood: Transformation in Masculinity from the Revolution to the Modern Era*. New York: Basic Books, 1993.

Said, Edward W. *Orientalism*. New York: Vintage Books, 1978.

Sappol, Michael. *A Traffic of Dead Bodies: Anatomy and Embodied Social Identity in Nineteenth-Century America*. Princeton, NJ: Princeton University Press, 2004.

Saxton, Alexander. *The Rise and Fall of the White Republic: Class Politics and Mass Culture in Nineteenth-Century America*. New York: Verso, 1990.

Schweiger, Beth Barton. *The Gospel Working Up: Progress and the Pulpit in Nineteenth-Century Virginia*. New York: Oxford University Press, 2000.

Scott, Joan W. "The Evidence of Experience." *Critical Inquiry* 17 (Summer 1991): 773–97.

Sexton, Jay. "Toward a Synthesis of Foreign Relations in the Civil War Era, 1848–1877." *American Nineteenth Century History* 5 (Fall 2004): 50–73.

Shade, William G. *Democratizing the Old Dominion: Virginia and the Second Party System, 1824–1861*. Charlottesville: University of Virginia Press, 1996.

Shrader, Richard Alexander. "William Lenoir, 1751–1839." Ph.D. diss., University of North Carolina at Chapel Hill, 1978.

Skinner, G. William. *Chinese Society in Thailand: An Analytical History*. Ithaca, NY: Cornell University Press, 1957.

Spector, Ronald H. "The American Image of Southeast Asia, 1790–1865." *Journal of Southeast Asian Studies* 3 (September 1972): 299–305.

Spivak, Gayatri Chakravorty. "Can the Subaltern Speak?" In *Marxism and Interpretation of Culture*, edited by Cary Nelson and Lawrence Grossberg, 271–313. Urbana: University of Illinois Press, 1988.

———. "The Rani of Sirmur: An Essay in Reading the Archives." *History and Theory* 24 (October 1985): 247–72.

Takaki, Ronald. *Iron Cages: Race and Culture in Nineteenth-Century America*. New York: Oxford University Press, 1990.

———. *Strangers from a Different Shore: A History of Asian Americans*. Rev. ed. Boston: Little, Brown, 1998.

Taylor, Jenny Bourne, and Sally Shuttleworth, eds. *Embodied Selves: An Anthology of Psychological Texts, 1830–1890*. Oxford, UK: Clarendon Press, 1998.

Tchen, John Kuo Wei. *New York before Chinatown: Orientalism and the Shaping of American Culture, 1776–1882*. Baltimore: Johns Hopkins University Press, 1999.

———. "Staging Orientalism and Occidentalism: Chang and Eng Bunker and Phineas T. Barnum." *Chinese America, History and Perspectives* (1996): 93–131.

Tejapira, Kasian. "Pigtail: A Pre-history of Chineseness in Siam." *Sojourn* 7 (February 1992): 95–122.

Terwiel, B. J. *Through Travellers' Eyes: An Approach to Early Nineteenth-Century Thai History*. Bangkok: Editions Duang Kamol, 1989.

Vella, Walter. *Siam under Rama III, 1824–1851*. Locust Valley, NY: J. J. Augustin, 1957.

Vinton, John Adams. *The Vinton Memorial: Comprising a Genealogy of the Descendants of John Vinton of Lynn, 1648*. N.p.: S. K. Whipple, 1858.

Wallace, Irving, and Amy Wallace. *The Two: A Biography*. New York: Bantam Books, 1978.

Walters, Ronald G. "The Erotic South: Civilization and Sexuality in American Abolitionism." *American Quarterly* 25 (May 1973): 177–201.

Wells, Jonathan Daniel. *The Origins of the Southern Middle Class, 1800–1861*. Chapel Hill: University of North Carolina Press, 2004.

Wu, Cynthia. *Chang and Eng Reconnected: The Original Siamese Twins in American Culture*. Philadelphia: Temple University Press, 2012.

———. "The Siamese Twins in Late-Nineteenth-Century Narratives of Conflict and Resolution." *American Literature* 80 (March 2008): 29–55.

Wyatt, David K. *Thailand: A Short History*. 2nd ed. New Haven, CT: Yale University Press, 2003.

Wyatt-Brown, Bertram. *Southern Honor: Ethics and Behavior in the Old South*. New York: Oxford University Press, 1983.

INDEX